Tourism and Crisis

The new millennium has been characterised by several crises ranging from dramatic acts of terror to natural disasters, as well as the most significant economic recession since the late 1920s. However, despite such challenges the global tourism system has in the main retained its past vitality although in some cases in a different form. This book investigates different kinds of 'crisis' and unpacks understandings of crisis in relation to various components in the contemporary tourism system.

The aim of this book therefore is to critically analyse the relationship between tourism and crises. The volume focuses on the roles and potential of tourism for development and relations between tourism, the environment and broad global processes of change at different levels of analysis, highlighting different types of 'crisis'. In particular it questions the general conviction that tourism-led development is a sustainable and necessarily solid platform from which to develop local, national and regional economies from a range of perspectives.

Written by leading academics in the field this book offers valuable insight into tourism's relationship with socio-cultural, environmental, economic and political crisis as well as the challenges facing future tourism development.

Gustav Visser is Professor of Human Geography at the University of the Free State, South Africa.

Sanette Ferreira is Associate Professor in Geography at Stellenbosch University, South Africa.

Routledge Critical Studies in Tourism, Business and Management

Series editors: Tim Coles, *University of Exeter, UK*, and
Michael Hall, *University of Canterbury, New Zealand*

This ground-breaking monograph series deals directly with theoretical and conceptual issues at the interface between business, management and tourism studies. It incorporates research-generated, highly specialised cutting-edge studies of new and emergent themes, such as knowledge management and innovation, that affect the future business and management of tourism. The books in this series are conceptually challenging, empirically rigorous, creative and, above all, capable of driving current thinking and unfolding debate in the business and management of tourism. This monograph series will appeal to researchers, academics and practitioners in the fields of tourism, business and management, and the social sciences.

Published titles:

Commercial Homes in Tourism (2009)
An international perspective
Edited by Paul Lynch, Alison J. McIntosh and Hazel Tucker

Sustainable Marketing of Cultural and Heritage Tourism (2010)
Deepak Chhabra

Economics of Sustainable Tourism (2010)
Edited by Fabio Cerina, Anil Markyanda and Michael McAleer

Tourism and Crisis (2013)
Edited by Gustav Visser and Sanette Ferreira

The Routledge Critical Studies in Tourism, Business and Management monograph series builds on core concepts explored in the corresponding Routledge International Studies of Tourism, Business and Management series. Series editors: Tim Coles, University of Exeter, UK, and Michael Hall, University of Canterbury, New Zealand.

Books in the series offer upper-level undergraduates and masters students comprehensive, thought-provoking yet accessible books that combine essential theory and international best practice on issues in the business and management of tourism, such as HRM, entrepreneurship, service quality management, leadership, CSR, strategy, operations, branding and marketing.

Published titles:

International Business and Tourism (2008)
Global issues, contemporary interactions
Tim Coles and Michael Hall

Carbon Management in Tourism (2010)
Mitigating the impacts on climate change
Stefan Gössling

Forthcoming title:

Tourism and Social Marketing
Michael Hall

Tourism and Crisis

Edited by
**Gustav Visser and
Sanette Ferreira**

Routledge
Taylor & Francis Group

LONDON AND NEW YORK

First published 2013
by Routledge
2 Park Square, Milton Park, Abingdon, Oxon OX14 4RN

Simultaneously published in the USA and Canada
by Routledge
711 Third Avenue, New York, NY 10017

Routledge is an imprint of the Taylor & Francis Group, an informa business

British Library Cataloguing in Publication Data
A catalogue record for this book is available from the British Library

Library of Congress Cataloging in Publication Data
Visser, Gustav.
    Tourism and crisis/Gustav Visser and Sanette Ferreira.
    p. cm.
    Includes bibliographical references and index.
    1. Tourism – Management.   2. Crisis management.
    I. Ferreira, Sanette.   II. Title.
    G155.A1V577 2013
    910.68′4 – dc23
    2012030930

ISBN: 978-0-415-53376-8 (hbk)
ISBN: 978-0-203-11404-9 (ebk)

Typeset in Times New Roman
by Florence Production Ltd, Stoodleigh, Devon, UK

Contents

Illustrations

Figures

Tables

Contributors

Tim Coles is a Professor at the University of Exeter, United Kingdom.

Larry Dwyer is a Professor at the University of New South Wales, Australia.

Sanette Ferreira is an Associate Professor at Stellenbosch University, South Africa.

C. Michael Hall is a Professor at the University of Canterbury, New Zealand.

Daniel Hammett is a Lecturer at the University of Sheffield, United Kingdom.

Holly Hunt is with the University of Johannesburg, South Africa.

John Kester is with the World Tourism Organization in Madrid, Spain.

Tanja Mihalič is a Professor at the University of Ljubljana, Slovenia.

Dieter K. Müller is a Professor at Umeå University, Sweden.

Christian M. Rogerson is a Professor at the University of Johannesburg, South Africa.

Jarkko Saarinen is a Professor at the University of Oulu, Finland.

Gustav Visser is a Professor at the University of the Free State, South Africa.

Anne-Kathrin Zschiegner is with the University of Exeter, United Kingdom.

Acknowledgements

Sanette Ferreira would like to thank the group of thirty-five international experts who made the effort to travel all the way to the southern part of the wine lands of South Africa – Stellenbosch – to discuss the relationship between tourism and development in the context of economic crisis and global change. This book is one of the outcomes of the conference that was held from 5–8 September 2010, which was organised by the Geography and Environmental Studies Departments of Stellenbosch University (SU) and the University of the Free State (UFS) on behalf of the International Geographical Union's (IGU) Commission of Tourism, Leisure and Global Change. A special word of thanks is due to our friends and core members of the Commission, Michael Hall, Allan Lew, Tim Coles, Jarkko Saarinen and Dieter Müller, who invited both of us – more than a decade ago – as 'geographers from the South' to become part of their group and discourse around tourism issues. Thanks for the confidence bestowed upon us to be the editors of this book.

For financial support for her research on tourism, Sanette Ferreira extends her thanks to the National Research Foundation, Pretoria, and the Stellenbosch University Research Committee. Lastly, she acknowledges the moral and intellectual support given by Dawie Ferreira and Gustav Visser.

Gustav Visser acknowledges financial support from the National Research Foundation and the University of the Free State Research Committee. He is also grateful for the personal and academic support of Sanette Ferreira and co-workers in the Department of Geography at the University of the Free State during the development of the conference on which this book draws.

1 Tourism and crisis

A never-ending story?

Gustav Visser and Sanette Ferreira

The global financial and economic downturn that has affected the tourism system since 2007 has cast significant attention on the role that crisis events play in tourism. The seeming increases in the impacts of economic downturns, political instability or natural disasters on tourism are arguably not a result of any increase in such events but instead illustrate the way in which the world's economies, transport systems, media and communication networks have now become so integrated that, when one destination (market) or region has been affected, then the impacts can reverberate through the entire system. Tourism is a global scale industry that increasingly impacts on the cultural, economic, social and environmental dimensions at the international, national, regional and local scale. In both developed and developing countries, tourism provides new opportunities such as employment and economic benefits to local communities. Currently, many countries see tourism development as an expedient and relatively inexpensive strategy by which to attract foreign direct investment through, for example, showcasing natural areas, cultural heritage sites and local indigenous cultures. As a result of growing tourism expansion as a key contributor to economies, many places in the world are increasingly tied to the tourism system and related cultural, social, economic and political networks.

At the same time, however, tourism is deeply influenced by its changing physical, economic and social contexts, and larger processes such as global climate change or financial instability, that present major challenges on a range of fronts. The current global economic credit crisis has underlined the impact of shifting economic fortunes on the tourism system and the vulnerability such a development strategy poses. However, the argument should be considered that 'crisis' and its relevance to tourism is potentially a continuous and ever changing challenge for places that focus on tourism-led development – economic or otherwise. What this book aims to demonstrate is that 'tourism and crisis' means different things to different people, with myriad meanings and impacts over space and through time.

The past five or so years have been framed as those of economic crisis. In many ways, this 'crisis' has been focused on the developed North. Whether or not the economic challenges of the developed North are a crisis for all, in terms of the global tourism system, needs to be considered carefully. It is suggested that, although 'the' or 'their' economic crisis is a global 'crisis' and something all countries or regions deploying tourism as a developmental tool ought to keep in mind, this is not a necessary outcome. It is equally important that the crisis has very diverse impacts on tourism systems that translate to crisis in some places but opportunities elsewhere and across different tourism product ranges.

The collection of essays assembled in this book started as a response to the 'initial' financial, or credit, crisis in the northern hemisphere during 2007. In many ways the longevity of this crisis was probably not anticipated by all when the Study Group of the International Geographical Union Commission on the Geography of Tourism and Leisure and Global Change decided to convene a meeting focusing on Tourism and Crisis at Stellenbosch in 2010. As organisers, and we dare say for many participants, we were not of the view at that time that the issues surrounding the crisis, particularly its economic dimensions and the tourism system, would last as long as they have. In some ways, it was assumed that the economies of the North would recover and that various tourism systems would be 'back in business as usual' relatively soon. Nevertheless, and as this collection of essays demonstrates, it was also evident at that meeting that there is a range of other crises that can and do impact tourism development and that are not being considered. What crises are we referring to, and where, and in which terms? A further theme of discussion was whether or not tourism might not perhaps always be in some sort of crisis, but depending on where you are and in terms of which variables we discuss crisis.

It has to be acknowledged that the response and preparedness of the tourism system to crisis has long been of interest to tourism scholars. Indeed, the significance of various crises for tourist behaviour and demand and their consequent effects on destinations has resulted in a substantial academic literature, with particular attention being given to issues of implications for crisis and risk management, assessment, forecasting, impact estimation, indicators, public relations, recovery strategies, communication and knowledge management, and security. The collection of essays in this book aims to make a modest contribution to the developing literature on tourism and crisis. It also reflects the concerns of only a handful of tourism scholars and their interests. Unlike some contributions to this field of research, we do not suggest this contribution to be definitive – by virtue of the topic at hand this book is part of an ongoing debate.

This book investigates some aspects of crisis, or more accurately crises, related to a range of tourism systems and argues that various tourism systems are always in crisis depending on where you are located, what tourism product is at stake and the temporal milieu of both a destination and the tourist-generating region. This investigation is deeply geographical for it considers spatio-temporal issues in the description and understanding of an economic system that is (or is not) always in some form of ongoing crisis. As demonstrated in this collection, there are many ways in which to view crisis in tourism. Tourism is inherently linked to capitalism and consumption: a crisis in capitalism will produce a crisis in tourism. Then again, such a statement can be tempered by specific and localised events. It might be that the world economy is growing, but there is no necessary or equal corresponding impact on the global tourism economy, and vice versa. Moreover, these impacts are locally specific and negotiated in myriad ways.

Key issues in this book are framed by C. Michael Hall in Chapter 2, which forms part of two conceptual and policy-oriented contributions. These two chapters deal in the main with the meta-environment in which the tourism system functions. Hall is of the view that there are limits to the environmental and socio-economic fixes that maintain capitalism's growth and reproduction. Indeed, the increased frequency of economic and financial crises together with growing opposition to the measures used to correct such problems suggest that some of those limits may be being reached. There are also ecological and social limits with respect to biodiversity and ecosystem loss. Tipping points appear closer than ever. But, argues Hall, from the majority of the tourism literature we would never know this to be the case. This situation may be because capitalism is not regarded as an issue, it is just there – and accepted by the academy, policy think tanks, government and consultants as such. Or, he suggests, it may be that, because the primary subjects of tourism – the tourist and their trips – are the wealthier elements of society in money and time, these commentators do not notice. Or it may be that so long as academic etc. salaries are being paid then we neither notice nor care.

Hall suggests that, while crises are seen as short term, the marketisation of everything and the continued loss of natural capital are long term – and do not fit into technical rational frameworks of crisis management and recovery. Yet even from a managerialist perspective there is a clear need to understand the way in which various crises interact with others and how this complicates the response to crisis at both a policy and business level. There is also a need to ask that, if crisis events are in fact a 'normal' part of doing business, should not industry then be the ones who respond from their own contingency funds and market actions?

In this chapter, it is argued that, although some crises appear to be recurring, it is also clear that issues keep emerging that challenge tourism. The current economic recession clearly provides many challenges and opportunities to destinations and businesses. The environment has also been an expressed concern for tourism for well over thirty years, yet there is little sign that it is becoming any more sustainable. Some natural disasters are hard to plan for, but the level of knowledge of the possibility of crisis events occurring means that contingencies can be made. The record of tourism industry learning with both the natural and economic environment is not good, however. The same old solutions are trotted out. Hall suggests that we face what might otherwise be described as a policy failure. In seeking to understand crises, far too much attention has been given to the assumption that a well-designed institution is 'good' because it facilitates cooperation and network development rather than a focus on norms, values and institutionalisation as the first and necessary steps in the assessment of what kind of changes institutional arrangements are promoting and their potential outcomes. This may be described as third-order change, or a paradigm shift. Yet any understanding of the potential for changing the framework by which we understand crisis needs to be grounded in research of the interrelationships between power, values, norms and interests and how they influence the selection of policy instruments, indicators and settings within broader frames of governance and change. This requires taking neoliberal capitalism from the background of tourism and making its interrogation essential to an understanding of contemporary tourism and its contribution and response to crisis.

In Chapter 3, Tim Coles takes these contentions further and they are made more concrete. He joins with Hall in demonstrating that the economic crisis of the past five or so years has had a profound effect on travel and tourism throughout the world, with significant implications for future tourism development. The ostensibly 'only economic' downturn has induced the restructuring and reorganisation of consumption, production and administration, the effects of which are only now beginning to be revealed and whose impacts should be more carefully considered in future research efforts as they unfold. Coles argues that terms such as 'global economic downturn', the 'financial crisis' or 'sovereign debt crisis' have been often and conveniently adopted as shorthand for the macro-economic downturn since 2007. This, however, he suggests, reflects a reductionist tendency to render the inherently complex much simpler. Umbrella terms like these imply that the effects of change have been ubiquitous, and that the same patterns of change have been – and indeed will be – experienced universally. This, Coles demonstrates, is not the case. There have been winners and losers within tourism as in other sectors of economic activity. This chapter notes that aggregated data and high-level forecasts derived from secondary sources serve an important purpose in offering, as they do, significant clues to possible trajectories for the sector. Nevertheless, and importantly so, in their coarseness they have the effect of obscuring more finely granulated features. Within the developed world, the financial crisis has dampened demand, thereby inducing a contraction in the time–space horizons of leisure tourists. Rationalisation of the supply side has accompanied this as businesses have struggled to maintain their competitiveness in altogether more testing operating environments. However, as important as raw demand may be, other more complex features related to the financial crisis, such as the availability and cost of credit, which often go unnoticed and which conspire with the unique features of many tourism enterprises, are also driving change. A more nuanced understanding is desirable – one that does not exclusively rely on modelling, and that instead also interrogates the social politics and political economy of travel and tourism.

Coles's contribution concludes with a set of issues that ought to be considered in future academic and policy research. He argues that, in relative terms, there has been far greater consideration of travel and tourism trends as they relate to the developed world, mainly in Europe and North America, since the onset of the financial crisis. In contrast, there has been far less attention on emergent markets, newly industrialised countries and states to the south of the Tropic of Cancer. In some cases, these economies appear to have been some of the (relative) beneficiaries from the redistributive effects of recent times. A more intensive spatio-temporal treatment of the current episode is proposed, and he highlights a range of issues that emanate from such a suggestion. In many of the contributions that follow, greater balance to such issues in the developing world is provided.

Chapter 4, and subsequent contributions, focus on more empirical interpretations and understandings of tourism and crisis. In addition, a number of the investigations aim to consider travel and tourism trends in the developing world context and against the backdrop of crisis. Daniel Hammett's contribution is concerned with forms of crisis in destination representations in the media in tourism-generating regions. This theme is of relevance to all tourism destinations, in both developed and developing countries. He frames his contribution with the observation that South Africa's transition from a pariah state to a consolidating democracy, reintegrated into the global community of nations, has been tremendously beneficial to the country's burgeoning tourism industry. Prior to 1994, South Africa's tourism sector was domestically orientated, constrained by international boycotts, hostile media framing and a negative destination image. Since 1994, the changing domestic socio-political situation as well as shifts in global geopolitics, advances in transport and technology and changes in the global economy have increased international travel overall, and to South Africa in particular. Consequently, South Africa has invested heavily in developing a tourism strategy that encompasses domestic, regional and international tourism and the promotion of a positive destination image through specific public relations campaigns, interactions with the media and the hosting of a series of spotlight or 'mega' events.

South Africa's destination image, like most countries and regions globally, is not purely constructed from the framing and content of these promotional practices. Tourists construct their image/imagination of potential destinations from a range of sources that are interpreted through existing knowledge and frames of reference. News media are one such important source of information about distant locations and potential tourist destinations. The content of news coverage is significant: the often politicised framing of reporting and content selection provides partial representations of people and places. These representational practices often utilise, implicitly or explicitly, discursive themes rooted in ideology and reiterating historical and colonial stereotypes and preconceptions. Potential travellers' conceptions of destinations are therefore produced through subjective processes of interpretation and negotiation that draw upon the information provided through media sources.

Hammett investigates the media framing and discursive representations of South Africa within British newspapers (keeping in mind that the UK is South Africa's main overseas source market). The hosting of the 2010 FIFA World Cup provided a moment of heightened press attention on South Africa, with the tourist industry hopeful that this coverage would produce a positive destination image. The South African government had hoped that successfully hosting this spectacle event would encourage new media framings of coverage of the country, instigating a shift away from (neo)colonial stereotypes and discursive constructs. Shifts in the framing and content of English media coverage of South Africa in the build-up to and duration of the tournament demonstrate that, despite continued salience of particular, self-perpetuating and discursive constructions and perceptions, there was evidence of a more positive media frame emerging in certain sections of the media. This emergent narrative acknowledged the success of South Africa's hosting of the tournament and witnessed the emergence of a more vocal, critical element directed towards FIFA's quasi-authoritarian control of the sport and major tournaments. The concern addressed in Hammett's contribution is how post-tournament British media framed South Africa in their reporting. As British media attention on South Africa declined after the tournament, were the discursive themes of crime and fear, pre-modernity and race still dominant – or was a more positive frame perpetuated? Newspaper content relating to South Africa is analysed for two two-month periods at six- and twelve-month intervals after the World Cup to ascertain the dominant discursive themes and media frames deployed. This analysis demonstrates a return towards a generally negative and self-perpetuating media frame, with negative implications for South Africa's destination image.

Retaining the focus on the World Cup theme, Chapter 5 investigates how this event has provided a real opportunity to give life to the ninth recommendation of the United Nations World Tourism Organization's (UNWTO) *Roadmap for Recovery*, namely 'to improve tourism promotion and capitalize on major events'. Sanette Ferreira untangles the role of this event during a time in which South Africa has not been immune to the effects of global economic recession. The global recession could not have come at a worse time for the South African hotel industry – while the supply of new hotel rooms surged by 10 per cent, demand dropped by 4 per cent. Average hotel occupancies fell to a ten-year low of 60.4 per cent in 2009, down from more than 70 per cent in the boom years of 2006–8. Although she paints a picture of inflated expectations, since winning the bid to host, the World Cup has helped the South African economy to resist some of the effects of the economic recession.

While the global travel industry experienced a decline of 4 per cent in 2009 as traveller markets reeled from the effects of the global financial crisis, the South African pre-World Cup context (or pregnancy effect) saw an increase in meetings, incentives, conferences and exhibitions (MICE) tourism, and the hosting of three sports events, among others, buffered South Africa from at least some of the effects of the world economic recession and postponed the real effect to the months following the event. The duration of the 'beneficial phase' had already started in the years before winning the bid, when South Africa was 'preparing and competing' to host the event and the country would be capitalising even more in the years to come on all the new infrastructure and tourism superstructure that were developed for the event. Ferreira explains the costs and long-term development goals, direct and indirect economic benefits, the oversupply of stadia and luxury hotel rooms, tangible and intangible benefits and missed opportunities. In her analysis, she reiterates that it will be a great omission to leave out the role of the Fédération Internationale de Football Association (FIFA). FIFA was able to extract much of the financial benefit of hosting the tournament from bidding countries – thinking of power relationships and political economy. South Africa as a developing country has taken all the risk, while FIFA banked the profit.

Chapter 6 considers the impact of low consumer confidence and its generation of crisis in regional tourism systems. Tanja Mihalič and her co-investigators work from the position that tourism is sensitive to financial and economic crisis on both its supply and demand sides. It is suggested that the global financial crisis has reduced tourism business and consumer confidence to almost record low levels. They argue that many studies using world-level data and some regional data have shown correlations among tourism flows, the economic crisis cycle and tourism confidence. This chapter attempts to study the current economic crisis impact on tourism flows and confidence in the UNWTO's largest (in a number of countries), yet developing tourism region. Its aim is to analyse the tourism crises caused by financial and economic factors, not only from quantitative and qualitative crisis perspectives, but from the side of the power potential of management tools for predicting tourism confidence in the circumstances of such a crisis. It studies the potential of the Tourism Confidence Index (TCI) to predict tourism demand and assesses its usefulness for tourism stakeholders. The results of this investigation generally confirm the usefulness of confidence surveys in predicting tourism demand. Yet, the regional-level analysis for Africa shows that African inbound tourism, in contrast to other regions and world tourism, did not follow the typical economic crisis cycle shape. Different African countries have reacted to the current economic crisis in various ways.

In Chapter 7, Dieter K. Müller continues the theme that, thus far, the inter-relationship between crisis and tourism is poorly understood and that there are many different inputs to such a position. He argues that, although there is substantial research on the impact of economic and financial downturns on tourism, it seems that there is a lack of understanding regarding what could be considered crisis and a 'normal state'. Joining Hall and Coles's contributions, it is argued that the interrelationship between crisis, particularly in the economic sector, and tourism is not unidirectional. Instead, tourism is often promoted as a solution to economic crisis, not least in peripheral areas, in both developed and developing world contexts. Drawing on Hall's suggestions it is also highlighted that this idea is not by any means new, but that tourism has often failed to deliver what has been promised. Moreover, even when tourism development is successful, there are warnings that it is just another staple industry in peripheral economies based on resource extraction and, thus, a dependency on extractive industries is simply exchanged for a dependency on tourism.

Müller argues that a common problem in this context is that research seldom acknowledges the long-term dynamics of industrial development. Instead, it focuses on crisis and its immediate impacts on communities, economy and other industries. This notion coincides with and is reminiscent of Hall's comment on the 'normal state of things'. For example, in economic history and economic geography, cyclical development is assumed to be the most common development of economies. Accordingly, a 'normal state' never occurs. Particularly with reference to peripheral economies dependent on the extraction of natural resources, boom and bust cycles have been recorded. Consecutively, periods of crisis and economic decline are frequently followed by periods of recovery or economic growth. Globalisation implies that peripheral economies are tied into complex global markets and networks with specific sets of rules and preconditions for different industries, hence causing different preconditions for innovation. Thus, a decline in one industry does not necessarily imply a decline in all others. Peripheral economies are traditionally based on the extraction of natural resources such as forests or minerals. This chapter aims to address the interrelationship between these industries and tourism from a labour market perspective. This is achieved by analysing labour market changes in northern Sweden from 1990 to 2007.

In Chapter 8, Gustav Visser retains the focus on tourism in the periphery of tourism in industrial and increasingly post-industrial societies. Against the backdrop of tourism as a keenly deployed developmental tool in the policies of a range of economies, this chapter demonstrates a crisis in the manner tourism products are marketed relative to stated national economic and tourism development strategies. The chapter assesses to what degree South Africa's marketing strategy has changed over the past decade and its potential to address a tourism space economy that is highly uneven. It is suggested that a decade after South African Tourism's (SAT's) commitment to a better distribution of tourists within the region there remains a significant schism between the marketing strategies and marketing information presented by SAT relative to the stated objectives and mandate of the organisation. It is suggested that SAT is still not encouraging the redress of the uneven South African tourism space economy through its current marketing material. In fact, the spatial implications of the contents of their marketing initiatives could potentially aggravate, rather than address, the development of an already highly uneven tourism space economy.

In Chapter 9, Tim Coles and Anne-Kathrin Zschiegner investigate responses to climate change mitigation during recessionary times. Their contribution examines this question in the context of a study of climate change mitigation and business innovation among accommodation providers in the Southwest of England, although this investigation's relevance is universal. In this contribution, it is argued that, through the Stern Report, the United Kingdom has occupied a prominent position in global discourse on climate change, and it has set itself targets for emissions that are more ambitious than its obligations under the Kyoto Protocol.

Coles and Zschiegner argue that a deeper understanding of mitigation among tourism businesses requires greater consideration of the political economy of climate change, and in particular how features in the macro-business environment, such as economic and electoral cycles, influence business responses. Whatever the precise nature and length of the current episode, a long-term environmental crisis, apparently requiring immediate response, has been running in parallel with a much shorter-term economic crisis. This chapter demonstrates that crises do not occur in isolation, and that they can be subtly and intricately connected. They can compound or ameliorate one another, resulting in outcomes that are not always obvious or predictable. Economic cycles in coming decades will influence the ability and willingness among businesses (and citizens) to respond to climate change, to meet the targets set by scientists and politicians, and hence to adapt to future change as it unfolds. Mitigation may have been the poor relation of adaptation so far in tourism studies, however current speculation on the long-term effects of climate change may be nothing more than that without a clearer understanding of the unfolding response from businesses in the tourism sector both currently and moving forward.

In Chapter 10, Holly Hunt and Christian M. Rogerson draw on the notion that a range of crises surrounding the adoption of outward-oriented neo-liberal development strategies, touted as an important source of outward-oriented growth in many parts of developing Africa, Asia and Latin America, should be acknowledged and anticipated critically. They highlight that during the 1990s international tourism garnered widespread currency in development literature as one of an array of new 'growth sectors' believed to exhibit much promise in developing countries based upon their so-termed 'comparative advantages'. Nevertheless, the development literature pointed also to several inherent dangers that accompanied the embrace of neo-liberal planning strategies. Past export-oriented development models had often been associated with vicious cycles of polarisation and repression. During the 1980s, dependency theories showed the existence of high rates of leakage associated with international tourism in developing countries. The appearance of such dangers highlights that national governments and policy makers must proceed cautiously with tourism-led development strategies, and especially so if growth in the volume of international tourism is not to be accompanied by many of the problems historically linked with outward-oriented development strategies.

Hunt and Rogerson argue that one challenge for tourism-led development strategies is to enhance the density of both intersectoral and local linkages by integrating tourism more closely into local, regional and national economic development. They draw on the idea that strong government actions may be required in order to devise and implement policies to secure the most benefits from potential intersectoral linkages. Against this backdrop, the aim of the chapter is to examine aspects of this important challenge and to present findings from recent empirical research concerning the extent and depth of linkages between the tourism and agriculture sectors in rural southern Africa. In this chapter, specific attention is upon the luxury safari lodge sector, one of the main assets for contemporary tourism-led economic development for several African countries. Their three country case studies are Botswana, South Africa and Zambia, all leading developing tourism economies in the southern African region.

Chapter 11 focuses on the role of tourism in, and its relations with, local communities. In this contribution, Jarkko Saarinen argues that, traditionally, the role and development impacts of tourism and related patterns of mobility and non-local consumption have been governed by market-driven industry and/or state authorities and other public sector institutions. Since the 1990s, however, there have been practically and theoretically driven attempts to transfer tourism growth towards the principles of sustainable development, and several models aiming for the devolution of power in development responsibilities have been proposed. These models try to give more authority to local actors, for example communities and other local institutions. The aim is to minimise negative impacts and maximise positive outcomes by providing local control over tourism development and resulting benefits. Especially in the Global South, tourism has been given an important role as a policy tool for community development, providing jobs and economic benefits for the poor and previously disadvantaged peoples. This kind of emphasis has highlighted the role of community-based natural resource management and especially community-based and pro-poor tourism initiatives. These models are based on partly different assumptions but, in general, they aim to promote the participation of local communities in tourism development.

Based on this background, the chapter evaluates the current main ideas and challenges of participation and benefit sharing in tourism development by utilising the basic premises of community-based and pro-poor tourism. The empirical examples are based on previous studies focusing on tourism operations and impacts in Kaokoland, northwest Namibia. The aim is to discuss the role of local people in tourism and the nature of tourism operations based on ethnic village tourism and the attractiveness of OvaHimbas (Himba). The OvaHimba communities have faced several environmental and socio-political crises in the past decades, which have made them vulnerable in nationally and internationally driven development processes. Here vulnerability refers to the degree to which a community is susceptible to, or even unable to cope with, the opposing effects of change, and how the effectiveness of certain adaptive mechanisms acts as a base for adaptive capacity. Thus, vulnerability influences the ability to adapt tourism and related changes and vice versa, and the relation between vulnerability and adaptation is defined by power issues between the industry and communities, for example.

The current economic recession has been foremost in the minds of many tourism researchers, policy makers, government officials, tourism service providers and those whose livelihoods are dependent upon the tourism system. However, as is suggested in this book, the investigatory net, insofar as the relationship between the tourism systems and crisis is concerned, needs to be cast wider. The tourism system is impacted by many factors: economic crisis is but one variable and clearly provides many challenges, but there are also opportunities for tourism destinations and related economic systems. Currently, the dimensions of the economic crisis in the developed North have morphed into increasing economic, social and political instability in a range of regions, not the least of which are Greece, Portugal and Spain – all of which are key role players in the global tourism system. As suggested in this collection, we need to be cautious in reducing those elements that impact tourism to mere economics. On the other side of the Mediterranean, the Arab Spring has thrown established tourism destinations such as Egypt and Tunisia into disarray. Again, it might be intuitive to suggest that, once the political environments of these countries have 'normalised', tourism will transcend the current crises there. On the whole, these are likely to be (relatively speaking) short-term crisis events.

The conceptual danger in the tourism and crisis debate is to assume that, once these particular crises are addressed, along with a range of other issues such as regional, cultural, religious or social instability, tourism will bounce back. The point that this book aims to underline is that this is not necessarily the case. Tourism is forever in crisis somewhere, and for different reasons that are separately – or collectively – bound to the realities of different locations globally.

There are, of course, long-term challenges that face the global tourism system and that will frame the tourism and crisis nexus globally, but their impacts are negotiated locally and in different ways. As seen in a number of contributions in this book, the broader economic system of capitalism is seen as currently unstable, inducing a range of crises in tourism systems in a range of settings. Some would argue that capitalism is in a process of reorganisation. However, whether there is lesser or greater emphasis on neoliberal capitalism as the outcome of such a transition will nevertheless impact the tourism system in a range of ways, many of which tourism studies have not yet contemplated. Whichever directions the transition in capitalism takes, it will nevertheless present both challenges and opportunities for different tourist destinations, tourism products and product providers – and for different reasons. A further long-term challenge, which will certainly present crises for a range of tourism systems, is related to climate change, an issue that has not received much attention in this collection. Again, the conceptual challenge is not to fall into the trap that climate change is a necessary crisis for the tourism system as a whole. We would argue that, while climate change as currently predicted will hold extraordinarily negative impacts for humanity as it currently functions, there are nevertheless opportunities in such a dismal context.

Tourism is a global system of production and consumption that, directly or indirectly, impacts the lives of hundreds of millions of people across the globe. We argue that there is an urgent need to extend our research, policy and management focus to understand the tourism and crisis nexus more fully.

2 Financial crises in tourism and beyond

Connecting economic, resource and environmental securities

C. Michael Hall

Introduction

The ongoing series of national and international financial crises and economic downturns since 2007 have affected tourism on a global scale. Although its effects were most noticeable in 2009 when the World Tourism Organization (UNWTO 2011) estimated that international tourist arrivals fell by 4 per cent, these effects have continued to play out at various destination, national and regional scales. Significantly, in the same period international tourism has also been affected by a number of other crises, including the impact of the ash cloud from the Eyjafjallajokull eruption in Iceland on trans-Atlantic and European aviation, the Japanese earthquakes and tsunami of 2011, the severe flooding in Thailand and the Christchurch, New Zealand, earthquake sequence of 2010–12 (Orchistron 2012; Rittichainuwat 2012). Such natural disasters are complemented by increased concerns over the effects of anthropogenic global environmental change, especially with respect to the impacts of high-magnitude weather events (Scott *et al.* 2012). Nevertheless, as Hall suggests, the seeming increase of crises in the form of economic and financial downturns, political instability or natural disasters on tourism

> are arguably not a result of any increase in such events but instead illustrate the way in which the world's economies, transport systems, and media and communication networks have now become so integrated that when one destination or region has been affected then the impacts can reverberate through the entire system.
>
> (2010a: 401)

Many of the crises that affect tourism are more correctly termed 'crisis events' that are of a specific duration and occur in an identifiable time and space, although they may have long-term impacts (Ren 2000). The notion of an event is significant because the limited duration of a high-impact crisis event only serves to enhance the attention a crisis may receive in the media and enhance the perception that the event is of concern and should be responded to (Smith 1990, 2005; Greening and Johnson 2007). The factors that contribute to a crisis may therefore be part of an issue–attention cycle, meaning that the elements that contribute to a crisis may exist on an ongoing basis but they do not constitute a crisis for a particular group of stakeholders until (a) they are aware of the elements, and/or (b) the crisis event occurs in a particular part of the global political-economic system (Hall 2002). Indeed, the longer a crisis occurs the more it becomes part of 'normal' affairs and instead becomes part of the everyday background. This is certainly the case with the political ecology of the news whereby major issues, such as biodiversity loss, climate change or famine, are never actually solved but rise and fall with respect to media coverage and public awareness.

The response and preparedness of the tourism industry with regard to crisis has long been of interest to tourism scholars. The significance of various crises for tourist behaviour and demand and their consequent effects on destinations has resulted in a substantial academic literature (Beeton 2001, 2002; Hall *et al.* 2004; Ritchie 2004, 2008, 2009; Laws and Prideaux 2005; Glaesser 2006; Mansfeld and Pizam 2006; Carlsen and Liburd 2007; Laws *et al.* 2007; Cohen and Neal 2010; Henderson 2010; Korstanje 2011), with particular attention being given to crisis, disaster and risk management (Anderson 2006; Pforr and Hosie 2007; Xu and Grunewald 2009), assessment (Tsai and Chen 2010), forecasting (Prideaux *et al.* 2003; Lean and Smyth 2009), impact estimation (Dwyer *et al.* 2006), indicators (Sausmarez 2007), public relations (Stanbury *et al.* 2005), recovery strategies (Scott *et al.* 2007), communication and knowledge management (Blackman *et al.* 2011) and security (Hall *et al.* 2004). This chapter provides another dimension of the tourism crisis literature by extending previous work on the relative emphasis given to the different types of crisis that are referred to in the tourism literature (Hall 2010a), but more particularly seeks to draw out some of the potential interplay between the different crises and their interdependencies.

Crisis events and hypermobility

Many of the crisis events that affect tourism have been occurring for millennia. Yet what has changed is the dramatic growth in the scale of tourism and related human movement to the extent that the developed world is often described as hypermobile. The definition of hypermobility as 'the maximization of physical movement' (Khisty and Zeitler 2001: 598) is a useful way to characterise the vast growth in temporary mobility in aggregate form in some societies as well as a relatively small number of extremely frequent travellers within them (Gössling *et al.* 2009).

There have been substantial changes in mobility since the development of mass commercial aviation in the late 1960s and early 1970s. This has meant that there has been a transition in aviation from being a luxury form of mobility available only for the wealthy few to being a relatively cheap means of mass transportation for many middle-class leisure and business travellers in industrialised countries (Gössling *et al.* 2009). Shifts in access as a result of improved affordability and availability also correspond with fundamental changes in perceptions of distance, place and space (e.g. Janelle 1969; Urry 2000; Gössling 2002; Adey *et al.* 2007). For many people, what was once a distant non-routine environment is now part of an everyday routine environment formed by both direct and virtual contact and experience (Hall 2005a, 2005b; Coles and Hall 2006). As Hall argued, the routinised space–time paths of those living at the start of this century

> are not the same as those of people in 1984 when Giddens was writing or in the 1960s when Hägerstrand was examining routine daily space–time trajectories. Instead, because of advances in transport and communication technology, for a substantial proportion of the population in developed countries or for elites in developing countries being able to travel long distances to engage in leisure behaviour (what one would usually describe as tourism) is now a part of their routine activities.
>
> (2005a: 24)

The significance of globalised mobility and new routine environments is that the more people participate in such long-distance movement and the more destinations and places depend on such relatively fast, large-scale movements in economic terms, the more perceptions of crisis develop when such 'normal' movement is stopped or slowed down. As Jenkins commented with respect to winter travel 'chaos' in the UK in December 2009 as a result of heavy snowfalls:

> My solution to winter travel chaos? Don't travel . . . Yet powered movement is a craving no government is willing to curb. Hypermobility is the totem of personal liberty . . . Before the invention of jet travel, the idea of a winter holiday was unthinkable for any but the very rich.
>
> (2009)

The notion of a crisis in tourism can therefore be partly understood in the context of the difficulties that tourists face in travelling or with respect to the problems facing tourism businesses (Ross 2005). But the term is arguably more widely used in conjunction with the effects of a crisis event at a destination (Gasperoni and Dall'Aglio 1992; Gunlu and Aktas 2006), sector (especially aviation) (Campiranon and Arcodia 2007; Niininen and Gatsou 2007) or at a national or global scale (Li *et al.* 2010). Yet the notion of a crisis in tourism, as with cognate terms such as 'security', cannot be seen in isolation.

Hall *et al.* (2003) stressed that the notion of security as an individual and collective political concept had expanded to include socio-economic and environmental issues. These include the economy (Gurr 1985), human rights, welfare and energy resources (Bielecki 2002), the environment (Myers 1993; Stern 1995), food (Cohen and Pinstrup-Andersen 1998) and water (Gössling *et al.* 2012) as part of the discourse on security (Hall *et al.* 2003). If security is the flipside of crisis, then we can also expect to see a number of different forms of crisis recognised in the academic and research literature. For example, there are extensive literatures on global crisis with respect to the financial system (Crotty 2009), economy

(Stiglitz 2000), energy (Li 2007), the environment (Saurin 2001; Wilshusen *et al.* 2002), food (Loewenberg 2008), health (Chen *et al.* 2004), population and demographics (Peterson 1999; Sinding 2000), water (Duda and El-Ashry 2000) and their interdependence, which is often also seen in political terms (Gills 2008). However, the connections between tourism crises and these broader understandings of crisis and security are usually not explored in the tourism literature (Hall *et al.* 2003). Therefore, the next section looks at the different ways in which tourism-related crises are perceived.

Tourism crises

International tourism arrivals had an average annual growth of 6.5 per cent between 1950 and 2005, although the overall average rate of growth has been gradually dropping, so that the average annual growth between 1990 and 2000 was 4.6 per cent and between 2000 and 2005 was 3.3 per cent. Given such growth levels Hall (2010a) suggested that any period where international tourism numbers increase by only 2 per cent or less often appears to be described as a crisis for the industry at the global level (WTO 1988; UNWTO 2006a; Papatheodorou *et al.* 2010). Hall's (2010a) observation reflects the extent to which the tourism industry, whether at the global, national or even destination scale appears to assume that growth is normal.

Although the relative growth in international and, to a lesser extent, domestic tourist arrivals provides an important benchmark for tourism, tourism crises are usually interrelated with other broader crisis events in economics and finance, politics and energy (Hall 2010a). Table 2.1 provides a timeline for various crisis events in tourism from the early 1970s to the present day. Tourism downturns are strongly related to economic recessions and financial problems at a global scale or in major travel markets, although there are often lag effects. That this link exists should not be surprising because of the role that levels of disposable income and economic confidence play in the capacity and willingness to travel (Hall 2005a). Indeed, a substantial weakness in much analysis of so-called crises in tourism is the extent to which they are related to broader business cycles, and the role that other events, particularly related to energy costs and political instability, may have in influencing those cycles (Schulmeister 1978; Dhariwai 2005; Guizzardi and Mazzocchi 2010).

Although there have been a substantial number of publications that have looked at the tourism crisis and how it should be managed, what has not been previously assessed is the extent to which different forms of crisis are identified in the tourism literature. Table 2.2, developed from the work of Hall (2010a), indicates the results of a content analysis of the CABI Leisure Tourism abstract database for publications on crisis, tourism crisis and other types of crises (financial, economic, environmental, ecological, biodiversity, energy, oil, political and water). Publications were counted in the table if the search term was found in the title, abstract or keyword information. As of April 2012, there were 118,000 records on the database. This was 8,000 more than in Hall's (2010a) analysis.

Table 2.1 Crisis events affecting international tourist arrivals

Year	International tourist arrivals (m.)	Change over previous year (%)	Economic recession/ financial crisis	Oil/energy issues	Political issues	Health issues	Natural/environmental disasters
1974	205.7*		W. Europe, N. America	1973–4 oil crisis	Arab oil embargo		
1975	222.3*	8.1					
1976	227.4*	2.3					
1977	246.1*	8.2					
1978	260.1•	5.7					
1979	272.1*	4.6		Energy crisis	Revolution in Iran; USSR invades Afghanistan		
1980	278.1*	2.0	US		Iraq/Iran war		
1981	278.6*	0.2	W. Europe, N. America				
1982	276.9	–0.6	W. Europe, N. America				
1983	281.8	1.8					
1984	306.8	8.9					
1985	320.1	4.3					
1986	330.2	3.2					
1987	359.7	8.9					
1988	385.0	7.0			1st intifada		
1989	410.1	6.5					
1990	439.5	7.2	Global	Oil shock	1st Gulf War		
1991	442.5	0.7	Global				

Year	Arrivals (millions)	Growth (%)	Region	Economic	Political	Health	Environmental
1992	479.8	8.4					Hurricane Andrew
1993	495.7	3.3	Global				
1994	519.8	4.9	Global				
1995	540.6	4.0					
1996	575.0	6.4					
1997	598.6	4.1	Asia				SE Asian haze
1998	616.7	3.0	Global				
1999	639.6	3.7					
2000	687.0	7.4			2nd intifada		
2001	686.7	0.0	Global		9/11 attacks	UK foot and mouth	
2002	707.0	2.9	Global			SARS	
2003	694.6	−1.7	Global		2nd Gulf War	SARS	
2004	765.1	10.1					Indonesian tsunami
2005	806.8*	5.5			Bali bombings		Hurricane Katrina; US heat wave; SE Asian haze
2006	842*	4.5			Israeli invasion of Lebanon		European heat wave
2007	898*	6.0	Global				
2008	917*	2.0	Global	Oil high of $147			
2009	882*	−4.0	Global			Swine flu pandemic	European and US cold wave
2010	939*	6.6*	Global	Oil back above $80			
2011	980*	4.4*	Europe, N. America			Potential Greek default and pressure on euro and EU	Japanese tsunami and earthquakes; New Zealand earthquakes
2012	>1,000*		Europe	Potential collapse of euro			

Sources: UNWTO (2006a, 2006b, 2007, 2008, 2009, 2011, 2012).
Notes: * Estimates only. Global recession: a slowdown in global growth to 3 per cent or less.

Table 2.2 Crises in relation to tourism in abstracts in the Leisure Tourism database

Year	Crises	Tourism crises	Financial crises	Economic crises	Environ-mental crises	Eco-logical crises	Bio-diversity crises	Energy crises	Oil crises	Political crises	Water crises
1977	2	–	–	–	–	–	–	1			
1978	5	–	–	–	–	–	–	5			
1979	1	–	–	–	–	–	–	2			
1980	7	–	–	–	–	–	–	4	2		
1981	7	–	–	1	–	–	–	4	1		
1982	12	–	1	2	–	–	–	1	3		
1983	9	–	–	6	–	–	–	1	2		
1984	9	–	–	2	–	–	–	1			
1985	12	–	–	5	–	–	–	1			
1986	7	–	1	1	–	–	–	–	–	1	
1987	9	–	–	1	–	–	–	–	2		
1988	15	–	–	4	–	–	–	–	1		
1989	11	–	–	3	–	–					
1990	20	–	–	1	1	–					
1991	28	–	1	1	1	–					
1992	21	1	–	–	–	1	–	–	–	1	
1993	20	–	1	3	–	–	–	–	–	1	

Year										
1994	10	–	1	–	1	–	–	–	–	1	1
1995	13	–	2	2	2	–	–	–	–	1	1
1996	10	–	–	2	–	–	–	–	–	1	1
1997	18	–	1	5	1	–	–	–	–	–	–
1998	18	1	4	3	–	–	–	–	–	1	–
1999	48	1	11	11	1	–	–	1	–	–	–
2000	18	–	4	6	–	–	–	–	1	–	–
2001	15	–	3	1	1	1	–	–	–	–	–
2002	41	2	4	2	1	1	–	–	–	1	1
2003	41	2	3	1	1	–	–	–	–	1	–
2004	30	6	–	3	1	–	–	–	–	1	1
2005	46	2	3	4	–	–	1	–	1	1	–
2006	79	9	10	4	–	–	–	–	1	–	–
2007	93	12	4	3	1	–	–	–	–	1	–
2008	52	1	4	4	1	–	–	–	–	1	1
2009	60	1	11	19	–	1	1	–	–	–	–
2010	117	5	26	33	1	–	4	–	–	1	2
2011	72	4	13	13	–	–	–	–	–	1	–
Total	966	47	108	146	13	3	6	20	13	12	6

Note: Abstract count as of April 2012.

Table 2.2 reinforces Hall's (2010a) findings that the majority of research in tourism on crisis concentrates on economic and financial crises. Given the interest in tourism on sustainability and global environmental change there are surprisingly few papers that explicitly focus on environmental crisis (Gössling and Hall 2006). Table 2.2 also suggests that research in some areas of crisis in tourism is significantly influenced by particular periods of recession or by crisis events such as the terrorist attacks of 9/11 or sudden oil shocks. However, this then raises significant questions as to the reactive nature of tourism research versus the development of greater predictive capacity and theory generation (Hall 2010a).

Despite the expansion of the security concept to include social and environmental concerns (Hall *et al.* 2003), no publications in the database have a significant focus on 'food crisis', 'population crisis' or 'climate crisis'. The latter is an interesting point given that, although climate change (for example) is a growing area of tourism research (Hall *et al.* 2012), it is not usually written of as being a 'crisis', although the separate effects of high-impact, low-frequency weather events may be (Scott *et al.* 2012). The reason for this may be that, for a crisis to be recognised, a particular event has to occur or a threshold has to be passed that specifically affects tourism, for example the loss of an attraction or extinction of charismatic megafauna or megaflora on which specific destinations may depend (Hall *et al.* 2011). Cumulative and gradual environmental change that does not attract media attention or politicians, although significant from an ecological perspective, does not necessarily constitute a significant, immediate crisis for tourism that may pose long-term issues with respect to specific attractions (Hall 2010b). Water issues also receive very limited attention (Araus 2004; Howard 2008; Gössling *et al.* 2012), while the notion of tourism's connection to an environmental crisis is also only given very limited recognition (Wilson 1992; Huntly *et al.* 2005; Remis and Hardin 2009), even though tourism is often portrayed as a major mechanism to prevent the loss of biodiversity (Hall 2010b). In terms of other areas of concern with resource security it is noticeable that literature that links tourism with an 'energy crisis' (Moncrief *et al.* 1977; Holder 1978; Waters 1980) or an 'oil crisis' (Wolfe 1982) primarily comes from research conducted in response to the oil shocks of the 1970s and 1980s and not more contemporary concerns with energy security and peak oil (Scott *et al.* 2012).

Natural disasters and anthropogenic environmental problems are given some significance because of their impacts on travel and tourism at various scales as well as their potential to affect perceptions of destinations (World Tourism Organization 1998). Crises covered include the Southeast Asian smoke haze (Henderson 1999a), earthquakes (Huang and Min 2002; Yang *et al.* 2008; Orchistron 2012), volcanoes (Aguirre 2007), tsunamis (Reddy 2005; Sharpley 2005; Carlsen and Hughes 2007; Calgaro and Lloyd 2008; Cohen 2010), cyclones (Prideaux *et al.* 2007), hurricanes (Baade and Matheson 2007) and bushfires (Armstrong and Ritchie 2007; Cioccio and Michael 2007). Concerns that arise at the interface of environmental and human-created crises include the role of tourism in the spread of pandemics and disease and the consequent effects of biosecurity measures.

Considerable attention has been given to specific crises, including the 2001 UK foot and mouth disease outbreak (Sharpley and Craven 2001; Frisby 2002; Miller and Ritchie 2003), SARS (Henderson 2003; Henderson and Ng 2004; Zeng *et al.* 2005; Gu and Wall 2007; Tew *et al.* 2008) and influenza (Page *et al.* 2006), as well as the development of biosecurity strategies that recognise the role of tourism (Hall 2003, 2005c; Peacock and Worner 2006; Trees 2009; Hall and Baird 2013).

The areas with the most substantial focus on crisis in tourism are finance and economics, although it is noticeable that the term 'financial crisis' did not really reach the lexicon of tourism until the Asian financial crisis of the late 1980s (Hall 2010a). Much of the research undertaken on the impacts of the Asian financial crisis on tourism was undertaken at a national or destination level (Funck 1999; Guo and Yao 1999; Henderson 1999a, 1999b, 2002; Prideaux 1999; Chen 2000; Gu 2000; King 2000; Law 2001a, 2001b; Rittichainuwat *et al.* 2002; Sausmarez 2003), although some research was also conducted at a sectoral scale (Henderson 1999c; Kontogeorgopoulos 1999; Raab and Schwer 2003). The terrorist attacks of 9/11 in the USA are also a significant area of research in terms of their financial impacts and subsequent recovery strategies (Enz and Canina 2002; Litvin and Alderson 2003; Blunk *et al.* 2006).

Research on economic crisis has gone hand in hand with major regional and global periods of recession and downturn in international tourism. Work has broadly occurred in three main periods: the economic downturn that occurred in Western Europe and North America in the early 1980s (Boerjan and Vanhove 1984; Clouston 1984; Gaullier 1985; Bodson and Stafford 1988; World Tourism Organization 1988), the recession of the late 1990s, which was first Asian in focus and then became global in scope, becoming entwined with the effects of 9/11 and the subsequent so-called 'war on terror' (Stafford and Sarrasin 2003; Akal 2005; Okumus and Karamustafa 2005) and the recession that has affected most of the world, but particularly Europe, since 2008 (Smeral 2009, 2010; Barda and Sardianou 2010; Papatheodorou *et al.* 2010; Ritchie *et al.* 2010; Song and Lin 2010). Curiously, the one recession and tourism downturn that did not attract significant academic analysis was that of the early 1990s, which was also associated with the effects of the first Gulf War and the accompanying oil shock, even though this attracted substantial industry concerns with respect to a crisis (Travel Industry Association of America 1991).

One of the topics that is relatively underexplored in tourism is that of political crisis and instability (Hall 1994; Jones *et al.* 1998; Ioannides and Apostolopoulos 1999; Bhandari 2004; Assaker 2008). Even though there is a substantial litera-ture on the effects of terrorism on tourism, these have usually been discussed more in terms of their economic and marketing issues rather than within a broader political science framework (Sönmez *et al.* 1999). This means that the potential contribution of tourism studies to policy making is usually framed in technical-rational terms (Blake and Sinclair 2003) rather than engaging with the way policy arenas actually operate, especially with respect to the manner in which different sets of crises or policy problems are highly interrelated (Richter 1999; Hitchcock and Putra 2005; Hall 2011). Indeed, the overall lack of awareness of processes of policy formulation and agenda setting in tourism (Hall 2002) and the focus on technical-rational solutions to crises means that many crisis events in tourism – and their potential solutions – seem destined to be repeated ad nauseam. For example, the solutions of the International Air Transport Association (IATA) (1992) to 'airlines in crisis' – deregulation, fewer taxes, and reductions in air traffic congestion – were the same in 1992 as they were in the economic and financial crises of the early and late 2000s.

Repeating crises: a never-ending story?

The repetition of responses, as well as the crises that underlie them, suggest that there are significant issues with the capacities to understand let alone solve tourism-related crises. Arguably, this situation occurs because of (at least) two related dimensions of much tourism scholarship. The first is the dominance of much of the tourism crisis literature by the technocratic ideology of managerialism, which views analytical tools, developed to help managers make decisions, as ends in themselves. The second is the need for more fundamental analysis of the relationships between different types of crises and the embeddedness of tourism within them, particularly its role in reinforcing socio-economic institutions, structures and relationships, that is, contemporary capitalism.

At the end of 2009, we were in the midst of the worst financial crisis since the Great Depression (Crotty 2009). This crisis is the latest phase of the evolution of financial markets under the radical financial and economic deregulation process that began in the late 1970s. This evolution has taken the form of cycles in which deregulation accompanied by rapid financial innovation stimulates powerful financial booms that end in crises (Crotty 2009). However, the crisis is also representative of the wider crises of capitalism in that it rests upon the perpetual search for surplus value (profit). As Harvey observes, 'The politics of capitalism are affected by the perpetual need to find profitable terrains for capital surplus production and absorption' (2012: 5). In this, to paraphrase Harvey, obstacles to such expansion must be overcome. If the scarcity of labour and wages is too high then, via technologically induced unemployment, reductions in the rights of organised labour and/or via new sources of labour, including migrants or export of capital to new locations, new means of production and new natural resources must be found as well as locations to dispose of wastes at low cost. If there is not enough purchasing power in a new market, then new markets must be found. If the profit rate is too low then changes in state regulation as well as the sphere of state intervention may be used to continue expansion.

If any one of the above barriers to continuous capital circulation and expansion becomes impossible to circumvent, then capital accumulation is blocked and capitalists face a crisis. Capital cannot be profitably reinvested, accumulation stagnates or ceases, and capital is devalued (lost) and in some instances even physically destroyed. Devaluation can take a number of forms. Surplus commodities can be devalued or destroyed, productive capacity and assets can be written down in value and left unemployed, or money itself can be devalued through inflation. In a crisis, of course, labour stands to be devalued through massive unemployment.

Tourism is both affected by and contributes to this crisis. The surplus commodities of event and other tourism-justified infrastructure are clear evidence of either state overdependency on an insecure market and/or unsustainable government borrowing for investment in unproductive tourism infrastructure (Hall 2010a). For example, the hosting of the 2004 Athens Summer Olympic Games in Greece at a cost ranging between 9 and 12 billion euros was undertaken by incurring substantial public debt with the 2004 budget deficit of over 6 per cent (Preuss 2004; Ikonomopoulos 2005). Tourism and its contribution to unsustainable construction and real estate speculation has similarly contributed to the economic problems facing Ireland, Spain and Portugal.

Perhaps ironically, in some countries, such as Greece, Spain and Iceland, tourism is also seen as a potential solution to economic crises. Jóhannesson (2010) discusses how tourism has been seen as a potential contributor to the Icelandic economy following the country's financial crisis and currency devaluation. However, as he notes, interest in tourism in public debates and policy seems to become prominent in times of economic crisis and wanes during years of economic growth (Jóhannesson 2010). Such an observation perhaps reflects broader concerns over the public and academic discourse that surrounds tourism. On one hand, tourism is promoted by academics and policy actors as an industry that demonstrates high rates of growth and is relatively resilient to economic downturn. Yet, on the other, it is also clearly associated with different forms of crisis and, like any industry, is subject to pressures in its economic, political and natural environment. Furthermore, it has long been recognised that, although international tourism has relatively high growth rates and is a major source of foreign currency receipts, earnings from tourism do not necessarily bring about a significant decrease in the instability of export earnings of most developing and industrialised countries. Indeed, tourism may even lead to a net increase in the instability of export earnings and be a particular problem in small, open developing economies (Sinclair 1990), where it could potentially worsen economic crises. This situation may be particularly significant for those small economies that are being encouraged to further liberalise and open up for foreign investment by such institutions as the UNWTO and the World Economic Forum (WEF) so as to become more 'competitive' tourism destinations (Hall 2007). Ironically, such measures are also used to promote pro-poor tourism policies while simultaneously also contributing to decline in natural capital and increased greenhouse gas emissions.

The Global Humanitarian Forum (GHF) (2009: 1) indicated that every year climate change already leaves over 300,000 people dead, with 325 million people seriously affected, and economic losses of USD 125 billion (more than all present world aid), primarily in the less developed countries. In all, four billion people are regarded as vulnerable to climate change, and 500 million people are at extreme risk with approximately half a million lives expected to be lost per annum to climate change by 2029. Given that tourism is conservatively recognised as contributing 5 per cent of greenhouse gas emissions (UNWTO and UNEP 2008; WEF 2009b), this means that in proportional terms tourism as a generator of greenhouse emissions was already responsible in 2009 for about 15,000 deaths, seriously affecting 8.25 million people, and producing economic losses of USD 6.25 billion. This figure is also significant given arguments by the UNWTO that tourism is a means to alleviate poverty in the less developed world, as the economic losses estimated by the GHF (2009) with respect to climate change in the developing world are already greater than the USD 5.42 billion of tourism expenditure in the 49 least developed countries (2006 figures in Hall 2010c). Tourism may possibly contribute to poverty alleviation but the benefits of tourism need to be weighed against all of its costs, including the effects of climate change (Zapata *et al.* 2011).

In tourism literature, the overall rundown of natural capital as a result of either resource exploitation, pollution or tourism-related global change is not regarded as a crisis. Instead, despite the apparent desire for more sustainable forms of tourism (at least in policy statements and academic writing), continued growth in international tourism and its impacts constitute business as normal. Unfortunately, much of the thinking about tourism, even if it does acknowledge economic costs, does not fully consider the extent to which the marginal benefits of economic growth relate to those costs. In particular, for all the talk about the importance of 'the environment' to tourism, tourism as an industry and, to a lesser extent as a subject of study, does not adequately deal with how tourism impacts natural capital and instead focuses on economic growth without fully considering the maintenance of the natural resources that allow such growth. Yet, 'any consumption of capital, manmade or natural, must be subtracted in the calculation of income' (Daly 2008: 10). Growth does not equal development. Similarly, increased consumption does not necessarily imply living better, even though most contemporary tourism marketing is geared towards encouraging increased consumption within a consumer society, and is embedded within both the ideologies and institutions of contemporary capitalism (Hall 2010c).

At the societal and destination level, crises in tourism cannot be fully understood unless placed within the context of capitalism and its inherent contradictions. Many of the crises that affect tourism occur as a result of the continued expansion of capitalism. In its current neoliberal variation, market expansion is ubiquitous. There is little, from the availability of health treatment through to the provision of food and education, that is now not considered in market terms – including tourism. Nature and its conservation are also increasingly regarded in neoliberal terms (Brockington and Duffy 2010), while even the loss of natural attractions becomes a tourist attraction to some (Hall and Saarinen 2010; Lemelin *et al.* 2010).

From crisis to tipping point

There are surely limits to the environmental and socio-economic fixes that maintain capitalism's growth and reproduction. Indeed, the increased frequency of economic and financial crises together with growing opposition to the measures used to fix such problems suggest that some of those limits may be being reached. There are also ecological and social limits with respect to biodiversity and ecosystem loss. Tipping points appear closer than ever. But from the majority of the tourism literature you would never know this to be the case. This situation may be because capitalism is not regarded as an issue, it is just there – and accepted by the academy as such. Or it may be that, because the primary subjects of tourism, tourists and their trips are the wealthier elements of society in money and time, the academy does not notice. Or it may be that so long as academic salaries are being paid then we neither notice or care.

Crises are seen as short term, while the marketisation of everything and the continued loss of natural capital is long term – and does not fit into technical, rational frameworks of crisis management and recovery. Yet even from a managerial perspective, there is a clear need to understand the way in which various crises interact with each other and how this complicates the response to crisis at both a policy and business level. And there is also a need to ask that, if crisis events are in fact a 'normal' part of doing business, should not industry then respond from their own contingency funds and market actions?

Although some crises appear recurring, it is also clear that issues keep emerging that challenge tourism. The current economic recession clearly provides many challenges and opportunities to destinations and businesses. The environment has also been an expressed concern for tourism for well over thirty years yet there is little sign that it is becoming any more sustainable (Hall 2010c). Some natural disasters are hard to plan for, but the level of knowledge of the possibility of crisis events occurring means that contingencies can be made. Yet the record of tourism industry learning with both the natural and economic environment is not good. The same old solutions are trotted out. We face what might otherwise be described as a policy failure (Hall 2011). In seeking to understand crises, far too much attention has been given to the assumption that a well-designed institution is 'good' because it facilitates cooperation and network development rather than a focus on norms, values and institutionalisation as first and necessary steps in the assessment of what kind of changes institutional arrangements are promoting and their potential outcomes. This may be described as third-order change, or a paradigm shift. Yet any understanding of the potential for changing the framework by which we understand crisis needs to be grounded in research of the interrelationships between power, values, norms and interests and how they influence the selection of policy instruments, indicators and settings within broader frames of govern-ance and change. This requires taking neoliberal capitalism from the background of tourism and making its interrogation essential to understanding contemporary tourism and its contribution and response to crisis.

References

Adey, P., Budd, L. and Hubbard, P. (2007) 'Flying lessons: exploring the social and cultural geographies of global air travel', *Progress in Human Geography*, 31: 773–91.

Aguirre, J.A. (2007) 'Tourism, volcanic eruptions and information: lessons for crisis management in national parks, Costa Rica, 2006', *PASOS: Revista de Turismo y Patrimonio Cultural*, 5: 175–92.

Akal, M. (2005) 'The impact of Turkey's economic crisis of February 2001 on the tourism industry in northern Cyprus', *Tourism Management*, 26: 95–104.

Anderson, B.A. (2006) 'Crisis management in the Australian tourism industry: preparedness, personnel and postscript', *Tourism Management*, 27: 1290–7.

Araus, J.L. (2004) 'The problems of sustainable water use in the Mediterranean and research requirements for agriculture', *Annals of Applied Biology*, 144(3): 259–72.

Armstrong, E.K. and Ritchie, B.W. (2007) 'The heart recovery marketing campaign: destination recovery after a major bushfire in Australia's national capital', *Journal of Travel & Tourism Marketing*, 23: 175–89.

Assaker, G. (2008) 'Rethinking international tourism in the face of the terrorist threat', *Espaces, Tourisme & Loisirs*, 257: 36–40.

Baade, R.A. and Matheson, V.A. (2007) 'Professional sports, hurricane Katrina, and the economic redevelopment of New Orleans', *Contemporary Economic Policy*, 25: 591–603.

Barda, C. and Sardianou, E. (2010) 'Analysing consumers' "activism" in response to rising prices', *International Journal of Consumer Studies*, 34: 133–9.

Beeton, S. (2001) 'Horseback tourism in Victoria, Australia: cooperative, proactive crisis management', *Current Issues in Tourism*, 4: 422–39.

Beeton, S. (2002) 'The cost of complacency: horseback tourism and crisis management revisited', *Current Issues in Tourism*, 5: 467–70.

Bhandari, K. (2004) 'Nepalese tourism: crisis and beyond Nepal's endeavor for tourism recovery', *Tourism*, 52: 375–83.

Bielecki, J. (2002) 'Energy security: is the wolf at the door?', *The Quarterly Review of Economics and Finance*, 42: 235–50.

Blackman, D., Kennedy, M. and Ritchie, B. (2011) 'Knowledge management: the missing link in DMO crisis management?', *Current Issues in Tourism*, 14: 337–54.

Blake, A. and Sinclair, M.T. (2003) 'Tourism crisis management: US response to September 11', *Annals of Tourism Research*, 30: 813–32.

Blunk, S.S., Clark, D.E. and McGibany, J.M. (2006) 'Evaluating the long-run impacts of the 9/11 terrorist attacks on US domestic airline travel', *Applied Economics*, 38: 363–70.

Bodson, P. and Stafford, J. (1988) 'Tourism, solution to third world debts', *Revue de Tourisme*, 43(2): 2–5.

Boerjan, P.A.R. and Vanhove, N. (1984) 'The tourism demand reconsidered in the context of the economic crisis', *Tourist Review*, 39(2): 2–11.

Brockington, D. and Duffy, R. (2010) 'Capitalism and conservation: the production and reproduction of biodiversity conservation', *Antipode*, 42: 469–84.

Calgaro, E. and Lloyd, K. (2008) 'Sun, sea, sand and tsunami: examining disaster vulnerability in the tourism community of Khao Lak, Thailand', *Singapore Journal of Tropical Geography*, 29: 288–306.

Campiranon, K. and Arcodia, C. (2007) 'Market segmentation in time of crisis: a case study of the MICE sector in Thailand', *Journal of Travel & Tourism Marketing*, 23(2/4): 151–61.

Carlsen, J.C. and Hughes, M. (2007) 'Tourism market recovery in the Maldives after the 2004 Indian Ocean tsunami', *Journal of Travel & Tourism Marketing*, 23(2/4): 139–49.

Carlsen, J.C. and Liburd, J.J. (2007) 'Developing a research agenda for tourism crisis management, market recovery and communications', *Journal of Travel & Tourism Marketing*, 23(2/4): 265–76.

Chen, J.S. (2000) 'Examining Asian outbound travelers' consumption patterns after the 1997 Asian economic crisis', *Journal of Hospitality & Leisure Marketing*, 7: 67–80.

Chen, L., Evans, T., Anand, S., Boufford, J., Brown, H., Chowdhury, M., Cueto, M., Dare, L., Dussault, G. and Elzinga, G. (2004) 'Human resources for health: overcoming the crisis', *The Lancet*, 364: 1984–90.

Cioccio, L. and Michael, E.J. (2007) 'Hazard or disaster: tourism management for the inevitable in northeast Victoria', *Tourism Management*, 28: 1–11.

Clouston, B. (1984) 'The tourism demand reconsidered in the context of the economic crisis', *Tourist Review*, 39(2): 2–11.

Cohen, E. (2010) 'Tourism crises: a comparative perspective', *International Journal of Tourism Policy*, 3: 281–96.

Cohen, E. and Neal, M. (2010) 'Coinciding crises and tourism in contemporary Thailand', *Current Issues in Tourism*, 13: 455–75.

Cohen, M.J. and Pinstrup-Andersen, P. (1998) 'Food security and conflict', *Social Research*, 66: 375–416.

Coles, T. and Hall, C.M. (2006) 'The geography of tourism is dead: long live geographies of tourism and mobility', *Current Issues in Tourism*, 9: 289–92.

Crotty, J. (2009) 'Structural causes of the global financial crisis: a critical assessment of the "new financial architecture"', *Cambridge Journal of Economics*, 33(4): 563–80.

Daly, H.E. (2008) *A Steady-State Economy*, London: Sustainable Development Commission.

Dhariwai, R. (2005) 'Tourist arrivals in India: how important are domestic disorders?', *Tourism Economics*, 11: 185–205.

Duda, A.M. and El-Ashry, M.T. (2000) 'Addressing the global water and environment crises through integrated approaches to the management of land, water and ecological resources', *Water International*, 25: 115–26.

Dwyer, L., Forsyth, P., Spurr, R. and Van Ho, T. (2006) 'Economic effects of the world tourism crisis on Australia', *Tourism Economics*, 12: 171–86.

Enz, C.A. and Canina, L. (2002) 'September 11, 2001: recovering hospitality at ground zero', *Cornell Hotel and Restaurant Administration Quarterly*, 43(5): 11–26.

Frisby, E. (2002) 'Communicating in a crisis: the British Tourist Authority's responses to the foot-and-mouth outbreak and 11th September, 2001', *Journal of Vacation Marketing*, 9: 89–100.

Funck, C. (1999) 'When the bubble burst: planning and reality in Japan's resort industry', *Current Issues in Tourism*, 2: 333–53.

Gasperoni, G. and Dall'Aglio, S. (1992) 'Crisis management in tourist destinations', *Visions in Leisure and Business*, 11(3): 25–33.

Gaullier, X. (1985) 'Economic crisis, work, leisure time: early retirement and departure from the labour force', *World Leisure and Recreation*, 27(1): 33–40.

Gills, B.K. (2008) 'The swinging of the pendulum: the global crisis and beyond', *Globalizations*, 5: 513–22.

Glaesser, D. (2006) *Crisis Management in the Tourism Industry*, Oxford: Butterworth-Heinemann.

Global Humanitarian Forum (GHF) (2009) *The Anatomy of a Silent Crisis*, London: Global Humanitarian Forum.

Gössling, S. (2002) 'Human-environmental relation with tourism', *Annals of Tourism Research*, 29: 539–56.

Gössling, S. and Hall, C.M. (eds) (2006) *Tourism and Global Environmental Change*, London: Routledge.

Gössling, S., Ceron, J.-P., Dubios, G. and Hall, C.M. (2009) 'Hypermobile travellers', in S. Gössling and P. Upham (eds) *Climate Change and Aviation*, London: Earthscan.

Gössling, S., Peeters, P., Hall, C.M., Ceron, J.-P., Dubois, G., Lehmann, L.V. and Scott, D. (2012) 'Tourism and water use: supply, demand, and security: an international review', *Tourism Management*, 33: 1–15.

Greening, D.W. and Johnson, R.A. (2007) 'Do managers and strategies matter? A study in crisis', *Journal of Management Studies*, 33: 25–51.

Gu, H. and Wall, G. (2007) 'SARS in China: tourism impacts and market rejuvenation', *Tourism Analysis*, 11: 367–79.

Gu, Z. (2000) 'The impact of the Asian financial crisis on Australian tourism', *Asia Pacific Journal of Tourism Research*, 5: 1–7.

Guizzardi, A. and Mazzocchi, M. (2010) 'Tourism demand for Italy and the business cycle', *Tourism Management*, 31: 367–77.

Gunlu, E.A. and Aktas, G. (2006) 'Vulnerability of coastal resorts to crises: probable scenarios and recovery strategies', *Tourism in Marine Environments*, 3: 3–13.

Guo, Y. and Yao, X. (1999) 'Tourism perspectives of the Asian financial crisis: lessons for the future', *Current Issues in Tourism*, 2: 279–93.

Gurr, T.R. (1985) 'On the political consequences of scarcity and economic decline', *International Studies Quarterly*, 29: 51–75.

Hall, C.M. (1994) *Tourism and Politics: Power, policy and place*, Chichester, UK: John Wiley.

Hall, C.M. (2002) 'Travel safety, terrorism and the media: the significance of the issue-attention cycle', *Current Issues in Tourism*, 5: 458–66.

Hall, C.M. (2003) 'Biosecurity and wine tourism: is a vineyard a farm?', *Journal of Wine Research*, 14(2/3), 121–6.

Hall, C.M. (2005a) *Tourism: Rethinking the social science of mobility*, London: Pearson Education.

Hall, C.M. (2005b) 'Reconsidering the geography of tourism and contemporary mobility', *Geographical Research*, 43: 125–39.

Hall, C.M. (2005c) 'Biosecurity and wine tourism', *Tourism Management*, 26: 931–8.

Hall, C.M. (2007) 'Tourism and regional competitiveness', in J. Tribe and D. Airey (eds) *Developments in Tourism Research: New directions, challenges and applications*, Oxford: Elsevier.

Hall, C.M. (2010a) 'Crisis events in tourism: subjects of crisis in tourism', *Current Issues in Tourism*, 13(5): 401–17.

Hall, C.M. (2010b) 'Tourism and biodiversity: more significant than climate change?', *Journal of Heritage Tourism*, 5(4): 253–66.

Hall, C.M. (2010c) 'Changing paradigms and global change: from sustainable to steady-state tourism', *Tourism Recreation Research*, 35(2): 131–45.

Hall, C.M. (2011) 'Policy learning and policy failure in sustainable tourism governance: from first and second to third order change?', *Journal of Sustainable Tourism*, 19: 649–71.

Hall, C.M. and Baird, T. (2013) 'Ecotourism, biological invasions and biosecurity, in R. Ballantyne and J. Packer (eds) *The International Handbook of Ecotourism*, Aldershot, UK: Ashgate.

Hall, C.M. and Saarinen, J. (2010) 'Last chance to see? Future issues for polar tourism and change', in C.M. Hall and J. Saarinen (eds) *Tourism and Change in Polar Regions: Climate, environments and experiences*, London: Routledge.

Hall, C.M., Timothy, D. and Duval, D. (2003) 'Security and tourism: towards a new understanding?', *Journal of Travel and Tourism Marketing*, 15(2–3): 1–18.

Hall, C.M., Duval, D. and Timothy, D. (eds) (2004) *Safety and Security in Tourism: Relationships, management and marketing*, New York: Haworth Press.

Hall, C.M., James, M. and Baird, T. (2011) 'Forests and trees as charismatic mega-flora: implications for heritage tourism and conservation', *Journal of Heritage Tourism*, 6(4): 309–23.

Hall, C.M., Becken, S., Buckley, R. and Scott, D. (2012) 'Tourism and climate change: a need for critical analysis', in T.V. Singh (ed.) *Critical Debates in Tourism*, Bristol, UK: Channelview.

Harvey, D. (2012) *Rebel Cities: From the right to the city to the urban revolution*, London: Verso.

Henderson, J.C. (1999a) 'Tourism management and the Southeast Asian economic and environmental crisis: a Singapore perspective', *Managing Leisure*, 4: 107–20.

Henderson, J.C. (1999b) 'Sustainable tourism or sustainable development? Financial crisis, ecotourism, and the "Amazing Thailand" campaign', *Current Issues in Tourism*, 2: 316–32.

Henderson, J.C. (1999c) 'Managing the Asian financial crisis: tourist attractions in Singapore', *Journal of Travel Research*, 38(2): 177–81.

Henderson, J.C. (2002) 'Managing a tourism crisis in Southeast Asia: the role of national tourism organizations', *International Journal of Hospitality & Tourism Administration*, 3(1): 85–105.

Henderson, J.C. (2003) 'Managing a health-related crisis: SARS in Singapore', *Journal of Vacation Marketing*, 10: 67–77.

Henderson, J.C. (2010) 'Natural disasters, tourism crises and marketing challenges: an Indonesian perspective', *International Journal of Tourism and Travel*, 3(1): 15–24.

Henderson, J.C. and Ng, A. (2004) 'Responding to crisis: severe acute respiratory syndrome (SARS) and hotels in Singapore', *International Journal of Tourism Research*, 6: 411–19.

Hitchcock, M. and Putra, I.N.D. (2005) 'The Bali bombings: tourism crisis management and conflict avoidance', *Current Issues in Tourism*, 8: 62–76.

Holder, J.S. (1978) *The Impact of the Energy Crisis 1973/74 on Tourism and some Consequences for Caribbean Development*, Vienna: Institute for Economic Research.

Howard, J.L. (2008) 'The future of the Murray River: amenity re-considered?', *Geographical Research*, 46: 291–302.

Huang, J. and Min, C.H.J. (2002) 'Earthquake devastation and recovery in tourism: the Taiwan case', *Tourism Management*, 23(2): 145–54.

Huntly, P.M., van Noort, S. and Hamer, M. (2005) 'Giving increased value to invertebrates through ecotourism', *South African Journal of Wildlife Research*, 35: 53–62.

Ikonomopoulos, H. (2005) 'Greece looks to PPPs to shrink state control', *International Financial Law Review*, Supplement, 53, August 24, retrieved 1 April 2010 from www.iflr.com/Article/1984753/Channel/193438/Greece-looks-to-PPPs-to-shrink-state-control.html.

International Air Transport Association (IATA) (1992) 'Apocalypse now – airlines in crisis', *IATA Review*, 6: 5–8.

Ioannides, D. and Apostolopoulos, Y. (1999) 'Political instability, war, and tourism in Cyprus: effects, management, and prospects for recovery', *Journal of Travel Research*, 38(1): 51–6.

Janelle, D.G. (1969) 'Spatial reorganization: a model and concept', *Annals of the Association of American Geographers*, 59: 348–64.

Jenkins, S. (2009) 'Don't blame the system for winter travel chaos. Stay put: hypermobility is now the opium of the people, an obsession that wrecks communities and planet. There are no free trips', *The Guardian*, 22 December, retrieved 22 December 2009 from www.guardian.co.uk/commentisfree/2009/dec/22/blame-for-winter-travel-chaos.

Jóhannesson, G.T. (2010) 'Tourism in times of crisis: exploring the discourse of tourism development in Iceland', *Current Issues in Tourism*, 13: 419–34.

Jones, G.W., Midmore, P., Haines, M. and Mackay, R. (1998) 'Tourism, terrorism, and political instability', *Annals of Tourism Research*, 25: 416–56.

Khisty, C.J. and Zeitler, U. (2001) 'Is hypermobility a challenge for transport ethics and systemicity?', *Systemic Practice and Action Research*, 14: 597–613.

King, B. (2000) 'Institutions, research and development: tourism and the Asian financial crisis', *International Journal of Tourism Research*, 2: 133–6.

Kontogeorgopoulos, N. (1999) 'The impact of the Asian financial crisis on Asian gaming activities: an examination of Las Vegas strip casino drops', *Current Issues in Tourism*, 2: 354–65.

Korstanje, M.E. (ed.) (2011) 'Narratives of risk, security and disaster issues in tourism and hospitality', *International Journal of Tourism Anthropology*, 1(special issue): 191–332.

Law, R. (2001a) 'The impact of the Asian financial crisis on Japanese demand for travel to Hong Kong: a study of various forecasting techniques', *Journal of Travel & Tourism Marketing*, 10: 47–65.

Law, R. (2001b) 'A study of the impact of the Asian financial crisis on the accuracy of tourist arrival forecasts', *Journal of Hospitality & Leisure Marketing*, 8(1/2): 5–17.

Laws, E. and Prideaux, B. (2005) Crisis management: a suggested typology, *Journal of Travel & Tourism Marketing*, 19(2/3): 1–8.

Laws, E., Prideaux, B. and Chon, K. (eds) (2007) *Crisis Management in Tourism*, Wallingford, UK: CABI.

Lean, H. and Smyth, R. (2009) 'Asian financial crisis, avian flu and terrorist threats: are shocks to Malaysian tourist arrivals permanent or transitory?', *Asia Pacific Journal of Tourism Research*, 14: 301–21.

Lemelin, H., Maher, P., Stewart, E.J., Dawson, J. and Lück, M. (2010) 'Last chance tourism: the boom, doom, and gloom of visiting vanishing destinations', *Current Issues in Tourism*, 13: 477–93.

Li, M. (2007) 'Peak oil, the rise of China and India, and the global energy crisis', *Journal of Contemporary Asia*, 37: 449–71.

Li, S., Blake, A. and Cooper, C. (2010) 'China's tourism in a global financial crisis: a computable general equilibrium approach', *Current Issues in Tourism*, 13: 435–53.

Litvin, S.W. and Alderson, L.L. (2003) 'How Charleston got her groove back: a Convention and Visitors Bureau's response to 9/11', *Journal of Vacation Marketing*, 9: 188–97.

Loewenberg, S. (2008) 'Global food crisis looks set to continue', *The Lancet*, 372: 1209–10.

Mansfeld, Y. and Pizam, A. (eds) (2006) *Tourism, Security and Safety: From theory to practice*, Amsterdam: Elsevier.

Miller, G.A. and Ritchie, B.W. (2003) 'A farming crisis or a tourism disaster? An analysis of the foot and mouth disease in the UK', *Current Issues in Tourism*, 6: 150–71.

Moncrief, L.W., Mouser, T.W. and Pitrak, P. (1977) 'The influence of gasoline price and availability upon recreation travel propensity', *Energy Communications*, 3, 431–47.

Myers, N. (1993) *Ultimate Security: The environmental basis of political stability*, New York: W.W. Norton.

Niininen, O. and Gatsou, M. (2007) 'Crisis management: a case study from the Greek passenger shipping industry', *Journal of Travel & Tourism Marketing*, 23: 191–202.

Okumus, F. and Karamustafa, K. (2005) 'Impact of an economic crisis: evidence from Turkey', *Annals of Tourism Research*, 32: 942–61.

Orchiston, C. (2012) 'Seismic risk scenario planning and sustainable tourism management: Christchurch and the Alpine Fault zone, South Island, New Zealand', *Journal of Sustainable Tourism*, 20: 59–79.

Page, S., Yeoman, I., Munro, C., Connell, J. and Walker, L. (2006) 'A case study of best practice: Visit Scotland's prepared response to an influenza pandemic', *Tourism Management*, 27: 361–93.

Papatheodorou, A., Rosselló, J. and Xiao, H. (2010) 'Global economic crisis and tourism: consequences and perspectives', *Journal of Travel Research*, 49: 39–45.

Peacock, L. and Worner, S. (2006) 'Using analogous climates and global insect pest distribution data to identify potential sources of new invasive insect pests in New Zealand', *New Zealand Journal of Zoology*, 33: 141–5.

Peterson, P.G. (1999) 'Gray dawn: the global aging crisis', *Foreign Affairs*, 78: 42–55.

Pforr, C. and Hosie, P.J. (2007) 'Crisis management in tourism: preparing for recovery', *Journal of Travel & Tourism Marketing*, 23(2/4): 249–64.

Preuss, H. (2004) *The Economics of Staging the Olympics: A comparison of the Games, 1972–2008*, Cheltenham: Edward Elgar.

Prideaux, B. (1999) 'Southeast Asian tourism and the financial crisis: Indonesia and Thailand compared', *Current Issues in Tourism*, 2: 294–303.

Prideaux, B., Laws, E. and Faulkner, B. (2003) 'Events in Indonesia: exploring the limits to formal tourism trends forecasting methods in complex crisis situations', *Tourism Management*, 24: 475–87.

Prideaux, B., Coghlan, A. and Falco-Mammone, F. (2007) 'Post crisis recovery: the case of after Cyclone Larry', *Journal of Travel & Tourism Marketing*, 23: 163–74.

Raab, C. and Schwer, R.K. (2003) 'The short- and long-term impact of the Asian financial crisis on Las Vegas strip baccarat revenues', *International Journal of Hospitality Management*, 22: 37–45.

Reddy, M.V. (2005) 'Commentary: tourism in the aftermath of the tsunami: the case of the Andaman and Nicobar Islands', *Current Issues in Tourism*, 8: 350–62.

Remis, M.J. and Hardin, R. (2009) 'Transvalued species in an African forest', *Conservation Biology*, 23: 1588–96.

Ren, C.H. (2000) 'Understanding and managing the dynamics of linked crisis events', *Disaster Prevention and Management*, 9: 12–17.

Richter, L.K. (1999) 'After political turmoil: the lessons of rebuilding tourism in three Asian countries', *Journal of Travel Research*, 38: 41–5.

Ritchie, B.W. (2004) 'Chaos, crises and disasters: a strategic approach to crisis management in the tourism industry', *Tourism Management*, 25: 669–83.

Ritchie, B.W. (2008) 'Tourism disaster planning and management: from response and recovery to reduction and readiness', *Current Issues in Tourism*, 11: 315–48.

Ritchie, B.W. (2009) *Crisis and Disaster Management for Tourism*, Bristol, UK: Channel View.

Ritchie, J.R.B., Amaya Molinar, C.M. and Frechtling, D.C. (2010) 'Impacts of the world recession and economic crisis on tourism: North America', *Journal of Travel Research*, 49: 5–15.

Rittichainuwat, B.N. (2012) 'Tourists' and tourism suppliers' perceptions toward crisis management on tsunami', *Tourism Management*, in press.

Rittichainuwat, B.N., Beck, J.A. and Qu, H.L. (2002) 'Promotional strategies and travelers' satisfaction during the Asian financial crisis: a best practice case study of Thailand', *Journal of Quality Assurance in Hospitality & Tourism*, 3: 109–24.

Ross, G.F. (2005) 'Tourism industry employee workstress: a present and future crisis', *Journal of Travel & Tourism Marketing*, 19(2/3): 133–47.

Saurin, J. (2001) 'Global environmental crisis as the "disaster triumphant": the private capture of public goods', *Environmental Politics*, 10(4): 63–84.

Sausmarez, N. de (2003) 'Malaysia's response to the Asian financial crisis: implications for tourism and sectoral crisis management', *Journal of Travel & Tourism Marketing*, 15: 217–31.

Sausmarez, N. de (2007) 'Crisis management, tourism and sustainability: the role of indicators', *Journal of Sustainable Tourism*, 15, 700–14.

Schulmeister, S. (1978) *Tourism and the Business Cycle*, Vienna: Institute for Economic Research.

Scott, D., Gössling, S. and Hall, C.M. (2012) *Tourism and Climate Change: Impacts, adaptation and mitigation*, London: Routledge.

Scott, N., Laws, E. and Prideaux, B. (2007) 'Tourism crises and marketing recovery strategies', *Journal of Travel & Tourism Marketing*, 23: 1–13.

Sharpley, R. (2005) 'The tsunami and tourism: a comment', *Current Issues in Tourism*, 8: 344–9.

Sharpley, R. and Craven, B. (2001) 'The 2001 foot and mouth crisis – rural economy and tourism policy implications: a comment', *Current Issues in Tourism*, 4: 527–37.

Sinclair, M.T. (1990) 'International tourism and export instability', *Journal of Development Studies*, 26: 487–504.

Sinding, S.W. (2000) 'The great population debates: how relevant are they for the 21st century?', *American Journal of Public Health*, 90: 1841–5.

Smeral, E. (2009) 'The impact of the financial and economic crisis on European tourism', *Journal of Travel Research*, 48: 3–13.

Smeral, E. (2010) 'Impacts of the world recession and economic crisis on tourism: forecasts and potential risks', *Journal of Travel Research*, 49, 31–8.

Smith, D. (1990) 'Beyond contingency planning: towards a model of crisis management', *Organization & Environment*, 4: 263–75.

Smith, D. (2005) 'Business (not) as usual: crisis management, service recovery and the vulnerability of organizations', *Journal of Services Marketing*, 19: 309–20.

Song, H. and Lin, S. (2010) 'Impacts of the financial and economic crisis on tourism in Asia', *Journal of Travel Research*, 49: 16–30.

Sönmez, S.F., Apostolopoulos, Y. and Tarlow, P. (1999) 'Tourism in crisis: managing the effects of terrorism', *Journal of Travel Research*, 38(1): 13–18.

Stafford, J. and Sarrasin, B. (2003) 'Post-war in Iraq: effects on international tourism', *Téoros, Revue de Recherche en Tourisme*, 22(1): 62–4.

Stanbury, J., Pryer, M. and Roberts, A. (2005) 'Heroes and villains – tour operator and media response to crisis: an exploration of press handling strategies by UK adventure tour operators', *Current Issues in Tourism*, 8: 394–423.

Stern, E.K. (1995) 'Bringing the environment in: the case for comprehensive security', *Cooperation and Conflict*, 30(3): 211–37.

Stiglitz, J.E. (2000) 'Capital market liberalization, economic growth, and instability', *World Development*, 28: 1075–86.

Tew, P.J., Lu, Z., Tolomiczenko, G. and Gellatly, J. (2008) 'SARS: lessons in strategic planning for hoteliers and destination marketers', *International Journal of Contemporary Hospitality Management*, 20: 332–46.

Travel Industry Association of America (1991) *Industry in a Crisis: The impact of the Persian Gulf War on the US travel industry*, Washington, DC: Travel Industry Association of America.

Trees, A.J. (2009) 'Disease threats from travelling pets', *British Veterinary Record*, 164: 28–9.

Tsai, C.-H. and Chen, C.-W. (2010) 'An earthquake disaster management mechanism based on risk assessment information for the tourism industry: a case study from the island of Taiwan', *Tourism Management*, 31: 470–81.

United Nations World Tourism Organization (UNWTO) (2006a) *The Impact of Rising Oil Prices on International Tourism*, Special Report No. 26, Madrid: UNWTO.

United Nations World Tourism Organization (UNWTO) (2006b) *International Tourist Arrivals, Tourism Market Trends: 2006 Edition – Annex*, Madrid: UNWTO.

United Nations World Tourism Organization (UNWTO) (2007) 'Another record year for world tourism', UNWTO Press Release, Madrid, 29 January, retrieved 1 April 2010 from www.unwto.org/newsroom/Releases/2007/january/recordyear.htm.

United Nations World Tourism Organization (UNWTO) (2008) 'World tourism exceeds expectations in 2007: arrivals grow from 800 million to 900 million in two years', UNWTO Press Release, Madrid, 29 January, retrieved 1 April 2010 from www.unwto.org/media/news/en/press_det.php?id=1665.

United Nations World Tourism Organization (UNWTO) (2009) 'International tourism challenged by deteriorating world economy', UNWTO Press Release, Madrid, 27 January, retrieved 1 April 2010 from www.unwto.org/media/news/en/press_det.php?id=3481&idioma=E.

United Nations World Tourism Organization (UNWTO) (2011) *UNWTO Tourism Highlights*, Madrid: UNWTO.

United Nations World Tourism Organization (UNWTO) (2012) 'International tourism to reach one billion in 2012', UNWTO Press Release, Madrid, 16 January, retrieved 1 April 2010 from http://media.unwto.org/en/press-release/2012-01-16/international-tourism-reach-one-billion-2012.

UNWTO and UNEP (2008) *Climate Change and Tourism: Responding to global challenges*, Madrid/Paris: UNWTO/UNEP.

Urry, J. (2000) *Sociology Beyond Societies: Mobilities for the twenty-first century*, London: Routledge.

Waters, S.R. (1980) 'Future development of tourism', *Tourist Review*, 35(2): 2–7.

Wilshusen, P.R., Brechin, S.R., Fortwangler, C.L. and West, P.C. (2002) 'Reinventing a square wheel: critique of a resurgent "protection paradigm" in international biodiversity conservation', *Society & Natural Resources*, 15: 17–40.

Wilson, A. (1992) *The Culture of Nature: North American landscape from Disney to the Exxon Valdez*, Cambridge: Blackwell.

Wolfe, R.I. (1982) 'Trends in the technology and economics of air transport', *Tourism Management*, 3: 291–3.

World Economic Forum (WEF) (2009) *Towards a Low Carbon Travel & Tourism Sector*, Davros: WEF.

World Tourism Organization (WTO) (1988) *Economic Review of World Tourism: Tourism in the context of economic crisis and the dominance of the service economy*, Madrid: WTO.

World Tourism Organization (WTO) (1998) *Handbook on Natural Disaster Reduction in Tourist Areas*, Madrid: WTO.

Xu, J. and Grunewald, A. (2009) 'What have we learned? A critical review of tourism disaster management', *Journal of China Tourism Research*, 5: 102–30.

Yang, W., Chen, G. and Wang, D. (2008) 'Impact of the Wenchuan earthquake on tourism in Sichuan, China', *Journal of Mountain Science*, 5: 194–208.

Zapata, M.J., Hall, C.M., Lindo, P. and Van der Schaeghen, M. (2011) 'Can community-based tourism contribute to development and poverty alleviation?', *Current Issues in Tourism*, 14(8): 725–49.

Zeng B., Carter, R.W. and de Lacy, T. (2005) 'Short-term perturbations and tourism effects: the case of SARS in China', *Current Issues in Tourism*, 8: 306–22.

3 Much ado about nothing?

Tourism and the financial crisis

Tim Coles

Introduction

During the current global economic downturn, the popular media have been replete with stories about the challenges faced by the travel and tourism industry. Conventional wisdom has been that demand has been depressed, fewer people have been travelling, and supply has been contracting. Once conditions ease, bookings will rise and business-as-usual will resume soon afterwards, aided and abetted by some high-profile casualties as well as some apparent signs of upturn, and on the whole this narrative seems pretty convincing. Of course, this is a gross simplification but it is not entirely dissimilar to how many global leaders in travel and tourism have portrayed circumstances or made sense of them for their audiences and stakeholders. For instance, the World Travel and Tourism Council noted how, just two years into the current crisis, global GDP generated by travel and tourism had declined by 4.8 per cent in 2009 with estimated job losses of almost five million (WTTC 2010: 7). Furthermore, as the 'world authority on travel and tourism' (WTTC 2012), it forecast that 'travel and tourism's recovery will be subdued in 2010 . . . [because] it was hit hard by the credit and housing market collapses last year [i.e. 2009] that triggered the deepest recession since the Great Depression' (WTTC 2010: 7). However, green shoots were visible and the situation would soon pick up again because 'the global economy has moved into a recovery phase, although the pick up in developed economies is expected to be gradual as households, corporations and governments do battle with their balance sheets'. As a result, 'Travel and Tourism Economy GDP is forecast to rise by just 0.5% in 2010 overall. But stronger second-half momentum will continue into 2011 to boost growth next year to 3.2%' (WTTC 2010: 7). In an attempt to put these figures into context, it observed that 'nevertheless, even in such a depressed year for activity as 2009, Travel and Tourism still employed over 235 million people across the world – 8.2% of all employment – and generated 9.4% of world GDP' (WTTC 2010: 7).

This endorsement – and other long-term prognoses for the growth of the global travel and tourism sector into the next decade – beg the question of whether there's much ado about nothing. Put more bluntly, why should we be bothered by the recent economic crisis in tourism? Recent disruption could be regarded as nothing more than a temporary interlude in an otherwise inexorable long-term trajectory of growth (Hall and Coles 2008; WTTC 2011a, 2012). One straightforward answer is that it is unclear exactly how long these conditions may last, how deep or prolonged their impacts may be, for how long tourism growth may be constrained, and hence what the consequences are likely to be. Conditions have, after all, been relatively turbulent, shifting in relatively short periods. As the WTTC later noted in November 2011, 'the global economic situation remains extremely challenging, with deteriorating financial conditions in the third quarter (Q3) of 2011, the continuing Eurozone debt crisis and threat of a return to recession in the United States' (2011b: 1). As a result, just six months after they were published 'a significant downgrading of prospects' was necessary from more bullish forecasts for the growth of the sector's contribution to GDP of 4.5 per cent in 2011 and 5.1 per cent in 2012 to 3.2 per cent and 3.3 per cent respectively (or back to where they had been when forecast in 2010).

There is, though, another reason rooted in epistemology and ontology. There is a growing body of knowledge based in economic modelling and forecasting that attempts to explain and predict likely trajectories. However, this currently dominant analytical approach paints only a partial picture. Inherently such estimates can only ever provide indications of what is unfolding (Scowsill 2011); the power of their predictions is limited by incomplete data sets or rationalising assumptions, and perhaps most importantly such models do not fully embrace the complexities and messiness in the social world that a finer, more granulated approach may reveal. The crisis is after all being played out by people; its effects are being experienced on a daily basis by citizens, consumers, business owners, voters and regulators; and it is the outcomes of their decisions at a micro level that forecasts at a macro level attempt to predict (and sometimes obscure) in their coarseness. Thus, another more interesting answer to the question is that the crisis has induced complex processes of restructuring and reorganisation in the consumption, production and administration of tourism that deserve to be unpacked further. This chapter makes the case for a more nuanced understanding of how recent macro-economic events and their associated conditions have impacted on tourism-related behaviours as well as the extent to which they may continue to do so in the coming years.

Beyond the conventional view

First of all, though, it is useful to consider some of the salient aspects of the recent – and still continuing – crisis as background to later discussions of its consequences on tourism consumption, production and administration. Many terms have been used in connection with the economic downturn around the world in the past five years, such as 'credit crunch', 'recession', 'downturn', the 'financial crisis', and the 'sovereign debt crisis', to name but a few. Elsewhere in this volume, more detailed accounts of the current crisis and its evolution are provided (see Chapters 1 and 2). Thus, it is unnecessary to repeat the substance of these historical accounts here. In essence, such terms all point to a period in which otherwise standard trajectories of growth have been suspended. The global economy has stagnated and economies of many states, especially in the industrialised, developed world have contracted. The major symptoms of this malaise are variously reported to have been restrictions in the availability of capital, increasing costs – especially in capital and raw materials, increased unemployment, falling property markets and reduced consumer demand (Buckley 2011).

Several attempts have been made to understand how this conspiracy of circumstances and conditions may impact on tourism demand. For instance, Smeral (2009) examined the demand for international travel among the pre-accession EU15 countries for 2009 and 2010. Through the lens of tourism imports at constant prices and exchange rates, he concluded that 'a dramatic collapse in international tourism demand [is] not unlikely, at least as long as there is a danger that the financial and economic crisis may be further intensified in the countries affected by it' (Smeral 2009: 12). In a later analysis of outbound demand from the EU15, Australia, Canada, Japan and the United States, he forecast a decline in aggregated demand of 11–12.5 per cent for foreign travel in the five source markets in 2009 and, as a result, that 'total world tourism spending on foreign travel might fall by about 10%' (Smeral 2010: 37). The situation was, though, less likely to be as bad in 2010. Papatheodorou *et al.* concurred with this assessment observing signs of recovery. In their view, '2010 may be the year of recovery at the global level' (2010: 44), whereas the situation in 2009 had been much worse, even than 2008. Nevertheless, there were signs of uneven development. Europe would be one of the regions to experience a more serious decline in tourism demand in 2010, whereas a revival in Asia was likely within a shorter period of time. Song and Lin (2010: 27) added detail to this prognosis. They noted that the economic crisis had had a significant negative impact on arrivals to Asia and expenditure by Asians outside Asia. Long-haul markets in both directions were especially vulnerable, but within Asia there was a need to concentrate on short-haul markets to compensate for the losses in long-haul visitors. Given the continuing growth of the Chinese economy there were reasonable prospects for demand substitution. Finally, both Brent Richie *et al.* (2010) and Page *et al.* (2011) have attempted to contextualise the effects of the financial crisis with the recent concurrent swine flu pandemic in the period of 2008–9. Within North America, Brent Ritchie *et al.* (2010: 5) argued that tourism in Canada and the United States had been (and would continue to be) more affected by the financial crisis, whereas Mexico had been more greatly impacted by the swine flu pandemic, exchange rates and weather conditions. In the case of the United States and Mexico, as bad as the situation had been during the economic crisis, previous events – 9/11 and natural disasters, respectively – had had a much greater effect (Brent Ritchie *et al.* 2010: 13). Page *et al.* (2011: 9) noted that both events had impacted negatively on fourteen source markets to the UK, with the greatest declines from European countries (Germany, Ireland, Spain) and the USA, whereas the smallest were from Asian markets. As a result of swine flu, visitor arrivals from China, Spain, South Korea and Russia declined significantly more than for other source markets.

As instructive as this emergent body of knowledge is, there are notable limitations associated with it. In part these are related to technical restrictions of the methods employed or the nature of the assumptions that limit the accuracy and hence power of the pronouncements. For instance, Smeral (2009, 2010) noted that his prognoses for a change in fortunes some time in 2010 or 2011 may be somewhat optimistic. In his later work, he mused about what the future may be because the global financial system remains fragile and the prospects for recovery, let alone growth, remain uncertain. For him, one 'consideration regarding the medium-term development is that the negative economic and social consequences of the crisis will accompany us for a long time', and he speculated further that the crisis may irreversibly alter consumption patterns and travel behaviours. Rather, in his view, the tourism industry 'may be faced with massive structural change as a "new" consumer with more limited financial and economic means might emerge from the crisis – a development that incidentally offers a stimulus for future research' (Smeral 2010: 37). Quite so. And it is necessary to progress from an exclusively demand-side reading of the crisis. Forecasts and modelling quite correctly point out that such conditions have not been experienced uniformly at an international scale (see also WTTC 2011a, 2011b, 2012). A political economy perspective would suggest that, in Europe at least, some of the economies that have been – and continue to be – most vulnerable to the financial crisis are also some of the most reliant on tourism as a mode of capital accumulation. As a result, further questions are raised about the nature and rate of recovery. For instance, the somewhat unflatteringly termed 'PIGS' states (Portugal, Ireland, Greece and Spain) are part of the 'pleasure periphery' of the European Union; however, each has encountered major economic difficulties since 2007 and, with the exception of Spain at the time of writing, has required a bailout (BBC 2011a; Featherstone 2012; Inman 2012). Domestic opposition within Germany to a second bailout for Greece in 2012, and the harsh austerity measures that accompanied this, appear to have resulted in greater reluctance among Germans to travel there (Neate 2012). Of course, it is unclear at this time how far this will impact on Greece or how long it will last. A supply-side reading would suggest that the specific conditions associated with the crisis increase the vulnerability of a great many tourism enterprises. For instance, among the SMTEs (small and medium-sized tourism enterprises) that dominate the sector (Hall and Coles 2008; Thomas *et al.* 2011), there are a considerable number of micro-enterprises and lifestyle businesses that are under-capitalised and in which domiciles double as premises and 'commercial homes' (Coles and Shaw 2006; Lynch *et al.* 2009). In this context, it is worth recalling that the origins of the current crisis are in the 'credit crunch' of 2007 (Buckley 2011). Numerous consequences have followed, including but not limited to: an increase in the cost of capital in both the wholesale and retail markets, greater lending risk aversion, greater requirement for associated collateral and guarantees, and a general unwillingness to lend to small and micro-enterprises that are in most need of investment. For many accommodation providers then, there is a double jeopardy. Not only has the cost of servicing their principal costs become more expensive, but also corrections in the market may have downgraded the value of businesses. As Coles and Shaw (2006) demonstrated, before the economic downturn, rising markets and property appreciation were a greater source of commercial gain than serviced accommodation for many SMTEs, and they offered the prospect of capital release for investment into renovation, upgrade and improvement.

Consumption

Thus, from a broader perspective of the social sciences, while forecasts offer insights into aggregate levels of behaviour, there is little sense of how the recession is experienced and understood by individual consumers or, for that matter, negotiated by particular social groups through their travel choices and behaviours. Within Europe, a contraction of travel in time and space has been observed (Olive Insight 2009). Beyond the temporarily mobile, travel patterns have changed notably. As Reinhardt notes, 'the average German's current approach . . . can be described in the following way: closer, shorter, cheaper' (2011: 27). Although the main point is still to get away from home, during the crisis German consumers are increasingly staying in-country, the length of trips is becoming shorter, and less money is being spent at destination. Over the period from 2004 to 2010, the proportion of Germans travelling for five or more days dropped under 50 per cent (3 per cent in total). The effects of the downturn have not been felt evenly through society. There were distinct variations in the proportion of urban (54 per cent) and rural (46 per cent) populations who went on holiday as well as among different vocational groups. Blue collar workers (41 per cent) were half as likely to travel as civil servants (80 per cent). Destinations such as Spain (13.2 per cent) and Turkey (6.6 per cent) maintained their popularity with travellers because of their climates and value for money, while long-haul markets waned as German consumers felt the pinch (Reinhardt 2011: 30). In many respects, this may be interpreted as an intensification of an earlier trend. During the earlier years of the 'noughties' (i.e. the decade of 2000–9), many Germans openly discussed taking their summer vacations in 'Balkonia' (a play on words to suggest travelling to a fictional country). Instead of frequenting their long-established hotspots on the French, Italian or Spanish coasts, many erstwhile regular travellers chose not to leave Germany. They stayed at home spending time typically on their balconies and at attractions close to their domiciles. The introduction of the euro in 2002 and its weakness against other major currencies reduced the erstwhile advantages German consumers had enjoyed from the previously stable and strong Deutschmark. Short-haul travel, especially to destinations that did not employ the euro, became comparatively more expensive and less attractive. This was notwithstanding the falling prices of international air travel facilitated by the unrelenting growth of the low-fare airlines (i.e. low-cost carriers) sector at that time (Francis *et al.* 2006).

Within the UK, a fragmented evidence base portrays a similar range of effects. Research conducted for VisitEngland (2011) suggests that, even in 2011 (when recovery was anticipated), high levels of concern remained over the economy and over 75 per cent of people felt the situation would get worse before it would get better. Accompanying this gloomy prognosis, 70 per cent of respondents now holidayed in England and only longer holidays were more likely to be taken overseas. Eccles (2011) reports the finding of a survey of 2,000 British consumers, over a quarter of whom intended to forgo their holidays altogether. Other middle-class (i.e. income) consumers, which comprise about thirteen million people based on Experian's definitions, preferred not to reduce the number of holidays. Instead, they looked for greater value by searching the internet for late, cheap deals. Price sensitivity (82 per cent) and customer service (66 per cent) were mentioned as principal drivers in decision making. Destinations in other parts of the UK appear to have benefitted as a result. VisitEngland (2011) identifies what it terms 'switchers' and 'extras' who comprise 30 per cent of consumers: the former take at least one holiday in England to replace a holiday that would have been taken abroad, while the latter took more domestic holidays than they had prior to the financial crisis. Hopes were unsurprisingly high for a bumper year for Scottish tourism in 2011 because of high-profile events and the growing preference among British people to stay at home for their vacations. So-called 'staycations' and a growing interest in domestic travel opportunities have been one of the welcome outcomes of the recent downturn that tourism managers believe will transcend the end of the financial crisis. VisitScotland, the national tourism body for Scotland, has attempted to capitalise on the trend through its recent marketing campaign under the tagline 'Surprise Yourself' and according to its chairman, Mike Cantlay, 'the interesting thing with the "staycation" trend is that it has become a habit. Scots are getting out and doing things they haven't before. They are having a good time and coming back' (Anonymous 2011: 16).

In a short space of time, a concept coined during the financial crisis has almost become an established part of the professional tourism lexicon and several definitions of 'staycation' now appear on the internet. These variously portray it more as a variant of domestic tourism or day visits, rather than a new mode of travel consumerism associated with a distinct set of socio-cultural conditions that deserves to be more completely understood. After all, its use is not restricted to the UK and the phenomenon is also widely discussed in popular media in the United States (Redbond 2008) and Canada (Bailey 2011). The original elements of social commentary and the irony it was intended to encapsulate have arguably been lost from some of the more anodyne definitions; a new term was required to help embattled consumers who could no longer afford to holiday away from their homes feel better about themselves. Even if the 'destination' was less fashionable, at least there was a new, exclusive term for those experiencing it! The need to preserve social status in a society that had, until 2007, been characterised by ever more conspicuous displays of consumption was also behind the emergence of so-called 'glamping', a contraction of 'glamorous camping', which entered the popular vernacular in 2009. Some social commentators noted that, for those who were really traumatised by the loss of their overseas holiday and the social stigma this may entail, 'glamping' represented the chance to save face. Higher-quality tents and camping equipment, in particular those supplied by marque brands, allied with 'glampsites' at trendy UK destinations such as Cornish coast offered opportunities for consumers to present themselves in a favourable light by holidaying at home with a (greater) degree of luxury (Knight 2011).

Time–space contractions in visitor travel horizons and behaviours are, therefore, an important geographical manifestation of the crisis. What is more, they have played an important role in reconfiguring the social relations of mobility. One of the fundamental geographical aspects of travel and tourism is that home and host, source and destination are connected in a systemic manner. Thus, a change to one part of the system will be reflected in another. Research on consumers travelling to the UK suggests that they were more likely to reduce their duration of stay as well as total spend rather than compromise the quality of the experience. Among Irish travellers (who had the gloomiest views of their future prospects), cutting costs in this manner was forecast to be much more frequent than among those from the Netherlands. Cost-cutting was more prevalent among those over forty-five years of age (Olive Insight 2009), with those receiving a pension looking to make it go further. There have been more unseemly dimensions of this relationship. Discontent in Greece in the summers of 2010 and 2011 manifested itself in civil unrest that impacted on the visitor economy (Panglos *et al.* 2010; Smith 2011). In Greece, where tourism was estimated to support 20 per cent of jobs, strikes by ferry workers targeted international tourists. The Portuguese resort of Albufeira on the Algarve coast came under the spotlight of the British media in the spring and summer of 2011 following attacks on tourists that left two men dead (*Independent* 2011). Although described as muggings and street robberies and reported as being conducted by foreigners, there was some (unfounded) speculation that they may have been provoked by the parlous economic situation in Portugal. Whatever the merit in this view, one correspondent noted heightened tensions between hosts and guests as a result of the financial crisis. As Henley (2011) reported, unemployment and the low value of wages created resentment among tourism workers, not least because many guests remained oblivious to the social problems during their stays. Of course, these are extreme and quite infrequent incidents that hit the headlines, but they point to the importance of not adopting static views of host–guest relationships, in particular those grounded in the social politics of macro-economic growth and stability.

Production

In addition to a reconfiguration of demand, the recent financial crisis has resulted in a consolidation on the supply side. As may have been expected, examples abound of business reorganisation, while sectoral restructuring has been commonplace as the operating environment has become more challenging. Ahead of the 2012 Olympics, the lack of robustness of many firms and whether they would be open as usual was a major topic for discussion. For example, in the period from 2008–10 the number of hotel firms that failed in the UK rose by 61 per cent despite the benefits of staycations (BBC 2010a). The rate of business failure and (the alleged lack of) resilience of remaining operators in 2010 was such that, rather than pay hotels and hospitality providers in advance for 2012 Olympic contract commitments, the *Financial Times* reported that escrow accounts had been introduced by PricewaterhouseCoopers (PwC) to ward off the risk of making early payment to businesses that may no longer be trading at the time of the games (Jacobs 2010). While some of the larger operators resisted this course of action, many of the smaller, independent businesses had less power to do so. They could see that money had been deposited by PwC's clients and they earned interest on it while it was held in trust, but it was only to be accessible in 2012.

Times have been testing for tour operators and travel management companies (TMCs). As Vorndran (2011: 231) notes, there has been a sharp drop in the volume of expenditure among business travellers. As a result of the financial crisis, business expenses were cut markedly with targets of 50 per cent not unusual. On the client side, this has manifested itself in travel embargos, redefinition of what is considered to be essential travel, and changes in booking classes while TMCs are driving down costs with transport and accommodation providers to secure the most competitive deals for their customers. There have also been several instances of major tour operators getting into difficulty. In October 2010, Europe's largest tour operator, TUI, found itself at the centre of a scandal, forcing the resignation of its Chief Financial Officer and triggering a 7 per cent drop in its share price (Kollewe 2010). In 2007, as part of the consolidation of the sector, it merged with First Choice. However, a £117 million 'hole' existed on its balance sheet as a result of 'failures to reconcile balances adequately in legacy systems' (English 2010: 43). Late in November 2011, Thomas Cook entered into talks with banks about its lending facilities. In order to improve its resilience in the face of a 'deterioration of trading', the company had already arranged one new credit agreement of £100 million. Announcements that it intended to apply for further credit of £100 million sparked unrest in the markets and a 75 per cent drop in its share amid uncertainty about its future, rumours that the management moved quickly to deny (BBC 2011b). According to one report, in 2010 alone 24 tour operators collapsed in the UK (DM 2011). Several high-profile failures were played out in the full glare of the media. The collapse of XL (2008), Goldtrail (2010), Sun4U (2010) and Kiss Travel (2010), all based in the UK, proved especially newsworthy because tourists were stranded either abroad or at home without the prospect of travelling. At a stroke, XL's failure left 85,000 passengers stranded, 1,700 staff without a job, and the taxpayer with a £20 million bill as a guarantor for a compensation scheme, not to mention many booking agents and overseas providers lacking commissions and payments (Brignall 2008). Goldtrail's demise left 16,000 British visitors in Greece and Turkey and a further 50,000 unable to take their summer holiday (BBC 2010b, 2010c). In some cases, the situation became tense as local hoteliers demanded that their visitors pay locally (a second time) for their holidays.

Aviation has not been spared. At the height of the financial crisis, oil reached USD 147 per barrel in July 2008 (compared to its current USD 110 per barrel) (Frigieri 2012). Even the previously inexorable expansion of low-fare carriers was halted, especially within Europe, as volatility in fuel prices compounded on other testing trading parameters. Sterling Air – a low-cost carrier covering Scandinavia – ceased operating in October 2008 partly as a result of the collapse of the financial system in Iceland where its major creditors were based (Done 2008). This was followed by SkyEurope and MyAir in 2009 (BBC 2009). Indeed, one listing suggests that, in 2008, as many as 52 airlines of various business models failed worldwide followed by a further 22 in 2009 (CAPA 2009). In the view of Michael O'Leary, the outspoken chief executive of Ryanair:

> what has happened in Europe in the last five years is that the industry is consolidating around four and a half [*sic*] airlines – BA, Air France, Lufthansa, Ryanair and easyJet trying but not really succeeding. As they consolidate, they're cutting routes and driving fares up.
>
> (Sibun 2011: n.p.)

Virtually all carriers have revised their operations to see them through tough trading conditions and in readiness for post-crisis scenarios (see Franke and John 2011); prominent among them are two of the flag carriers O'Leary deemed to have reasonable future prospects. British Airways has merged with Iberian in order to reduce its cost base and to increase its reach (BBC 2010d). Late in 2011, the German carrier Lufthansa announced its intention to sell British Midland (BMI) to British Airways, which wanted to take advantage of the consolidation to acquire more landing slots at a congested London Heathrow (BBC 2011c). Within the low-fares sector, others have defied O'Leary's predictions. Vueling and Clickair merged in 2008, while British-based Flybe acquired a 60 per cent controlling interest in Finncomm (Finnish Commuter Airlines) in a joint venture with Finnair to export its business model to short-haul and domestic aviation around the Baltic (Flybe 2011). Other carriers have cancelled routes or reduced the frequency of scheduled flights, including Ryanair (Robertson 2010), despite O'Leary's argument that it is 'growing capacity – although at a slower rate – and keeping fares low' (Sibun 2011: n.p.).

Finally, there has been a complex response within the accommodation sector. Research in the United States suggests that output performance metrics have been strongly correlated with the state of macro-economic conditions. Woodworth (2009: 407) reports a fall in total demand of 1.8 per cent in 2008 and an 8 per cent decline in June 2009 year-on-year. Some respite was forecast with an upturn hypothesised for 2011 (Smith 2010). Decline in business travel budgets, especially in 2009 (Kiessling *et al.* 2009), as well as willingness to pay among private travellers are routinely cited explanations for the depressed average room rate and occupancy levels. For example, Woodworth (2010: 154) notes that average occupancy was at 55.1 per cent in 2009, or 11.5 per cent below the long-run average of 62.7 per cent. According to Smith's (2010: 149) analysis, this represents significant development. Operators had attempted to weather the financial storm by improving efficiency and average break-even occupancy was 50 per cent. Nevertheless, in this context, an average occupancy of 55 per cent makes uncomfortable reading. Reduced profitability manifested itself in decline in the growth of new rooms entering the market and the trading of property assets. In the case of the latter, for instance, Pechlaner and Frehse (2010: 35) demonstrate a dramatic decline in hotel transaction volumes within Europe from a peak of over €20 billion in 2006 to around €5 billion in 2009, or the level previously experienced in 2002. In the case of the former, Smith (2010: 150) notes that investment decisions made before the onset of the recession meant that, by the end of 2008, 185,000 rooms were under construction in the United States, while in 2009 the figure was 97,000. Strongest growth had been in the luxury chain scale group mainly geared towards high net worth individuals, which increased by 13.2 per cent in 2009. A similar trend was observed in Europe as several brands attempted to capitalise on greater affluence among the BRIC countries (Brazil, Russia, India, China). Expansion in this segment had been curtailed by the credit crunch, not least because less debt was available for investors, but overall investments were considered robust because of the nature of the primary target consumers (Kiessling *et al.* 2009: 22). Recent data for the UK indicate that, unsurprisingly, the budget market has also been a stimulus for growth, suggesting a polarisation in the market. Despite the ongoing recession, the British Hospitality Association (BHA) expected 106 hotels to open in 2011 with 11,800 new rooms, to be followed by a further 170 hotels with 21,500 rooms in 2012. Of these, 7,100 (60.2 per cent) and 14,575 (69.4 per cent) in 2011 and 2012 respectively would be in budget accommodation (BHA 2011). Various reasons exist for such counter-cyclical investments, including postponements, renegotiations and enhanced preparedness for recovery. As Woodworth has argued confidently with respect to the US market, 'history tells us that extraordinary declines lead to above-average recoveries, and such will be the case with the current episode' (2009: 411).

Adminstration, management and governance

Consumption and production are obvious subjects to consider when exploring the relationship between tourism and the economic downturn. Both are suggestive of straightforward 'cause-and-effect' type relationships that can be empirically observed: the economic downturn is the cause, and the effects are to be seen in adjustments to the patterns of consumption, as well as the restructuring and reorganisation of production. In this conceptualisation, consumption and production are viewed almost as dependent variables, whereas the potential for the tourism sector to contribute to recovery from crisis is ignored. Shortly after the election of the Coalition Government in 2010, in his first major speech on tourism, the new British Prime Minister, David Cameron, argued that tourism should be central to rebalancing the UK economy. In principle, this idea has much to commend it in states such as the UK, which have major structural deficits between what they earn and what they spend. As a major form of economic activity and source of export earnings, a boost in tourism-related activity also significantly contributes to the taxation base and reduces the welfare bill. As Cameron put it:

which industry is our third highest export earner behind chemicals and financial services? Manufacturing? IT? Education? No, it's tourism. And it's not just a great export earner. There's also a huge domestic market too . . . Tourism presents a huge economic opportunity. Not just bringing business to Britain but right across Britain driving new growth in the regions and helping to deliver the rebalancing of our national economy that is so desperately needed.

(2010: n.p.)

In keeping with such immaculate logic, destinations of varying scales have used the recent economic downturn as an opportunity to reform tourism administration with a view to boosting productivity and aiding the recovery. By reforming state involvement in tourism in the short term, they hope to capitalise on what they hope will be a more competitive offer in the post-recessionary period. For example, the city authorities in Vienna argued that the city was not spared the effects of the recession when performance in 2009 brought six years of record growth to an end. In their view, though, the key to their resilience and hence to their recovery was a longer view, not short-term expediency. Rather than cutting investment in tourism as tax revenues fell, instead the city injected a further €1.5 million in the marketing effort and a new concept was developed to encourage the addition of €100 million and one million bednights by 2015. As they noted, it is essential 'for a destination with such a small domestic market to pitch its marketing as internationally as possible in order to spread the risk' (WTV 2009: 9). Stockholm, one of Vienna's benchmark competitors, had taken a similar view. The city had become cheaper in comparison to competitors nearby because of the weakening of the krona during the crisis (Euromonitor 2010). However, the marketing effort had been reorientated to higher value creation from a smaller group of key overseas markets and by investing in the development of the website and new social media to enhance the experience of future visitors (SVB 2010).

Counter-cyclical investment is evident at the national level. For example, the Federal Government of Germany has committed itself to providing an annual budget of €27.7 million for the Deutsche Zentrale für Tourismus (DZT) for marketing Germany, primarily in foreign markets. It sees this role as especially important in supporting smaller enterprises that would not otherwise have the resources necessary to reach such audiences (BMWI 2012a, 2012b). Nevertheless, in some states public sector support for tourism has been reduced. Perhaps most ironically, it would appear that some of the greatest reductions in public sector support for tourism are in fact taking place in the UK, in spite of Cameron's championing of the sector and the desire to capitalise on the imminent 2012 Olympic Games (Penrose 2011). Tourism administration with Britain functions on two levels. VisitBritain exists (now) primarily as an overseas marketing organization for inbound visitors to the UK as a whole. Public sector responsibility for tourism administration is devolved to each of the four home 'nations' which has its own national tourism body; moreover, within England tourism is a non-statutory obligation for local government. This means that unlike issues such as health, welfare and education, which are a legal obligation to provide, support for tourism is discretionary. As a result of the 2010 Comprehensive Spending Review which set public sector spending up to 2014–15, funding to support tourism was cut noticeably. Central government support for VisitBritain and VisitEngland, the national tourism body, were cut by 34 per cent (Hunt 2010). VisitBritain's budget will fall from £26.5 million to £21.2 million by 2014, while VisitEngland's will fall from £9.2 million to £7.3 million over the same period. The latter is compounded by the fact that £5 million is to be ring-fenced as its contribution to a national transition/challenge fund leaving an effective operating budget of £2.3 million.

Put in context, the prima facie central government investment for tourism in the UK is similar to the German Federal Government's (BMWI 2012a). However, whereas the latter has pledged to continue enhancing the competitiveness of (and marketing effort for) Germany, the former is committed to reducing its involvement progressively in the operation of markets. In its subsequent tourism policy, central government argued in especially strong terms that 'stronger more focused tourism bodies' (Penrose 2011: 19) are necessary, especially at the local level. This is because the state's involvement in tourism management – particularly in marketing – was portrayed as an unacceptable and unaffordable instance of market failure. As the minister noted, 'we shouldn't expect taxpayers to pay for the marketing budget of any other sector of our economy, let alone an industry as large and successful as this one', furthermore noting that the sector is characterised by '"free riding" by firms which don't participate but which nonetheless benefit from everyone else's joint investments' (Penrose 2011: 19). Prior to the publication of this policy, it had been announced that regional tourist boards, where they still existed, were to be wound up as part of an existing commitment to abolish regional development agencies (Cable and Pickles 2010). In their place, destination management organisations (DMOs) were to work with their effective replacements, local enterprise partnerships (LEPs), in public–private partnerships to provide services and solutions that are appropriate to local conditions (and, it may be added, resourcing levels). While this may appear logical in principle, in practice the experience has been somewhat different. Local authorities have assumed the role of key intermediaries insofar as they are expected to be key players in the LEPs and they are already key stakeholders (not to say investors) in many DMOs. However, settlements to local government were also cut by an average of 7.1 per cent as a result of the 2010 Spending Review (BBC 2010e). Not surprisingly then, as Dinan *et al.* (2011) reported, 68 per cent of DMOs had experienced reductions in their financial resources; however, a more concerning effect had been the loss of capacity and tacit knowledge as a result of staff cuts. Moreover, it appears as though public and private sector actors in the tourism sector may not be able to rely on LEPs to provide the sort of leadership that will leverage significant future investment for tourism. Only seven of thirty-five LEPs that were established in July 2010 explicitly identified tourism as a strategic priority in their accompanying documentation.

Discussion and conclusion

The recent economic crisis has had a profound effect on travel and tourism throughout the world. The downturn has induced the restructuring and reorganisation of consumption, production and administration, the effects of which are only now beginning to be revealed and whose impacts should be more carefully considered in the future research effort as they unfold. Terms such as 'global economic downturn', 'financial crisis' or 'sovereign debt crisis' have often and conveniently been adopted as shorthand for the macro-economic downturn since 2007. However, they reflect a reductionist tendency to render the inherently complex much simpler. Umbrella terms like these imply that the effects of change have been ubiquitous, and that the same patterns of change have been – and indeed will be – experienced universally. This is clearly not the case. There have been winners and losers within tourism as in other sectors of economic activity. As this chapter has noted, aggregated data and high-level forecasts derived from secondary sources serve an important purpose, offering as they do significant clues to possible trajectories for the sector. Nevertheless, in their coarseness, they have the effect of obscuring more finely granulated features. Within the developed world, the financial crisis has dampened demand, thereby inducing a contraction in the time–space horizons of leisure tourists. Rationalisation of the supply side has accompanied this as businesses have struggled to maintain their competitiveness in altogether more testing operating environments. However, as important as raw demand may be, other more complex features related to the financial crisis, such as the availability and cost of credit, which often go unnoticed and which conspire with the unique features of many tourism enterprises, are also driving change. A more nuanced understanding is clearly desirable – one that does not exclusively rely on modelling and instead also interrogates the social politics and political economy of travel and tourism.

It is somewhat predictable to end with a call for future research, not least by pointing to the limitations of the current contribution. In the case of the latter and, as the preceding account makes clear, in relative terms there has been far greater consideration of travel and tourism trends as they relate to the developed world, mainly in Europe and North America, since the onset of the financial crisis. In contrast, there has been far less attention paid to emergent markets, newly industrialised countries and states to the south of the Tropic of Cancer. In some cases, these economies appear to have been some of the (relative) beneficiaries from the redistributive effects of recent times. A more intensive spatio-temporal treatment of the current episode is also desirable for two general reasons. First, it is central to developing a useful body of knowledge for academics, policy makers and practitioners of the future. Within the past two decades there has been a surge in academic interest in tourism. The majority of research has examined tourism in times of growth and relative economic stability (Hall and Coles 2008). While short-term, mainly localised crises have attracted attention, in contrast the effects of comparatively more prolonged periods of economic downturn have yet to be fully researched. For instance, the end of the last major financial crisis in the UK in the early 1990s largely pre-dates the sustained growth in tourism scholarship. Recessionary periods or episodes of economic stagnation may be shorter or more infrequent than periods of growth; however, economies are characterised by their cyclical performance and periods of expansion are followed by periods of decline. Superficially at least, the study of growth may be more attractive than decline, but both are necessary to a more complete understanding of the fluctuating dynamics of the tourism sector. Second and somewhat pragmatically then, if the effects of the downturn are to be more fully appreciated, a more intensive research effort, engaging with people, is required while these conditions persist – not after the fact. What is more, it is by no means certain that the worst is over and that some markets will not slide into another downward phase in a 'double dip'. Other changes, such as counter-cyclical marketing reforms or structural adjustments to state support, have yet to do their work through the system. Perhaps most importantly, it is simply unrealistic to assume that some notional view of business-as-usual (i.e. business-as-before) will resume at some time in the future. Business is very rarely usual and both producers and consumers continually have to respond to (and manage) change. The recent crisis is likely to have more far-reaching and enduring effects because its origins are in the credit crunch and subsequent crisis in the financial markets. Precisely the same types of institutions that induced the current crisis are those that tourism operators around the world in various forms and sizes look to for finance, advice and assistance. They are the same ones that provide loans and mortgages for millions of customers and drive the availability of disposable income. The real crisis for tourism development lies, therefore, in the assumption that conditions will revert back to precisely how they were – or how we understood them – before 2007, and that stakeholders in the tourism sector will fail to recognise or learn the lessons from the processes of restructuring and reorganisation that continue to unfold.

Acknowledgements

The author would like to thank the Economic and Social Research Council for its support in the form of a Business Placement (RES-185–31–0002), which contributed to part of this chapter. Oliver Weigel and Markus Pillmayer provided helpful insights on the situation in Germany. The usual caveats apply.

References

Anonymous (2011) 'Hopes high for bumper year for Scottish tourism', *Destination*, 40 (May/June): 16.
Bailey, G. (2011) 'Ridgeway: the perfect "staycation"', retrieved 14 March 2012 from www.edmontonsun.com/2011/10/31/ridgeway-the-perfect-staycation.
Brent Ritchie, J.R., Molinar, C.M.A. and Frechtling, D.C. (2010) 'Impacts of the world recession and economic crisis on tourism: North America', *Journal of Travel Research*, 49(1): 5–15.
Brignall, M. (2008) 'XL: travel firm's collapse may land taxpayer with £20m bill', retrieved 14 March 2012 from www.guardian.co.uk/business/2008/sep/13/theairlineindustry.travelleisure.

British Broadcasting Corporation (BBC) (2009) 'Airline collapse hits passengers', retrieved 24 March 2012 from http://news.bbc.co.uk/1/hi/8232362.stm.

British Broadcasting Corporation (BBC) (2010a) 'Hotels closing down despite rise in UK "staycations"', retrieved 14 March 2012 from http://news.bbc.co.uk/1/hi/uk/8657540.stm.

British Broadcasting Corporation (BBC) (2010b) 'Goldtrail collapse leaves Britons in Greece and Turkey', retrieved 14 March 2012 from www.bbc.co.uk/news/uk-10671063.

British Broadcasting Corporation (BBC) (2010c) 'Goldtrail collapse: travellers' stories', retrieved 14 March 2012 from www.bbc.co.uk/news/uk-10672853.

British Broadcasting Corporation (BBC) (2010d) 'British Airways and Iberia sign merger agreement', retrieved 24 March 2012 from http://news.bbc.co.uk/1/hi/8608667.stm.

British Broadcasting Corporation (BBC) (2010e) 'Spending Review 2010: key points at-a-glance', retrieved 21 March 2012 from www.bbc.co.uk/news/uk-politics-11569160.

British Broadcasting Corporation (BBC) (2011a) 'Portugal reaches deal on EU and IMF bail-out', retrieved 24 March 2012 from www.bbc.co.uk/news/business-13275470.

British Broadcasting Corporation (BBC) (2011b) 'Thomas Cook shares dive 75% on news of bank talks', retrieved 24 March 2012 from www.bbc.co.uk/news/business-15832438.

British Broadcasting Corporation (BBC) (2011c) 'British Airways owner IAG buys BMI from Lufthansa', retrieved 24 March 2012 from www.bbc.co.uk/news/business-16298167.

British Hospitality Association (BHA) (2011) 'Hotel construction continues into the future', retrieved 24 March 2012 from www.bha.org.uk/2011/12/08/new-hotel-construction-continues-into-the-future/.

Buckley, A. (2011) *Financial Crisis: Causes, context and consequences*, Harlow, UK: FT Prentice Hall.

Bundesministerium für Wirtschaft und Technologie (BMWI) (2012b) 'Wirtschaftsfaktor Tourismus Deutschland. Kennzahlen einer umsatzstarken Querschnittsbranche', retrieved 26 March 2012 from http://bmwi.de/BMWi/Navigation/Service/publikationen,did=474112.html.

Bundesministerium fürWirtschaft und Technologie (BMWI) (2012a) 'Tourismuspolitik', retrieved 21 March 2012 from www.bmwi.de/BMWi/Navigation/Tourismus/tourismus politik.html.

Cable, V. and Pickles, E. (2010) Letter on Local Enterprise Partnerships, retrieved 22 June 2011 from http://centreforcities.typepad.com/centre_for_cities/2010/06/cablepickles-letter-on-local-enterprise-partnerships.html.

Cameron, D. (2010) PM's speech on tourism, retrieved 22 June 2011 from www.number 10.gov.uk/news/speeches-and-transcripts/2010/08/pms-speech-on-tourism-54479.

CAPA – Centre for Aviation (2009) 'Airline failures 2009: where and why: the CAPA list', retrieved 24 March 2012 from www.centreforaviation.com/analysis/european-regions-airlines-association-warns-of-further-bankruptcies-in-2009-11005.

Coles, T.E. and Shaw, G. (2006) 'Tourism, property and the management of change in coastal resorts: perspectives from South West England', *Current Issues in Tourism*, 4(1): 46–68.

Destination Marketer (DM) (2011) '2010 UK tour operator failures', retrieved 24 March 2012 from http://destinationmarketer.wordpress.com/2011/02/17/2010-uk-tour-operator-failures/.

Dinan, C.R., Hutchison, F. and Coles, T.E. (2011) *The Changing Landscape of Public Sector Support for Tourism in England: Insights from local enterprise partnerships and destination management organizations (DMOs) in England*, Exeter, UK: University of Exeter, Centre for Sport, Leisure and Tourism Research.

Done, K. (2008) 'Budget carrier Sterling collapses', retrieved 24 March 2012 from www.ft.com/cms/s/0/d3607a82-a5bd-11dd-9d26-000077b07658.html#axzz1ps2QfKHm.

Eccles, C. (2011) 'How Middle Britons face downturn', *Destination*, 40 (May/June): 1.

English, S. (2010) 'Finance Boss quits over TUI over £117m "hole"', *Evening Standard*, 21 October: 43.

Euromonitor (2010) *City Briefing Report – Stockholm*, retrieved 23 March 2012 from www.euromonitor.com/city-travel-briefing-stockholm/report.

Featherstone, K. (2012) 'Are the European banks saving Greece or saving themselves?', retrieved 23 March 2012 from www.guardian.co.uk/commentisfree/2012/mar/22/greece-european-banks-eurozone.

Flybe (2011) 'Acquisition of Finncomm Commuter Airlines in joint venture with Finnair', retrieved 24 March 2012 from www.flybe.com/corporate/media/news/1107/01.htm.

Francis, G., Humphreys, I., Ison, S. and Aicken, M. (2006) 'Where next for low cost airlines? A spatial and temporal comparative study', *Journal of Transport Geography*, 10(1): 15–21.

Franke, M. and John, F. (2011) 'What comes next after recession? Airline industry scenarios and potential end games', *Journal of Air Transport Management*, 17(1): 19–25.

Frigieri, G. (2012) 'Oil prices since 1998', retrieved 24 March 2012 from www.guardian.co.uk/business/interactive/2008/sep/18/oilprice.

Hall, C.M. and Coles, T.E. (2008) 'Introduction: tourism and international business – tourism as international business', in T.E. Coles and C.M. Hall (eds) *International Business and Tourism: Global issues, contemporary interactions*, London: Routledge, pp. 1–26.

Henley, P. (2011) 'Hunting for jobs in Portugal's recession-hit resorts', retrieved 14 March 2012 from www.bbc.co.uk/news/world-europe-13084426.

Hunt, J. (2010) Letter on the Spending Review Settlement to Chair of VisitBritain, retrieved 12 May 2012 from www.culture.gov.uk/images/publications/Rodrigues_Visit_Britain.pdf.

Independent (2011) 'Tourist dies after Portugal attack', retrieved 14 March 2012 from www.independent.co.uk/news/world/europe/tourist-dies-after-portugal-attack-2290951.html.

Inman, P. (2012) 'Ireland back in recession as global slowdown hits exports', retrieved 23 March 2012 from www.guardian.co.uk/business/2012/mar/22/ireland-recession-global-slowdown-exports.

Jacobs, R. (2010) 'PwC ring fences Olympic cash to protect against bankruptcies', *The Financial Times*, 20 September: 16.

Kiessling, G., Balekjian, C. and Oehmichen, A. (2009) 'What credit crunch? More luxury for new money: European rising stars and established markets', *Journal of Retail and Leisure Property*, 8(1): 3–23.

Knight, J. (2011) 'Ten of the best glamping sites in the UK', retrieved 24 March 2012 from www.guardian.co.uk/travel/2011/may/24/camping-glamping-uk-campsites-england.

Kollewe, J. (2010) 'TUI travel finance chief to quit after accounts glitch', retrieved 24 March 2012 from www.guardian.co.uk/business/2010/oct/21/tui-travel-finance-chief-to-quit.

Lynch, P., McIntosh, A.J. and Tucker, H. (eds) (2009) *Commercial Homes in Tourism: an international perspective*, London: Routledge.

Neate, R. (2012) 'Greeks try to keep peace with their dwindling German tourists', retrieved 23 March 2012 from www.guardian.co.uk/world/2012/mar/02/greeks-keep-peace-germany-tourists.

Olive Insight (2009) 'Impact of economic downturn on attitudes and behaviour of international tourists to Britain', retrieved 14 March 2012 from www.visitengland.org/insight-
statistics/market-research/Economic_Downturn_and_the-Staycation/index.aspx.

Page, S.J., Song, H. and Wu, D.C. (2011) 'Assessing the impacts of the global economic
crisis and swine flu on inbound tourism demand in the United Kingdom', *Journal of
Travel Research*, 51(2): 142–53.

Panglos, P., Bond, W. and Charter, D. (2010) 'Strikes in Spain and Greece raises fears for
summer tourism in southern Europe', *The Times*, 30 June: 29.

Papatheodorou, A., Rossello, J. and Xiao, H. (2010) 'Global economic crisis and tourism:
consequences and perspectives', *Journal of Travel Research*, 49(1): 39–45.

Pechlaner, H. and Frehse, J. (2010) 'Financial crisis and tourism', in R. Conrady and
M. Buck (eds) *Trends and Issues in Global Tourism 2010*, Berlin/Heidelberg: Springer,
pp. 27–38.

Penrose, J. (2011) *Government Tourism Policy*, retrieved 20 April 2011 from www.
culture.gov.uk/images/publications/Government2_Tourism_Policy_2011.pdf.

Redbond, M. (2008) 'Staycation nation: destination tourism at home', retrieved 14 March
2012 from http://blog.compete.com/2008/09/10/staycation-summer-in-state-travel/.

Reinhardt, U. (2011) 'Closer, shorter, cheaper: how sustainable is this trend?', in
R. Conrady and M. Buck (eds) *Trends and Issues in Global Tourism 2011*, Berlin/
Heidelberg: Springer, pp. 27–36.

Robertson, D. (2010) 'Ryanair cuts winter flights to Europe', *The Times*, 30 June: 35.

Scowsill, D. (2011) 'Global travel and tourism in 2012: resilience amidst revolution and
recession', *Tourism Society Journal*, 148: 10.

Sibun, J. (2011) 'Ryanair chief Michael O'Leary on why airlines should handle the ash
cloud crisis', retrieved 14 March 2012 from www.telegraph.co.uk/finance/newsbysector/
transport/8545247/Ryanair-chief-Michael-OLeary-on-why-airlines-should-handle-the-
ash-cloud-crisis.html.

Smeral, E. (2009) 'The impact of the financial and economic crisis on European tourism',
Journal of Travel Research, 48(1): 3–13.

Smeral, E. (2010) 'Impacts of the world recession and economic crisis on tourism: forecasts
and potential risks', *Journal of Travel Research*, 49(1): 31–8.

Smith, H. (2011) 'Greek tourism hit by recession but still seen as recovery hope', retrieved
14 March 2012 from www.guardian.co.uk/world/2011/aug/04/greek-tourism-recession-
recovery-hope.

Smith, R.A. (2010) 'Surviving the first half of 2010 is foremost on hoteliers' minds', *Cornell
Hospitality Quarterly*, 51: 149–52.

Song, H. and Lin, S. (2010) 'Impacts of the financial and economic crisis on tourism in
Asia', *Journal of Travel Research*, 49(1): 16–30.

Stockholm Visitors Board (SVB) (2010) *Facts about Stockholm's Tourism Industry:
Statistics for 2010*, retrieved 24 March 2012 from www.investstockholm.com/Global/
Investment promotion/Dokument/Fakta_turism_ENG/520-11.pdf.

Thomas, R., Page, S. and Shaw, G. (2011) 'Understanding small firms in tourism: a perspective on research trends and challenges', *Tourism Management*, 32(5): 963–75.

VisitEngland (with Olive Insight) (2011) *The Staycation – 2011 and Beyond*, retrieved
14 March 2012 from www.visitengland.org/insight-statistics/market-research/Economic_
Downturn_and_the-Staycation/index.aspx.

Vorndran, S. (2011) 'Business travel management: everything remains different! Post-crisis
strategies', in R. Conrady and M. Buck (eds) *Trends and Issues in Global Tourism 2011*,
Berlin/Heidelberg: Springer, pp. 231–5.

Wiener Tourismusverband (WTV) (2009) *Tourismusbilanz: Tourism review 2009*, Vienna: WTV.

Woodworth, R.M. (2009) 'The recession is over (maybe!) Now what?', *Cornell Hospitality Quarterly*, 50(4): 407–12.

Woodworth, R.M. (2010) 'Record low occupancies', *Cornell Hospitality Quarterly*, 51: 153–7.

World Travel & Tourism Council (WTTC) (2010) *Progress and Priorities, 2009–2010*, London: WTTC.

World Travel & Tourism Council (WTTC) (2011a) *Travel and Tourism 2011*, retrieved 24 March 2012 from www.wttc.org/site_media/uploads/downloads/traveltourism2011.pdf.

World Travel & Tourism Council (WTTC) (2011b) *Economic Impact of Travel and Tourism: Update November 2011*, retrieved 24 March 2012 from www.wttc.org/site_media/uploads/downloads/4pp_document_for_WTM_RGB.pdf.

World Travel & Tourism Council (WTTC) (2012) *Travel and Tourism Economic Impact 2012*, retrieved 3 February 2012 from www.wttc.org/research/economic-impact-research/.

4 South Africa's destination image

Media framing and representational crises

Daniel Hammett

Introduction

South Africa's transition from a pariah state to a consolidating democracy, reintegrated into the global community of nations, has been tremendously beneficial to the country's burgeoning tourism industry. Prior to 1994, South Africa's tourism sector was domestically orientated, constrained by international boycotts, hostile media framing and a negative destination image. Since 1994, the changing domestic socio-political situation as well as shifts in global geopolitics, advances in transport and technology and changes in the global economy have increased international travel overall, and to South Africa in particular. Consequently, South Africa has invested heavily in developing a tourism strategy that encompasses domestic, regional and international tourism (Rogerson 2011a) and the promotion of a positive destination image through specific public relations campaigns, interactions with the media and hosting of a series of spotlight or 'mega' events (see Avraham 2003; Ferreira 2011).

South Africa's destination image is not purely constructed from the framing and content of these promotional practices. Tourists construct their image/imagery of potential destinations from a range of sources that are interpreted through existing knowledge and frames of reference. News media are one such important source of information about distant locations and potential tourist destinations. The content of news coverage is significant: the often politicised framing of reporting and content selection provides partial representations of people and places. These representational practices often utilise, implicitly or explicitly, discursive themes rooted in ideology and reiterate historical and colonial stereotypes and preconceptions. Potential travellers' conceptions of destinations are therefore produced through subjective processes of interpretation and negotiation that draw upon the information provided through media sources.

This chapter analyses the media framing and discursive representations of South Africa, a former colony, within English (the former colonial power) newspapers. The hosting of the 2010 FIFA World Cup provided a moment of heightened press attention on South Africa, with the tourist industry hopeful that this coverage would produce a positive destination image. The South African government had hoped that successfully hosting this spectacle event would encourage new media framings of coverage of the country, instigating a shift away from (neo)colonial stereotypes and discursive constructs. Shifts in framing and content of English media coverage of South Africa in the build-up before, and duration of, the tournament demonstrate that, despite continued salience of particular, self-perpetuating, discursive constructions and perceptions, there was evidence of a more positive media frame emerging in certain sections of the media. This emergent narrative acknowledged the success of South Africa's hosting of the tournament and witnessed the emergence of a more vocal, critical element directed towards FIFA's quasi-authoritarian control of the sport and major tournaments (see Hammett 2011). The concern addressed here is how post-tournament English media coverage framed South Africa in their reporting. As English media attention on South Africa declined after the tournament, were the discursive themes of crime and fear, pre-modernity and race still dominant – or was a more positive frame perpetuated? Newspaper content from *The Guardian, The Times*, the *Daily Mail* and the *Daily Star* relating to South Africa is analysed for two two-month periods at six and twelve months after the World Cup to ascertain the dominant discursive themes and media frames deployed. This analysis demonstrates a return towards a generally negative and self-perpetuating media frame, with negative implications for South Africa's destination image.

The chapter proceeds through a discussion of South Africa's emergent tourism industry in relation to destination image concerns and media framing theory, and the importance of the 2010 FIFA World Cup to the cultivation of South Africa's destination image. A short methodological comment follows, before a discussion of the ways in which English media reporting of South Africa has (and has not) shown signs of change and of the continued dependence upon particular discourses and framings in this reporting. The chapter then goes on to question the extent to which the legacy of the FIFA World Cup has been to improve South Africa's destination image.

South Africa and destination imaging

South Africa's emergence as a vibrant tourist destination has been aided by shifting global geopolitical relations and expansion of transport links. The country's flora and fauna, diverse cultures and historical interest are marketed to a range of potential travellers, from business travellers to backpackers (George 2010; Rogerson 2011b, 2012). With tourist visits approaching ten million per annum by 2008/2009 (George 2010; Ferreira 2011), this sector is a governmental development priority, viewed as an ideal vehicle for economic expansion and pro-poor development (Rogerson and Visser 2011a, 2011b; Visser and Hoogendoorn 2011). The government has invested heavily in improvements to infrastructure and efforts to promote a positive destination image through international marketing campaigns, notably around the 2010 FIFA World Cup. However, these efforts are not travellers' only source of information; place scripting and destination images are also informed by news media coverage, popular culture and personal recommendations (see Nelson 2005; de Jager 2010).

Tourists' negotiation of these information streams are informed by their pre-existing knowledge and perceptions, meaning their constructions of destination image are framed by prior knowledge. Similarly, the frame within which information is relayed and presented to the public is itself shaped by prior knowledge and experience, and tailored to anticipated audience dispositions and tacit knowledge (see Downing 1990). The construction of destination image is therefore a composition of the hosts' efforts to construct specific (often sanitised) images and experiences of a 'tourist bubble' that minimise risks (and perceptions of risk) while emphasising specific benefits and attractions (van Beek 2007) and visitors' negotiations of these idealised projections through a frame informed by existing knowledge and a range of alternative information sources to (re)produce particular socio-cultural constructions of place (Pritchard and Morgan 2000; Jenkins 2003; Nelson 2005). These constructions are integral to broader negotiations of place, identity and behaviour that encompass understandings of the risks and rewards perceived as offered by the destination (Visser 2004; Cornelissen 2005; Su 2010). Thus, while South Africa benefits from a range of cultural and natural tourist attractions, perceptions of the country as crime-ridden and unsafe undermine the country's destination image: as George observes, South Africa 'has received negative media attention as a tourist destination following several high profile cases involving crime against tourists' (2010: 806; also Donaldson and Ferreira 2009).

The media is a powerful 'text of tourism' (Crang 2004: 77), contributing through text and images to practices of place scripting (Edensor 1998; Avraham 2003). The media's penetration into everyday consciousness, through print, broadcast, digital and social media, means this remains a powerful factor in our construction of destination images. The production processes involved, including practices of selective and subjective authority ordering, selection of 'newsworthy' material and ideological framing, provide networks of reference that are implicated in the negotiations through which we construct understandings of and engagements with the world around us (Avraham 2003; Boykoff and Boykoff 2007). Within the news media, these framings play an important role in shaping audience dispositions towards news stories (Dell-Orto *et al.* 2004) and in symbiotically (re)confirming existing frames of understanding. Thus, as Santos (2004: 123–4) recognises, when tourists have not yet experienced a destination, the media coverage of this place and its peoples acts as the dominant frame for popular understanding and perception.

International news coverage of South Africa plays an important role in constructing popular perceptions of the (in)security of the country and its destination image. This coverage is often informed by broader media framing of the African continent, which perpetuates the myth of the 'Dark Continent' through episodic reporting of misleading and formulaic content coalesced around disasters, conflict and disorder (Kothari 2010: 209). The media's dependence upon networks of gatekeepers, journalists and informants, allied to the prioritisation of content by journalistic norms of personalisation, dramatisation and novelty (Boykoff and Boykoff 2007: 1192), contributes to the perpetuation of normative views through sensationalised representations of Africa in Western media (Kothari 2010). In this regard Campbell (2007) and Kothari (2010) demonstrate how the processes behind media reporting and framing of the Darfur conflict produce particular under-standings of the region in relation to conflict, while Brookes (1995) outlines broader media practices implicated in the perpetuation of neocolonial and racist depictions of Africa.

The continued salience of discourses of Afro-pessimism and Afro-essentialism within sections of the English media are noted as being utilised to juxtapose negative images of an 'othered' South Africa against an idealised English self (Hammett 2011). In Zimbabwe, similar practices were noted in the private press, while state-owned newspapers promoted a more positive, Pan-African framing of the economic success of the World Cup for the continent as a whole (Chari 2010). The representations seen within the English press coverage are common in the place scripting of many semi-peripheral and/or ex-colony states. Rooted in colonial histories and the selective and strategic silences over, and inclusions of, histories, peoples and places, these scriptings invoke images, imaginaries and stereotypes of exoticism, primitivism, savagery and ethnicity (Crang 2004; d'Hauteserre 2004; Cornelissen 2005; Gruley and Duvall 2010). These understandings result in a perception of (South) Africa that is simultaneously alluring and terrifying, instantiating a desire to 'be there' and experience this exoticism while also 'not being there' so as to avoid the perceived risks and dangers of the post-colony (see Brooks 2005; Hammett and Jayawardane 2009). The presence of such themes, notably surrounding crime and security, in much of the English media coverage prior to the 2010 FIFA World Cup in South Africa was criticised by FIFA and South Africa as unfairly tarnishing the country's reputation and destination image, underlining how 'any threat to the safety of a tourist (i.e. criminal activities against tourists) along with associated media publicity (i.e. news reporting, government travel warnings) is likely to negatively affect a specific location' (George 2010: 807) and remains a key challenge to South Africa's image in the international tourist market (see Cornelissen and Swart 2006; Donaldson and Ferreira 2009; Ferreira 1999).

Methodological note

South Africa's hosting of the 2010 FIFA World Cup garnered intense international media attention prior to and during the tournament and provided an opportunity to address the extent to which media framing of the host country changed as a result. While a few observations from analysis of media coverage during this period (1 January 2010 to 13 July 2010) are provided, the chapter focuses upon the framing evident in media coverage from December and January 2010/2011 (six months after the tournament) and June and July 2011 (twelve months after the tournament). These samples allow for consideration of changes in media discourse and framing evident as a legacy of the World Cup, since the hosting of such spectacle events is often viewed as a key tool in efforts to improve destination imaging (Avraham 2003). A cross-section of English newspapers was identified to provide a range of editorial positions and targeted audiences. The *Daily Mail* (and its Sunday version *The Mail on Sunday*) is a conservative compact paper, with a high circulation figure, targeted at the conservative lower-middle classes. The *Daily Star* (and *Daily Star Sunday*) is a populist right-wing tabloid with a primarily working-class target audience. *The Times* (and *The Sunday Times*) is a centre-right compact/broadsheet targeting a middle-class audience, while *The Guardian* (and its Sunday version *The Observer*) is a centre-left Berliner/ broadsheet with a liberal editorial policy and is targeted at a middle-class readership. For each paper articles, editorials and opinion columns relating to South Africa were identified through the papers' own websites and cross-referenced with Newsbank archives for the three periods. Articles focused on food and drink, travel supplements and sports reporting were excluded.

A total of 888 articles were identified, catalogued and coded, comprising 701 articles for the first period, 114 for the second sample window and 73 in the third period. Articles were subjected to discourse analysis and, through an iterative process informed by existing work on media framing and post-colonial understandings of representations of South Africa (Edensor 1998; Hammett and Jayawardane 2009), fourteen key thematic categories were identified and articles coded according to these themes (see Tables 4.1–4.3 for numbers of articles and Tables 4.4–4.6 for percentage coverage).

Overview comments

Prior to and during the 2010 World Cup tournament, the broadsheet press dominated English newspaper coverage of South Africa: *The Guardian* carried 262 relevant stories and *The Times* 180, the *Daily Mail* 176, and the *Daily Star* 83. In the post-tournament sample periods, the *Daily Star* had the least South Africa-related reporting (22 stories), while the *Daily Mail* carried the most (65) ahead of *The Times* (56) and *The Guardian* (44). However, the *Daily Mail*'s coverage was less substantive than that of *The Times* and *The Guardian*, whose Johannesburg-based correspondent filed regular interest pieces. Thematically, the *Daily Star* and *Daily Mail* maintained higher levels of coverage of 'crime and security' across the first two sample periods and of 'celebrity and gossip' stories throughout the three sample windows. *The Times* and *The Guardian* provided greater coverage throughout of 'politics and history', 'economy', 'race' and 'general interest' stories. These differing foci would be expected given the target audiences and expected readership interests of the tabloid/compact (*Daily Mail*, *Daily Star*) and broadsheet (*The Times*, *The Guardian*) press.

A decline in media coverage is evident after the World Cup, coverage before and during the tournament averaging 3.6 articles per day before declining to 1.8 and 1.2 articles per day for the six- and twelve-month post-tournament samples

Table 4.1 Number of articles by thematic code, pre- and tournament period

	Nature	Crime and fear	Politics and history	Sex	Health	Threats to fans/tourists	Celebrity and gossip	Economy	Race	General interest	Problems and chaos	Critique UK	Tradition	Society	Total of articles examined
Daily Mail	27	78	27	7	14	38	40	15	13	42	15	7	10	19	176
Daily Star	3	48	8	5	7	25	18	6	6	21	7	2	5	2	83
Times	4	67	29	15	19	32	23	30	21	43	4	2	14	20	180
Guardian	10	74	50	19	24	45	20	48	28	112	5	2	7	52	262
Totals	**44**	**267**	**114**	**46**	**64**	**140**	**101**	**99**	**68**	**218**	**31**	**13**	**36**	**93**	**701**

Table 4.2 Number of articles by thematic code, six-month post-tournament period

	Nature	Crime and fear	Politics and history	Sex	Health	Threats to fans/tourists	Celebrity and gossip	Economy	Race	General interest	Problems and chaos	Critique UK	Tradition	Society	Total of articles examined
Daily Mail	3	29	3	4	3	3	8	1	1	27	0	2	0	2	40
Daily Star	0	12	1	0	4	7	3	0	0	7	0	0	0	0	15
Times	2	23	9	2	8	5	1	2	2	27	0	0	1	3	34
Guardian	4	10	6	0	5	2	0	1	3	18	0	0	1	8	25
Totals	**9**	**74**	**19**	**6**	**20**	**17**	**12**	**4**	**6**	**79**	**0**	**2**	**2**	**13**	**114**

Table 4.3 Number of articles by thematic code, twelve-month post-tournament period

	Nature	Crime and fear	Politics and history	Sex	Health	Threats to fans/tourists	Celebrity and gossip	Economy	Race	General interest	Problems and chaos	Critique UK	Tradition	Society	Total of articles examined
Daily Mail	0	2	3	1	3	1	13	1	1	12	0	0	1	1	25
Daily Star	2	2	0	0	2	0	3	0	0	3	0	0	1	0	7
Times	4	4	10	1	2	3	4	5	0	13	0	0	0	3	22
Guardian	0	4	7	0	1	0	6	1	1	16	0	0	0	9	19
Totals	**6**	**12**	**20**	**2**	**8**	**4**	**26**	**7**	**2**	**44**	**0**	**0**	**2**	**13**	**73**

Table 4.4 Percentage of articles by thematic code, pre- and tournament period

	Nature	Crime and fear	Politics and history	Sex	Health	Threats to fans/tourists	Celebrity and gossip	Economy	Race	General interest	Problems and chaos	Critique UK	Tradition	Society
Daily Mail	15	44	15	4	8	22	23	9	7	24	9	4	6	11
Daily Star	4	58	10	6	8	30	22	7	7	25	8	2	6	2
Times	2	37	16	8	11	18	13	17	12	24	2	1	8	11
Guardian	4	28	19	7	9	17	8	18	11	43	2	1	3	20
Average	**6**	**38**	**16**	**7**	**9**	**20**	**14**	**14**	**10**	**31**	**4**	**2**	**5**	**13**

Table 4.5 Percentage of articles by thematic code, six-month post-tournament period

	Nature	Crime and fear	Politics and history	Sex	Health	Threats to fans/tourists	Celebrity and gossip	Economy	Race	General interest	Problems and chaos	Critique UK	Tradition	Society
Daily Mail	8	73	8	10	8	8	20	3	3	68	0	5	0	5
Daily Star	0	80	7	0	27	47	20	0	0	47	0	0	0	0
Times	6	68	26	6	24	15	3	6	6	79	0	0	3	9
Guardian	16	40	24	0	20	8	0	4	12	72	0	0	4	32
Average	**8**	**65**	**17**	**5**	**18**	**15**	**11**	**4**	**5**	**69**	**0**	**2**	**2**	**11**

Table 4.6 Percentage of articles by thematic code, twelve-month post-tournament period

	Nature	Crime and fear	Politics and history	Sex	Health	Threats to fans/tourists	Celebrity and gossip	Economy	Race	General interest	Problems and chaos	Critique UK	Tradition	Society
Daily Mail	0	8	12	4	12	4	52	4	4	48	0	0	4	4
Daily Star	29	29	0	0	29	0	43	0	0	43	0	0	14	0
Times	18	18	45	5	9	14	18	23	0	59	0	0	0	14
Guardian	0	21	37	0	5	0	32	5	5	84	0	0	0	47
Average	**8**	**16**	**27**	**3**	**11**	**5**	**36**	**10**	**3**	**60**	**0**	**0**	**3**	**18**

respectively. The post-tournament coverage was skewed by extensive coverage of two key stories – the murder of Anni Dewani and the marriage of Prince Albert II of Monaco and Charlene Wittstock, a former South African Olympic swimmer. Across the three periods, certain trends, with implications for South Africa's destination image, are evident in the English press coverage. First, there is a continued preoccupation with 'crime and security' stories across all three sample periods, peaking in the December 2010/January 2011 period due to coverage of the murder of tourist Anni Dewani. The sustained coverage of 'crime and security' stories suggests this media frame is self-perpetuating, rooted in negative stereotypes and perceptions of (South) Africa as dangerous and perpetuated through enhanced focus upon this theme (see Hammett 2011). While South Africa had hoped that hosting a mega-tournament as a 'showcase for [the] country' (*Daily Mail*, 15 January 2010) would provide an opportunity to project a positive destination image, this potential was undermined by pre-existing media framing and perception.

'Celebrity and gossip' content remained significant in the tabloid press through-out the sampled periods. The notable increase in June/July 2011 was associated with Prince Albert and Princess Charlene's troubled wedding. A dramatic increase in the proportion of 'general interest' stories after the tournament (from 31 per cent to 69 per cent and 60 per cent) is in part linked to the decrease in attention to 'threats to fans/tourists' and 'problems and chaos' as the World Cup surge in interest and travellers passed. Second, many of these stories were related to the shifting framing of the Anni Dewani murder case, as the accused (Shrien Dewani) became the focus of content and South Africa the backdrop to these stories. Finally, many of these stories also overlapped with the increase in the 'politics and history' theme as the broadsheet press carried obituaries of leading South African figures and anti-apartheid struggle stalwarts, including Kader Asmal, Zim Ngqwana, Magnus Malan, Therese Maingard, Jean Middleton, David Kitson and Albertina Sisulu. Similarly, coverage of Nelson Mandela's health scare in January 2011 contributed to themes of 'health', 'politics and history' and 'general interest', as these articles noted the importance of Mandela's political activities and noted the sombre mood of the nation as 'one of the world's most revered statesmen, was taken to hospital yesterday amid growing concerns over his health' (*The Times*, 27 January 2011) and 'Tears, prayers and a country on edge as Mandela is treated for "collapsed lung"' (*The Times*, 28 January 2011).

Tournament build-up

Although the dominant themes in English media coverage prior to and during the tournament have been examined elsewhere (see Hammett 2011), a brief summary is necessary. The first discursive frames to note are Afro-pessimism and Afro-essentialism: Western media are often criticised for portraying Africa as homogeneously violent, corrupt and dangerous (Kothari 2010). South African complaints of Afro-essentialism and pessimism in English media stories, notably after the attack on the Africa Cup of Nations in Angola and fears for post-tournament xenophobic violence, were complicated by the utilisation of discourses of Pan-African renaissance in the bidding process and promotion of the World Cup as 'Africa's tournament' by the organisers (Black and van der Westhuizen 2004; Cornelissen 2004; Desai and Vahed 2010; Ndlovu 2010). English media coverage drew on these discourses in paradoxical ways, but generally 'inter-racial harmony and Pan-Africanism were held up as beacons of hope until divisions were apparent, whereupon pre-existing and latent prejudices within the media re-surfaced through negative coverage' (Hammett 2011: 67).

Pre-existing stereotyping and prejudices were also evident in discourses of primitivism and exoticism through coverage of Jacob Zuma's polygamous lifestyle, with a column in *The Times* (6 March 2010) claiming that 'everyone thinks that having multiple wives is sick, primitive, hypocritical and immoral, and sets the man who indulges in it no higher than the animals'. Such vitriolic commentaries and hostile media framing 'wrote the essentialised African into the (urban) South African experience as a threatening pre-modern being' (Hammett 2011: 69). This practice continued through journalistic norms of personalising and sensationalising stories (Boykoff and Boykoff 2007), notably those surrounding fears of crime and security, including 'Ballykissangel star Victoria Smurfit shot at on "Kill a tourist day" in South Africa' (*The Mail on Sunday*, 11 January 2010), 'England fans could be caught up in a machete race war' (*Daily Star*, 5 April 2010) and 'On sale: Body armour with "team colours of your choice" for World Cup 2010 in South Africa' (*Daily Mail*, 14 January 2010). More broadly, the exoticism and sexualisation of the 'other' present in colonial and neocolonial imagery permeated the themes of sex – in relation to health and threats/risks from the levels of HIV prevalence in South Africa (*Daily Star*, 9 January 2010) and of sexual violence (*Daily Mail*, 22 June 2010). Throughout such coverage, a generally negative place scripting of South Africa was evident, promoting a negative destination image.

FIFA and the tournament's Local Organising Committee complained that such reporting was producing an unfairly negative image of South Africa prior to the tournament. The self-sustaining nature of such coverage was evident in the prominence given to the fears of British media personalities ahead of the tournament (e.g. 'Adrian Chiles "terrified" of South Africa ahead of World Cup' (*Daily Star*, 28 May 2010) and Frank Skinner's column in *The Times* (11 June 2011), 'I'm off to the World Cup. I've updated my will') – stories that themselves served to (re)instil fear and trepidation of South Africa as a dangerous tourist destination. However, a gradual shift in framing during the tournament, away from overt pessimism towards a cautious congratulation, was noted in the broadsheet press. *The Guardian* noted, 'Sceptics drowned out by another rainbow nation miracle' (11 July 2010) and that 'As a public relations job, the 2010 World Cup looks like paying off in the intangible currency of image and reputation' (12 July 2010), with positive connotations for the country's destination image. However, did this more positive tone continue in coverage after the tournament or did the British press return to 'portraying simplified, de-contextualised images of a country, a continent and its people' (Hammett 2011: 71)?

Post-tournament framings

Nature and wildlife are central to South Africa's tourist marketing strategies and the commodification of nature has been integral to the growth of this industry (Brooks 2005; Brooks *et al.* 2011). *The Times* picked up on this commodification of nature, with articles addressing the growth of hunting safaris and attraction of North American tourists (12 June 2011) as well as the dangers posed to South Africa's wildlife by poaching and the illegal trade in highly valued elephant tusks and rhino horns for the Chinese market (8 January 2011). This concern with poaching conveyed a second theme that is increasingly prominent in Western media coverage of Africa – the growing role of (and perceived threat posed by) China in Africa, in this case with South Africa's wildlife an alluring commodity threatened by the excesses of Chinese development (see Mawdsley 2008). The paradoxical relationship of African nature as both alluring and threatening to Western travellers was a prominent theme during and after the World Cup. Coverage of celebrities and nature continued to provide content for the tabloid press, as *Daily Star* readers were informed that '[Kylie] Minogue took time out from her world tour to go on safari in South Africa . . . [and] she wasted no time in soaking up its infamous wildlife' (8 July 2011). However, newspaper readers were also warned of the threats posed by the 'wilderness' to travellers, as actress Hermione Norris's fear for her family while on safari was dramatised and personalised: 'I've got visions of my children being eaten by lions, trampled on by elephants . . . I've been having nightmares' (*Daily Mail*, 29 January 2011). This framing combines the desire of 'being there' to experience the 'wilds of Africa' with the fear of these same objects of desire (see van Beek 2007).

The *Daily Star* went further, writing of the danger of the 'wilds of Africa' encroaching into urban areas with the headline 'Rats devour slum babies' before detailing 'Giant rats are eating children in squalid and overcrowded townships' (4 June 2011). The framing of this story dramatised the content while reinforcing perceptions of (urban) South Africa as a disorderly and dangerous place. Without due consideration of the socio-political and economic history and context of the development of South Africa's townships, such coverage fails to engage questions of social and environmental justice and replicates the view of South Africa as disorderly and dangerous.

Media framing emphasising the dangers of the urban post-colony, often through the writing of the 'pre-modern' Africa(n) into the 'modern' urban space, has been noted as a problematic trend in English newspaper reporting of South Africa during the World Cup (Hammett 2012). In the post-tournament period, coverage of the murder of the tourist Anni Dewani (née Hindocha) in Gugulethu, Cape Town, provided further insights into the ways in which media framing of crime and security concerns invoked particular spatial representations and place scriptings of South Africa. The murder of Anni Dewani on 12 November 2010 and subsequent court case in December 2010 received extensive coverage in the English media as Anni's husband, Shrien Dewani, is British and was named as a suspect in the case. A high-profile violent crime involving a tourist can be expected to negatively affect South Africa's international destination image (George 2010) and the specifics of the media coverage highlight important dynamics and framings.

The first aspect to consider is the ways in which spatialities of (in)security are inscribed and linked to negative stereotypes of (South) Africa. The ways in which Gugulethu was described in newspaper coverage of the case reinforced expectations and (racialised) imaginings of poor urban South Africa as disorderly and dangerous: 'Gugulethu, a notoriously dangerous area' (*Daily Star*, 8 December 2010), 'the notorious township of Gugulethu' (*Daily Star*, 11 December 2010) and 'a dangerous black township' (*Daily Mail*, 4 December 2010). The racialisation of this urban danger was extended beyond Gugulethu in the *Daily Mail*'s reporting, as a story outlined the route taken by Anni and Shrien Dewani on the day Anni was murdered along 'the N2 motorway, which threads its way through the notoriously dangerous black townships dotted around Cape Town' (4 December 2010). These 'notoriously dangerous' spaces are also located as being the 'real Africa' in the *Daily Mail*'s interview with Shrien Dewani who explained that:

> She [Anni] had never been to Africa before, so she suggested we should have a look at the 'real Africa'. The stop was on the way back here [their hotel], and was intended so that we could experience a township.
>
> (4 December 2010)

A circular logic emerges, as the 'real Africa' is 'notoriously dangerous' and racialised, re-inscribing paradoxical relations of attraction and fear and contributing to a negative international perception of South Africa. This process was more evident in the tabloid press, as the broadsheet papers used less evocative language, talking of 'Gugulethu township, which visitors are warned to avoid at night' (*Guardian*, 8 December 2010). The one instance when *The Guardian* prefaced Gugulethu as 'notorious' is telling, however, as the story did not have a reporter's byline but was taken directly from the Press Association. Given the processes of news reporting and production, it appears that, while *The Guardian* tried to avoid sensationalist reporting, the Press Association's use of evocative terminology in their releases contributed to broader discursive constructions and place scripting (see Kothari 2010).

More broadly, English media reporting of crime issues in South Africa tended to portray a homogeneous picture of insecurity in South Africa, with stories such as '[Actress Helen] Baxendale's knifeman scare in South Africa' (*Daily Star*, 13 December 2010), personalising and dramatising incidents in ways that generalised the severity and spatiality of crime. The specific resonance of these concerns for tourists was clearly explicated in *The Times* in a commentary on the murder of an Irish tourist in Mauritius, which switched focus to South Africa and the dangers faced by tourists in a country with 'the second highest murder rate per capita in the world (with 49.6 murders per 100,000 population)' (16 January 2011). (An article in *The Times* (11 December 2010) also notes these figures, dramatically presenting them as 'some of the worst crime statistics in the world . . . except for countries such as Mexico and Colombia where drug wars are raging'.) The article continues to caution tourists of the perils of visiting South Africa and disparages the criminal justice system: 'Clear-up rates for crime in South Africa are also woeful and the police force is notoriously corrupt . . . In Cape Town unsolved murders are legion.' The article notes how 'South Africans take their personal security seriously and, if you are staying with them, insist that you do too', and juxtaposes this against the (unintentional) risks taken by tourists in the same settings:

> Yet tourists wander round largely unaware of the dangers. While locals take care to walk on Table Mountain in groups (afraid of robbery or rape) and would never go into the townships after dark . . . travellers on high-end breaks all too often put themselves unwittingly at risk.
>
> (16 January 2011)

In the touristic imagination, Cape Town and South Africa are written as dangerous and risky destinations.

As coverage of the Dewani case continued, an interesting discourse emerged in the press and was mobilised by Shrien Dewani's lawyers: that efforts to prosecute Shrien were due to attempts to shift focus away from high crime levels in South Africa. In December 2010 a surge of media stories carried this allegation, with *The Times* reporting Shrien's defence lawyer as arguing that 'the case against Mr Dewani had been cooked up', adding that the murder would 'seriously damage the reputation of South Africa if it were merely the work of a local gang' and that a story was put together to 'put blame on someone else' (9 December 2010), and the *Daily Mail* suggesting that 'police in South Africa have mishandled the investigation into the "honeymoon murder" of Anni Dewani, offering reduced sentences to the killers after they implicated her "madly in love" husband, Shrien, thus switching the blame away from crime-infested South Africa' (20 December 2010). A similar discourse was evident in South Africa, where concerns spread that negative, sensationalised international press coverage of the case was negatively affecting the country's image and tourist sector: 'Many South Africans believe that it is their country on trial. The crime has drawn attention to its high murder rate and has apparently deterred tourists' (*The Times*, 8 December 2010). Certainly the investment of police time and resources in solving the case would suggest that the South African authorities are aware of the potential damage to the country's destination image the Dewani case could have/has caused. While efforts to resolve the case quickly and recover from negative reporting may fit a broader strategy for tourism development, a sense of inequitable policing has angered some in South Africa, as evidenced in a letter from a South African resident published in the *Daily Mail*:

> There is rising public anger in South Africa at the priority afforded to the murder investigation of a British tourist when every day 50 South Africans are murdered and 40 killed on the roads by speedsters and drunk drivers

with no such priority given to saving lives or arresting the killers . . . The South African public demands that the murders, rapes and road killings of South Africans receive the same priority as the murder of a single foreigner.

(3 December 2010)

The concerns and risks raised in the letter are noted as themes in pre-tournament English media reporting on South Africa (see Hammett 2011), while the sense of injustice in policing effort implicitly demonstrates South African authorities' awareness of reporting norms (see Boykoff and Boykoff 2007) and the importance of media reporting in shaping destination image (see George 2010).

Testimonies presented in *The Times* (11 December 2011) from South African crime experts noted that 'the murder had done "severe damage" to the country's tourist industry' and that township tourism had been particularly badly affected. Rather than consider the specific dynamics of crime and (in)security in South Africa, locating this in terms of continuing socio-economic issues and emphasising that violence against tourists is uncommon, this reporting personalised the content around Shrien Dewani and, in so doing, implicitly entrenched a sense of 'us' and 'them' – of South Africans as the dangerous 'other':

If Shrien Dewani is extradited he will need special protection and would most likely have to be held in solitary confinement. Many South Africans have convicted him already . . . Mr Dewani is now widely seen as public enemy number one, followed closely by the British media, which initially also highlighted the country's crime rate.

(*The Times*, 11 December 2011)

The hostility reported in such content, as well as comments made by Bheki Cele, South Africa's National Police Commissioner, in which he described Shrien Dewani as a 'monkey' (*The Sunday Times*, 12 December 2010) led to claims reported in the *Daily Mail* that 'given the xenophobic nature of the case, they [Shrien's family] also claim Shrien will not receive a fair trial' (15 January 2011). The mobilisations of this allegation and concern with xenophobia are intriguing, not only because the *Daily Mail*'s editorial line is strongly anti-immigrant, but also because the paper made no mention of broader concerns with actual and potential xenophobic violence in South Africa against non-British nationals. In this context, xenophobia is a vehicle for the *Daily Mail* to assert the juxtaposition between British and foreign interests/behaviours (see Hammett 2012). Coverage of fears over xenophobic attacks surrounding the World Cup were reported in the broadsheet press, as were developments in June 2011:

Fears are rising that South Africa could face a new wave of xenophobic violence as mock eviction notices are issued to foreign traders in townships around Johannesburg, the scenes of bloody violence in May 2008 . . . Now a graphic video has emerged this weekend showing a mob beating to death an innocent Zimbabwean man.

(*The Guardian*, 5 June 2011)

As the article reports, because of the previous eruption of xenophobic violence in May 2008, 'South Africa's image as the rainbow nation took a hard knock' and coverage of growing concerns in 2011 will have compounded this negative influence on the country's destination image.

One theme more consistently present in tabloid coverage of the Dewani case was sex, including sensationalised coverage of allegations that Shrien had slept with a male prostitute ('Police interview male prostitute over Dewani claim', 16 December 2010), but more substantively surrounding unfounded claims that Anni Dewani had been sexually assaulted before being killed ('Honeymoon murder victim "was assaulted"', 6 December 2010). When these allegations were proven to be false, a subtle reframing served to continue to inscribe fear and the risk of sexual violence into popular imagination:

> The medic who attended the crime scene went on to claim that the nature of the hijacking was extremely unusual for the notorious South African township of Khayelitsha, where Mngeni and Qwabe [the men convicted of Anni's murder] come from . . . 'In Khayelitsha they would have definitely raped her. And they [the police] would never have found her.'
>
> (*The Mail on Sunday*, 26 December 2010)

and:

> Dewani's lawyers said he should not be extradited to South Africa because he would be at risk of being raped while on remand by gangs who are HIV positive. Miss Montgomery said that South African prisons were often controlled by violent gangs who use sexual violence on inmates they disliked.
>
> (*Daily Mail*, 19 July 2011)

The framing of this content reflects the evolution of the Dewani coverage, demonstrating a gradual shift in primary focus, from South Africa to Shrien Dewani. The stories therefore increasingly shifted towards general interest content with the crime and South Africa as background, as personalisation of the story was key to retaining reader interest (see Boykoff and Boykoff 2007).

The personalisation of coverage was also evident in the tabloid press reporting of British banker Thomas Heathfield's initiation as a *sangoma*, as were neocolonial discursive framings that juxtaposed 'pre-modern Africa' against 'modern Britain' in pejoratively framed stories of 'Banker switch to witch doctor' (*Daily Star*, 2 July 2011). The contrasts of modernity/pre-modernity were further inscribed in the *Daily Mail*'s coverage: 'going without sleep for three days, putting himself in a trance and drinking goat blood Mr Heathfield, 32, has given up his suit, laptop and his office to train as a witchdoctor' (2 July 2011). A broader sense of South Africa as a primitive and inferior society was implicit as the article reported that 'More than 50 per cent of South Africans use traditional healing – which involves the use of herbs, bones and chants – including many educated professionals', implying that even the 'civilised' and 'Westernised', educated South Africa remains primitive and pre-modern. The continued salience of such framings was also evident in *The Mail on Sunday*'s interview with American actress Jennifer Hudson regarding her filming in South Africa for a forthcoming film about Winnie Mandela, which perpetuated a sense of inferiority/superiority through Western paternalism (10 July 2011). More sensitive handling of local history, context and tradition was evident in broadsheet reporting, including a story detailing the revival of the traditional sport of stick fighting in Cape Town's townships as an antidote to excesses of modernity and criminality. Headlined 'Stick fighting returns as township young turn their backs on gangs and guns' (*The Guardian*, 31 January 2011), the story reported how Xhosa youth were using this sport as an alternative outlet for energies and conflict resolution, resonating with continued efforts in the UK to use sport and community organisations as tools to reduce gangsterism and violence.

The reporting of a broader range of general interest stories in the broadsheet press was aided by *The Guardian*'s Africa correspondent filing regular stories from Johannesburg, covering events from calls for government investigations into deaths by lightning (5 January 2011) through cultural adaptations of Shakespeare (23 January 2011) to acclamation of growing numbers of university graduates – and black graduates in particular – as a sign of the growth and progress of South Africa's higher education sector (20 January 2011). While a significant proportion of such stories reported more positive aspects of South Africa's democratic consolidation, other content from *The Guardian* picked up on otherwise over-looked criminality, from the theft of SIM cards from traffic lights in Johannesburg (7 January 2011), through the case of a surrogate mother in South Africa 'holding a couple "to ransom"' for more money before handing over the baby she carried for them (22 January 2011), to reporting that 'a fugitive French couple who used their survival training to elude South African police for six days have died in a hail of bullets after a "Hollywood-style" last stand' after they had killed one policeman and wounded another (21 January 2011). Throughout this coverage, however, critical reflections on the context framing the events and an avoidance of pejorative language and framing is notable, reducing the likelihood of these stories having a negative influence on South Africa's destination image.

Despite *The Guardian* having a correspondent based in South Africa a year after the World Cup, the paper did not offer a retrospective analysis of the tournament and its legacies. Given the predominance in coverage of social and environmental justice issues prior to and during the tournament, this absence is notable. Instead, *The Times* was the one paper to offer a critical reflection at the one-year anniversary, in two detailed articles, both of which offer rather mixed conclusions. Where the articles do question the benefits of the tournament, the criticisms are balanced between 'how to weigh up the obvious pride in an event successfully and peacefully staged, defying the dire warnings of half-finished stadiums and countless muggings, against the reality that a quarter of the nation's 17 million labour force remain unemployed and more than 50 per cent live below the poverty line' (*The Times*, 11 June 2011) and the tensions between long-term infrastructural investment and benefits versus 'Fifa's demand for new stadiums rather than tarted-up existing venues'. In this regard, a main focus of the commentators' ire is FIFA rather than South Africa, fitting within a broader hostility within the English media (and beyond) towards FIFA's authoritarian control of the game and perceptions of Sepp Blatter treating FIFA as his personal fiefdom. Critics remain of South Africa's decision to spend billions of rand on 'a spectacularly successful World Cup, [when] the country seems no closer to providing basic services for most of its citizens' (*The Times*, 11 June 2011).

At the same time, they acknowledge that successfully hosting the tournament 'undoubtedly helped South Africa's image' (11 June 2011), although as is evident from the coverage discussed above English media framing of South Africa remains mixed but largely dominated by neocolonial stereotypes. Certainly the Local Organising Committee for the tournament would argue that popular perceptions have changed, 'the transformation in perceptions of his country had, alone, made it all worthwhile. "The first question people asked you internationally was about crime," he said. "That question is done"' (*The Times*, 11 June 2011), although the rhetoric surrounding the Dewani case would indicate that this change in perception is less notable than suggested. On the other hand, as *The Times* reports:

> There were fewer visitors than expected last summer, nearer 300,000 than the 450,000 envisaged. Yet those who did come left largely with very positive experiences. According to South African Tourism, arrivals from the United States increased by 22.6 per cent in 2010 and have continued to rise over 18 per cent into 2011. It is why some, like Jordaan [head of the Local Organising Committee for the tournament], continue to insist that the World Cup was worth the investment for showing what the African continent could achieve.
> (11 June 2011)

Conclusions

The 2010 FIFA World Cup offered South Africa an opportunity to improve its destination image. Despite a growing tourism industry, South Africa has suffered from a problematic destination image (Hammett 2011) as '[South] Africa is more often than not presented to the international travel market in overwhelmingly negative terms' (Visser 2004: 338). For South Africa, this coverage has been framed by broader neocolonial discourses and negative media framing of the continent as a whole (see Kothari 2010), while international opinion has shifted from viewing South Africa as Africa's 'poster child' for democratic transformation and peaceful prosperity towards a more concerned view of the country's continuing socio-political transformation (Berger 2010).

The location of South Africa in the English media imagination remains heterogeneous and contested. Media coverage of South Africa dropped dramatically once the spectacle event had passed, with the gains made in a subtly more positive portrayal of the country for successfully hosting the World Cup also rapidly lost. The foci of post-tournament coverage demonstrate a continued fascination with specific aspects of South African life and the self-perpetuating biased media frame. Interest in the personal and dramatic dominates – notably in relation to crime, but also through celebrity and wildlife content. The broadsheet press, as expected, maintained a greater engagement with South Africa (as part of their world news focus) and addressed a broader range of general interest stories. On the one hand, *The Guardian* attempted to provide contextual depth and critical analysis of the background to lead stories, while on the other *The Times* often maintained a critical, neocolonially informed agenda. This agenda often overlapped with the sensationalised and dramatised coverage of the tabloid press, not necessarily in terms of content but in disposition, to implicitly perpetuate a sense of Afro-pessimism and to maintain a media frame antithetical to the promotion of a positive destination image for South Africa. This continued bias and framing leave South Africa's tourist industry facing a crisis of representation it is largely powerless to address.

References

Avraham, E. (2003) *Behind Media Marginality: Coverage of social groups and places in the Israeli press*, Lanham, MD: Lexington Books.

van Beek, W. (2007) 'Approaching African tourism: paradigms and paradoxes', in P. Chabal, U. Engel and L. de Haan (eds) *African Alternatives*, Boston: Brill, pp. 145–72.

Berger, G. (2010) 'Image revisions: South Africa, Africa and the 2010 World Cup', *Ecquid Novis: African Journalism Studies*, 31(2): 174–90.

Black, D. and van der Westhuizen, J. (2004) 'The allure of global games for "semi-peripheral" polities and spaces: a research agenda', *Third World Quarterly*, 25: 1293–309.

Boykoff, M. and Boykoff, J. (2007) 'Climate change and journalistic norms: a case-study of US mass-media coverage', *Geoforum*, 38: 1190–204.

Brookes, H. (1995) '"Suit, tie and a touch of juju" – the ideological construction of Africa: a critical discourse analysis of news on Africa in the British press', *Discourse & Society*, 6(4): 461–94.

Brooks, S. (2005) 'Images of "Wild Africa": nature tourism and the (re)creation of the Hluhluwe game reserve, 1930–1945', *Journal of Historical Geography*, 31(2): 220–40.

Brooks, S., Spierenburg, M., van Brakel, L., Kolk, A. and Lukhozi, K. (2011) 'Creating a commodified wilderness: tourism, private game farming and "third nature" landscapes in KwaZulu-Natal', *Tijdschrift voor Economische en Sociale Geografie*, 102(3): 260–74.

Campbell, D. (2007) 'Geopolitics and visuality: sighting the Darfur conflict', *Political Geography*, 26: 357–82.

Chari, T. (2010) 'Press representation of the 2010 World Cup soccer extravaganza in two Zimbabwean newspapers', *Ecquid Novis: Africa Journalism Studies*, 31(2): 205–24.

Cornelissen, S. (2004) '"It's Africa's turn!": the narratives and legitimations surrounding the Moroccan and South African bids for the 2006 and 2010 FIFA finals', *Third World Quarterly*, 25, 1293–309.

Cornelissen, S. (2005) 'Producing and imagining "people" and "place": the political economy of South African international tourist representation', *Review of International Political Economy*, 12(4): 674–99.

Cornelissen, S. and Swart, K. (2006) 'The 2010 Football World Cup as a political construct: the challenge of making good on an African promise', *Sociological Review*, 54(2): 108–21.

Crang, M. (2004) 'Cultural geographies of tourism', in A. Lew, C. Hall and A. Williams (eds) *A Companion to Tourism*, Oxford, Blackwell, pp. 74–84.

Daily Mail/Mail on Sunday (2010–11) Various issues, 11 January 2010–19 July 2011.

Daily Star/Sunday Star (2010–11) Various issues, 9 January 2010–8 July 2011.

Dell-Orto, G., Dong, D., Schneeweis, A. and Moore, J. (2004) 'The impacts of framing on perceptions of foreign countries', *Ecquid Novis: African Journalism Studies*, 25(2): 294–312.

Desai, A. and Vahed, G. (2010) 'World Cup 2010: Africa's turn or the turn on Africa?', *Soccer and Society*, 11: 154–67.

Donaldson, R. and Ferreira, S. (2009) '(Re-)creating urban destination image: opinions of foreign visitors to South Africa on safety and security', *Urban Forum*, 20: 1–18.

Downing, J. (1990) 'US media discourse on South Africa: the development of a situation model', *Discourse & Society*, 1(1): 39–60.

Edensor, T. (1998) *Tourists at the Taj: Performance and meaning at a symbolic site*, London: Routledge.

Ferreira, S. (1999) 'Crime: a threat to tourism in South Africa', *Tourism Geographies*, 1(3): 313–24.

Ferreira, S. (2011) 'South African tourism road to economic recovery: 2010 FIFA Soccer World Cup as vehicle', *Tourism Review International*, 15, 91–106.

George, R. (2010) 'Visitor perceptions of crime-safety and attitudes towards risk: the case of Table Mountain National Park, Cape Town', *Tourism Management*, 31(6): 806–15.

Gruley, J. and Duvall, C. (2012) 'The evolving narrative of the Darfur conflict as represented in The New York Times and The Washington Post, 2003–2009', *GeoJournal*, 77(1): 29–46.

Guardian/Observer (2010–11) Various issues, 11 July 2010–5 June 2011.

Hammett, D. (2011) 'British media representations of South Africa and the 2010 FIFA World Cup', *South African Geographical Journal*, 93(1): 63–74.

Hammett, D. (2012) 'A crisis of representation? British media framing of South Africa's destination image', *Tourism Geographies*, in press.

Hammett, D. and Jayawardane, N. (2009) 'Performing the primitive in the post-colony: Nyoni's Kraal in Cape Town', *Urban Forum*, 20(2): 216–33.

d'Hauteserre, A.-M. (2004) 'Postcolonialism, colonialism and tourism', in A. Lew, C. Hall and A. Williams (eds) *A Companion to Tourism*, Oxford: Blackwell, pp. 235–45.

de Jager, A. (2010) 'How dull is Dullstroom? Exploring the tourism destination image of Dullstroom', *Tourism Geographies*, 12(3): 349–70.

Jenkins, O. (2003) 'Photography and travel brochures: the circle of representation', *Tourism Geographies*, 5(3): 305–28.

Kothari, A. (2010) 'The framing of the Darfur conflict in the New York Times: 2003–2006', *Journalism Studies*, 11(2): 209–24.

Mail on Sunday (2010–11) Various dates, 3 December 2010–19 July 2011.

Mawdsley, E. (2008) 'Fu Manchu versus Dr Livingstone in the Dark Continent? Representing China, Africa and the West in British broadsheet newspapers', *Political Geography*, 27: 509–29.

Ndlovu, S. (2010) 'Sports as cultural diplomacy: the 2010 FIFA World Cup in South Africa's foreign policy', *Soccer and Society*, 11: 144–53.

Nelson, V. (2005) 'Representations and images of people, place and nature in Grenada's tourism', *Geografiska Annaler B*, 87(4): 131–43.

Pritchard, A. and Morgan, N. (2000) 'Constructing tourism landscapes: gender, sexuality and space', *Tourism Geographies*, 2(2): 115–39.

Rogerson, C. (2011a) 'Urban tourism and regional tourists: shopping in Johannesburg, South Africa', *Tijdscrhift voor Economische en Sociale Geographie*, 102(3): 319–30.

Rogerson, C. (2011b) 'Youth tourism in Africa: evidence from South Africa', *Tourism Analysis*, 16(2): 105–20.

Rogerson, C. (2012) 'Niche tourism policy and planning: the South African experience', *Tourism Review International*, 15(1–2): 199–211.

Rogerson, C. and Visser, G. (2011a) 'African tourism geographies: existing paths and new directions', *Tijdschrift voor Economische en Sociale Geographie*, 102(3): 251–9.

Rogerson, C. and Visser, G. (2011b) 'Rethinking South African urban tourism research', *Tourism Review International*, 15: 77–90.

Santos, C. (2004) 'Framing Portugal: representational dynamics', *Annals of Tourism Research*, 31(1): 122–38.

Su, X. (2010) 'The imagination of place and tourism consumption: a case study of Lijiang Ancient Town, China', *Tourism Geographies*, 12(3): 412–34.

Times/Sunday Times (2010–11) Various issues, 6 March 2010–11 December 2011.

Visser, G. (2004) 'The world wide web and tourism in South Africa: the case of open Africa', in C. Rogerson and G. Visser (eds) *Tourism and Development Issues in Contemporary South Africa*, Pretoria: Africa Institute of South Africa, pp. 335–54.

Visser, G. and Hoogendoorn, G. (2011) Current paths in South African tourism research, *Tourism Review International*, 15: 5–20.

5 Hallmark events as a counter to economic downturn

The 2010 FIFA Soccer World Cup

Sanette Ferreira

Introduction

Over the last six months of 2008, at a global level, international tourist arrivals decreased to 2007 levels and hotel occupancy rates declined by at least 10 per cent. According to the International Monetary Fund (IMF), global gross domestic product (GDP) shrunk by 1.3 per cent in 2009 – the most dramatic decline since the Second World War (Hall 2010; Van Schalkwyk 2010). Tourism, though resisting decline better than other sectors, has not been immune to the deteriorating economic conditions. This economic situation, combined with additional uncertainties brought about by the influenza (AH1N1) outbreak in April 2008, the Icelandic volcanic eruption (April 2010) and the earthquake in Japan (March 2011), is expected to continue impacting tourism demand – at least over the short term. Though decline rates eased during 2009, growth was negative in all regions except Africa. Tourism earnings suffered more than arrivals as consumers tend to trade down, stay closer to home (staycation) and travel for shorter periods.

Despite the gloomy global picture of tourism over the past months, sport and mega events can play a powerful role in stimulating local tourism economies and the 2010 FIFA World Cup was no exception. The year 2010 started with the Winter Olympics in February in Vancouver, and with the FIFA World Cup in June in South Africa, the World Expo from May to October in Shanghai and the Commonwealth Games in October in New Delhi, the tourism calendar was being re-energised across the globe, fuelling global economic activity, employment and confidence. Moreover, it is increasingly apparent that these events not only have to respond to the changing global sustainability norms and development imperatives, but can themselves be drivers of change.

Unfortunately, net gains from hosting mega events are usually grossly overestimated and, in most cases, they are worse investments for developing countries than for industrialised countries (Matheson and Baade 2004). There was therefore little guarantee that the realised effects would meet the expectations of one in every three South Africans to personally benefit from employment-creation opportunities through the 2010 FIFA World Cup (Pillay 2010). Notwithstanding the unrealistic expectations, the FIFA World Cup had provided a real opportunity to give life to the ninth recommendation of the UNWTO's (2009) *Roadmap for Recovery*, namely 'to improve tourism promotion and capitalize on major events'.

This chapter reflects on: first, the existing body of knowledge on mega sport events and the tangible and intangible benefits and costs for host societies; second, the inflated expectations of South Africa since winning the FIFA 2010 bid in May 2004; third, 2009 as the build-up phase towards hosting the FIFA 2010 World Cup by using three other mega sport events and disclosing their contributions to the local economy; fourth, the political will of the South African government to invest in long-term tourism developmental goals by exposing the size of investments made in large-scale superstructural and infrastructural projects; and, lastly, unveiling the golden-egg contribution of this mega event during tough economic times.

Mega events and the tangible and intangible benefits for host societies

In the past decade, academic analyses of mega sport events and their legacy have significantly increased in number. According to Preuss, 'It is interesting that it is rarely the sport legacy that is stressed in discussing the legacy, but rather the economic and tourism legacies' (2007: 209). Preuss has listed a number of objectives that hosting countries have on their non-sporting agendas (2000: 89). These include: putting the country 'on the map'; showcasing the region; promoting the political system; creating new trading partners; attracting investment; boosting tourism; creating jobs and business opportunities; urban renewal including housing and infrastructure; and building a legacy of sports infrastructure (Hiller 1998; Cornelissen and Swart 2006; Matheson 2006). Benefits from mega sport events range from visible superstructure such as new airports and sport stadiums, urban regeneration and hard and soft landscaping along major access roads connecting airports with the hosting cities, to less visible intangible legacies such as enhanced international reputation, re-creation of tourism destination image, increased tourism, additional employment, more local business opportunities, opportunities for city marketing, renewed community spirit, better inter-regional cooperation, opportunities for education, emotional experience, and nation building (Cashman 2005; Kesenne 2005; Smith and Fox 2007; Donaldson and Ferreira 2009). In contrast to these positive legacies there are also 'negative legacies such as debts from construction, high opportunity costs, unneeded infrastructure, temporary crowding out, loss of the "repeater visitor", increases in property rental and socially unjust displacement of people' (Haußermann and Simons 2000: 71). Notwithstanding these latter negative legacies, 'politicians still follow "event strategies", because mega-events can also spread a general spirit of optimism, create combined visions, attract exogenous resources and accelerate city development' (Preuss 2007: 207).

Although the short-term benefits of large-scale sporting events are very attractive for cash-strapped developing countries, city and regional leadership should aspire to long-term economic growth that requires a constant influx of 'outside' money.

This, according to Preuss, can only be reached if the mega event has 'changed the host city's structure' (2007: 213). Therefore, politicians should use the mega event to piggyback infrastructural changes that improve the host city's tourism spaces and supporting facilities for future use. This could be the upgrading of the necessary infrastructure (airports, roads, railway stations and public transport) and also tourism superstructure (hotels, museums, promenades, waterfronts and restaurants).

Faulkner *et al.* (2000), Kasimati (2003), Crompton (2006) and Preuss (2007) all suggest that political will in itself is an important contributor to the success of event-related initiatives and investments. In particular, it can lead to the securing of additional 'exogenous resources' (Preuss 2007: 219) that would otherwise have been unavailable to the sector. As such, major events such as the Olympic Games, FIFA Football World Cup and IRB Rugby World Cup have the potential to generate additional resources for particular projects in the sport and health sectors. On the negative side, political will can lead to economic impact evaluations being compromised as there can be both political and economic pressure on evaluators to demonstrate a positive impact (Kasimati 2003; Crompton 2006).

Unfortunately, there exists a great deal of controversy around the validity of economic-impact studies of sporting events. Economists widely believe that studies sponsored by professional franchises and large sporting-event organisers exaggerate the economic impact of these events on local communities (Lee 2001; Szymanski 2002; Kasimati 2003; Cashman 2005; Preuss 2007). Most of these studies ignore the substitution, crowd-out and leakage effects (Matheson 2006) that can exist during these events. One method that can be used to determine the accuracy of economic impact studies is '*ex post* comparisons of predicted economic gains to actual economic performance of cities hosting sporting events' (Matheson 2006: 1). According to Matheson there is enough evidence to

> believe that economic impact studies of large sporting events may overstate those events' true impact. In addition, evidence suggests that in practice the *ex ante*[1] estimates of economic benefits far exceeded the *ex post* observed economic development of communities that host mega-events or stadium construction.
>
> (2006: 3)

Ex post analyses generally confirm the criticisms of economic impact studies that *ex ante* studies routinely exaggerate the benefit of mega events often by a factor of 10 (Dwyer *et al.* 2006). Reinforcing Kasimati's (2003) point that most evaluations are *ex ante* predictions, Faulkner *et al.* note that the lack of *ex post* or long-term evaluations

> may reflect a form of 'policy fatalism'. That is, having committed public resources to the event on such a large scale, the responsible politicians and their advisors regard any evaluation of the outcomes of this investment as being superfluous or, more importantly, potentially politically embarrassing.
>
> (2000: 235)

Within the latter context, Jago *et al.* stress that 'the evaluation of mega-events needs a serious rethink . . . and . . . [should] cover the real lifecycle from bid to legacy, including stated economic and development priorities. This is particularly important in times of volatile economies' (2010: 5).

In the process of untangling the costs and benefits associated with the World Cup it will also be a very great omission to leave out the role of the Fédération Internationale de Football Association (FIFA). As a monopolist facing a competitive group of bidders, FIFA is able to extract much of the financial benefit of hosting the tournament from bidding countries (Maenning and Du Plessis 2007). In South Africa, this 'price' paid for hosting the World Cup and the likely negligible direct economic benefits have only recently entered the public debate. The major revenue stream of the World Cup is the television and marketing rights to which FIFA lays claim. Major expenditures by FIFA include payment to thirty-two participating teams in the form of prize money and compensation for travel and preparation costs. According to Maenning and Du Plessis 'the reported costs for the World Cup 2006 in Germany were about 5,300 million ZAR (530 million Euro) while FIFA earned a profit of 14 billion ZAR (1.4 billion Euro)' (2007: 3).

The prospect of hosting a successful mega event and the positive spin-offs and opportunities that this might create through international publicity (Jeong and Faulkner 1996; Donaldson and Ferreira 2007) often cause host communities to ignore negative impacts that might occur (Kim *et al.* 2006; Bird and Donaldson 2009). Hosting a major event might raise the positive perceptions of the city so that it becomes a 'world-class' city (Preuss 2007) and travel destination, but the presence of a mega event is also accompanied by intangible costs. For example, the publicity associated with a sporting event may not always place a city in a positive light (such as high prices charged by hotels, exaggerated crime situations, strikes by low-paid workers, bribery and terrorist attacks).

Inflated expectations since winning the bid – 'bread and circuses'[2]

In a socio-economic context, South Africa is the most unequal country in the world – worse now than it was before the end of apartheid. It has the world's twenty-fourth biggest economy, but ranks 129th out of 182 on the UN's Human Development Index. Almost one in four adult South Africans is unemployed, and one in three lives on less than $2 a day (Intelligence 2010: 1). In May 2004, South Africa emerged as the winner of the bid to host the 2010 FIFA World Cup. This was a momentous occasion, particularly given that it was the first time that a country on the African continent was chosen to host such a prestigious mega event.

In the aftermath of the failed Olympic bid of 1997, positive developmental expectations of this 2010 mega event were again very high. Could the soccer World Cup rejuvenate a fading 'rainbow nation dream'[3] and give new hope as the poor majority in South Africa still wondered whether they would ever see any of the gold at the end of the rainbow? The event was considered an opportunity to maximise tourism value, to enable African countries to draw benefit from the event, to maximise the opportunity to brand South Africa as a tourism destination, and to have a positive impact on the country's social legacy through advancing tourism competitiveness to support the objectives of creating employment, growth and equity (DEAT 2005: 5).

Contrasting the latter expectations of the South African government's Department of Economic Development and Tourism, the 'critical voices' from community-based grassroots organisations and alternative and conventional media prophesied that the tournament would not 'benefit the poor and the disadvantaged . . . and that the expenditure of billions of rands on the World Cup constitutes a misdirection of resources needed to meet a wide range of pressing social needs' (Ngonyama 2010: 169). To strengthen this side of the argument, the chairperson of the Young Communist League, David Masonda, asked the question, 'How will poor South Africans react upon realizing that the World Cup brought them no significant tangible benefit?' (Ngonyama 2010: 170). In this regard, the Anti-Privatization Forum (APF) had plans for well-coordinated campaigns to put pressure on the authorities to deliver on the expectations and promises they had created (McKinley 2008). Yet, when 70,000 construction workers went on national strike in July 2009, the majority of whom earn less than R3,000 per month, their action received negative media coverage. Some media reports referred to the striking workers as disgruntled, while the South African Federation of Civil Engineering Contractors (SAFCEC) held that a 65 per cent increase was unthinkable (Cottle 2009: 8). Peter Alegi (2007) refers to the realities of ownership in the context of soccer's political economy as 'how South Africa's engagement with global capitalism is not mitigating apartheid's . . . legacy of racism . . . and poverty'.

On another front, great noise was made that 'Africa's time had come', this event was a first for Africa, and Africans would share the opportunity to attend the sixty-three World Cup matches. Unfortunately, by mid-April 2010, only 2 per cent of the tickets that were sold belonged to foreign Africans (*International Business Times* 2010: 1). Three weeks before the opening match between Mexico and South Africa on 11 June, organisers had revised their estimates for the World Cup visitors down to 200,000 from an original figure of 750,000. Reasons for revising their once-optimistic tourism goals were the poor economy worldwide, anecdotes about inflated prices in South Africa, and the country's high crime rate – which the British newspaper *The Observer* said included fifty murders a day. The rigid internet-based ticketing system used by FIFA, the federation that manages international soccer as well as the World Cup, was also blamed (Baxter 2010: 1).

The projected R34.2 billion ($6 billion)[4] impact of the World Cup for South Africa in 2002 suggested that the soccer games and the ancillary activities would represent over 4 per cent of the entire GDP of the country in the year of the event. At the time of the tournament bid in 2004, the South African delegation budgeted R818 million ($144 million) for stadium development (FIFA

Table 5.1 2010 FIFA World Cup stadiums

Stadium	Location	Capacity	ZAR (billion)	US$ (million)
Soccer City	Johannesburg	94,500	3.3	440
Cape Town	Cape Town	66,000	4.4	600
Loftus Versfeld*	Pretoria	49,365	0.099	25.7
Moses Mabhida	Durban	69,957	3.4	450
Nelson Mandela Bay	Port Elizabeth	46,082	2.5	270
Royal Bafokeng	Rustenburg	44,530	0.25	20.4
Free State*	Bloemfontein	45,058	0.305	34.1
Mombela	Nelspruit	43,589	1.5	140
Peter Mokaba	Polokwane	45,264	1.24	150
Ellis Park*	Johannesburg	61,639	0.24	29.2
Totals			17.4	2,159.4

Source: MediaClubSouthAfrica (2010).
Note: * Upgraded existing stadium.

2004b: 65). Since 2004, the South African government substantially increased the budgeted amount for investment in stadiums and related infrastructure. In the October 2006 Medium Term Budget Policy Statement, the Minister of Finance budgeted R15 billion to finance World Cup-related investments, of which R8.4 billion was earmarked for stadiums and R6.7 billion for infrastructure (Manuel 2006). Though these budgeted allocations were much higher than previously allowed, they fell short of the Minister of Transport's claim that transport infrastructure to an amount of R14.9 billion would be required leading up to the World Cup (though presumably not all of this would be directly associated with the tournament) (Phasiwe 2006). According to current information, a total invest-ment of R17.4 billion on stadiums (Table 5.1) represented a 757 per cent increase on the original estimate (Cottle 2009: 8), for which the South African government was almost exclusively accountable.

An understanding of the way in which events impact upon the quality of life of local residents is critical for the success and ultimate legacy of any mega sport event. Research shows that, if disparities exist between pre- and post-event perceptions, local residents are likely to adjust their perceptions and attitudes towards hosting events in the future (Fredline and Faulkner 2002). Recent research in South Africa (Cornelissen 2010; Pillay 2010) shows a wide range of government, industry and personal assumptions of the legacy outcomes, which will need to be carefully managed. It has also showed that the legacy of the event must be realistically communicated. Two weeks before the 'kick off' of the 2010 World Cup, South Africa was plagued with strikes; for two weeks Transnet workers paralysed the public rail and bus transport system as well as the fruit and vehicle export system. Was this the beginning of a disillusioned mass protest against unfulfilled expectations?

2009 as 'build-up' phase to the 2010 World Cup

In 2009, there were 9,933,966 foreign arrivals to South Africa, which represented an additional 342,138 arrivals to the 9,591,828 in 2008. The 3.6 per cent growth was well above the global average decline of –4.3 per cent. Tourism to South Africa had been growing steadily since 2001 but growth in 2009 was slower than in the previous three years due to the global economic crisis that affected mainly overseas arrivals. Due to the crisis, overseas arrivals fell by 4 per cent while arrivals from Africa grew by 5.7 per cent, resulting in an overall growth in arrivals in 2009. There is no doubt that the South African tourism industry has also been challenged by the economic downturn and some tourists have also been deterred by the strong rand against source market currencies. In November 2009, Kamil Karrim, managing director of Pam Golding Tourism and Hospitality Consulting, told delegates to the annual Hospitality Investment Conference Africa (HICA) in Sandton:

> the global recession could not have come at a worse time for the South African hotel industry, while the supply of new hotel rooms surged by 10%, demand has dropped by 4%. He further admits that average hotel occupancies have fallen to a 10-year low of 60.4% in 2009, down from more than 70% in the boom years of 2006–2008. Hotel revenues (revenue per available room RevPar) simultaneously dropped 10% from January to August 2009 year-on-year.
>
> (Müller 2009: 1)

There is only enough demand to fill about 35,000 graded hotel rooms, while South Africa's room supply (awaiting World Cup 2010) swelled to approximately 60,000, translating into a 25 per cent oversupply. By June 2010, about 2,500 new five-star rooms were added to Cape Town alone, bringing the city's total supply of five-star rooms to 14,000 (Müller 2009: 1).

Considering the legacy in the widest possible terms, the duration of the 'beneficial phase' can stretch from the years before winning the bid (where countries are 'preparing and competing' to host the event) until many years after the event (where the country can capitalise on all the new infrastructure and tourism superstructure). Weed (2008) refers to the phase after winning the bid as the 'pregnancy effect'. When this metaphor is explained within the context of South Africa, from 2004 South Africa was very fortunate to capitalise on expecting the FIFA World Cup in June 2010: 'South Africa's hosting of the 2010 FIFA world Cup was one of the most important keys in the short term to help the country ride out the recessionary storm' – in early March (2010) these words were uttered by the South African Minister of Tourism, Marthinus van Schalkwyk, when he participated in a debate on the UN World Tourism Organization document on *Travel and Tourism: Stimulus for G20 economies*. While the global travel industry experienced a decline of 4 per cent in 2009 as traveller markets reeled from the effects of the global financial crisis (UNWTO 2010), the South African pre-World Cup context (or pregnancy effect) saw an increase in MICE[5] tourism and the hosting of three events (among others) buffered South Africa from at least some of the economic effects of the world economic recession or maybe only postponed the real effect, which would only be clear in the months following the event.

In April 2009, the Indian Premier League (IPL) event was relocated to South Africa, due to the possible political instability during the Indian national election. Within twenty-one days, South Africa had organised this mega sport event. The IPL cricket tournament had drawn 800,000 spectators to watch the fifty-nine games at eight stadiums throughout South Africa. The IPL 'spectacle' brought a total spend in South Africa of about R1.5 billion. It was a welcome boost for tourism during the international economic downturn, selling an extra 25,000 hotel room nights and 6,000 extra flights over a forty-day tournament (Oosthuizen 2010: 4). A special complementing benefit accruing from the success of this event was the strengthening of sporting, trade and political relationships between South Africa and India.

From 14–28 June 2009, eight national soccer teams contested in the FIFA Confederations Cup in South Africa. The 2009 FIFA Confederations Cup was hailed as successful by all major role players. The four stadiums, namely Ellis Park, Loftus Versfeld, Mangaung and Royal Bafokeng, were completed well on time and the host cities of the tournament benefited from a financial, marketing and tourism perspective (Parliamentary Monitoring Group 2009: 1). Thousands of media people had arrived in South Africa with a 'magnifying-glass attitude' – to inspect the 'dress rehearsal' and to make sure that South Africa was ready to host the FIFA World Cup in 2010. This tournament had also provided the opportunity to train 5,000 volunteers for the 2010 World Cup (Parliamentary Monitoring Group 2009).

South Africa also hosted a successful rugby series between the Springboks and the British and Irish Lions in 2009. According to a study commissioned by SA Rugby, the arrival of 37,000 overseas visitors generated R1.47 billion in direct and indirect value to the GDP. The six-week tour produced close to 9 per cent of South Africa's annual tourism GDP (based on 2008 figures). In a study done in 2009 by Kamilla-SA consulting on the Lions Tour, 800 respondents expressed high levels of satisfaction; it was also found that supporters spent on average R44,622 during the series and stayed for an average of sixteen days. In Cape Town in June 2009, despite only hosting two rugby matches, the British and Irish Lions Tour alone gave the hotel industry a welcome break from the declines of the previous months. The revenue per available room (revPAR) in Cape Town jumped 14.3 per cent, breaking five consecutive months of revPAR decline (Deloitte 2009).

The hosting of the FIFA Confederations Cup, the IPL cricket and the British Lions Tour contributed to South Africa's performance in the international arena in 2009, with a growth in foreign arrivals of 3.6 per cent.

Political will of the South African government to invest in long-term development goals

The very nature of the hallmark event as an image-building exercise creates a situation in which personal and institutional interests receive a high degree of publicity and visibility. Hallmark events are 'first and foremost, political events'

(Syme *et al.* 1989: 219). In a macro-political perspective, hallmark events act as a means to enhance a destination's image and ideology – in the South African context, the post-apartheid government's ideology. At a micro-political level, politicians have the opportunity to use such events to support their individual political ambitions and goals. Over the last few years, the political will of the South African government to invest in long-term development goals can be seen in the ratio of investment to GDP. In 2002, South Africa's ratio of investment to GDP was only 14 per cent, whereas the global norm was 25 per cent. What South Africa was spending was not enough even to maintain existing infrastructure, let alone develop new projects for a rapidly growing economy. By 2009, the ratio had increased to 22.4 per cent, thanks largely to the 2010 FIFA World Cup and a need to put the country's best foot forward (Fisher-French 2010). The economic activity associated with staging hallmark sporting events can create significant economic impact benefits for the host destination (or city). As the FIFA 2010 World Cup slogan said, 'Africa's time has come', and with the hosting of the world's largest sporting event came the expectation of pumping a projected R93 billion into the South African economy and the creation of 159,000 jobs as well as the biggest multi-billion rand post-democracy infrastructure investment (Grant Thornton 2010a).

Unfortunately, the South African government's commitment to the hosting of a successful World Cup also included a more than R120 million splurge on World Cup soccer tickets (Table 5.2) (Azzakani 2010; Pressly 2010). The 'known' figure

Table 5.2 Rent-a-crowd tickets

Government departments/ semi-government institutions	Amount in ZAR	Number of tickets
SAA	23,000,000	1,749
Department of Trade and Industry	16,000,000	3,054
Manguang Municipality (Free State Provincial Government	15,000,000	
PetroSA	12,500,000	1,000
Industrial Development Corporation	12,000,000	
Transnet	11,500,000	
Eskom	12,000,000	1,110
City of Johannesburg	4,500,000	
Gauteng Provincial Government	4,000,000	4,613
SABC	3,300,000	2,190
Development Bank of South Africa (DBSA)	2,300,000	
Broadcast signal regulator/Sentech	1,700,000	96
Central Energy Fund	1,400,000	
Post Office	800,000	500
Council for Scientific Industrial Research (CSIR)	314,990	
Public Investment Corporation (PIC)	109,200	
Public Service and Administration	65,000	25
Government Employees Medical Scheme	65,400	
Total	120,554,590	

Source: Azzakani (2010); Govender (2010); Pressly (2010).

applies to money collectively spent by state departments, utilities and parastatals on tickets. State-owned entities and government departments spent money to 'rent a crowd'. In terms of the legislation governing these matters, the Public Finance Management Act (PFMA), accounting officers must ensure in advance that fruitless, wasteful or irregular expenditure does not take place: 'The question is why those who are placed well to be able to afford tickets are now getting state-subsidised tickets, when many ordinary South African have been unable to get tickets' (Govender 2010: 1).

Golden egg or wind egg? Valuing the 2010 World Cup in South Africa

When valuing the 2010 World Cup in South Africa, the economic dividends of the hosting of the event are plenty: some short- and long-term development goals were conquered, but unfortunately there were also other costs, realities and challenges. Some of the benefits were more visible than others and there were also opportunities that were missed. The following paragraphs will discuss some of these issues by distilling/synthesising some of the facts and arguments of previous paragraphs.

Costs and long-term development goals

The cost of hosting the event had, predominantly, been borne by all South African taxpayers (eleven million taxpayers in 2007) via the government's financing of the event. The direct and indirect economic impact of more than R100 billion expenditure on infrastructure, superstructure and security equipment by the national government had impacted positively on development in general. The South African government's support for infrastructure development such as transport (roads, airports, harbours and railway and taxi stations), telecommunication services and energy generation, as well as a specific expenditure focus on urban regeneration, have contributed significantly to the longer-term development of the region and country as a whole. In the cases of the Cape Town and Ellis Park stadiums, the newly built Cape Town stadium and upgraded Ellis Park were part of a broader urban redevelopment strategy, which resulted in precinct upgrades around stadiums, beautified through extra illumination, with hard and soft land-scaping and a seamless integration with other transport interchange stations and leisure spaces. Improvements included more parking space and pedestrian access that would benefit the whole region. The latter strategies reflect the current government's commitment to creating liveable urban space.

Economic benefit: new money from outside the system?

In May 2010, an analysis by Grant Thornton (2010a), a firm of accountants, predicted that the World Cup might boost GDP by an additional 0.5 per cent, confirming the estimate put out earlier by the National Treasury in February 2010.

Grant Thornton's predictions increased substantially from R21 billion since winning the bid in 2004, to R93 billion in May 2010, with 62 per cent expected to be generated pre-2010, and 38 per cent during the course of the year. The majority of the economic expenditure came from the national government's spend on infrastructure and some operational expenditure. Foreign tourism would account for 16 per cent of the gross impact (Grant Thornton 2010b).

The direct income from tourist expenditure was estimated as R18.5 billion ($2.5 billion).[6] The approximately 500,000 international tourists that had finally arrived to watch the World Cup spent on average R36,300 ($5,000) (excluding tickets). This was still dwarfed by FIFA's pre-event profit of R24 billion ($3.3 billion), generated in pre-Cup (chiefly commercial) activities, for example television and marketing rights (Sharife 2010: 1).

Indirect economic benefit: investment climate

Good organisation and infrastructure would definitely promote further investment in South Africa. According to a study by Deloitte, *Partnering for Value*, 77 per cent of senior business executives surveyed in the United States believed that, over the following five years, infrastructure – both public and private – would become a more important factor in determining where they locate their operations to accommodate for expected growth (Deloitte 2010). And with the massive infrastructure investment of more than R100 billion that poured into South Africa ahead of the World Cup, the picture is far larger than a thirty-day football tournament.

Realities or challenges

South Africa received 250,000 fewer international tourists than had been estimated in 2004 (Grant Thornton 2010a). Among other reasons, the global recession and the African soccer supporters' reluctance to use (or unfamiliarity with) the internet booking system of FIFA were blamed for the low number of ticket sales to the potential African market. But other realities such as the geographical distance of South Africa from some of the more lucrative markets in the world need to be part of the explanation equation. South Africa is located at the tip of Africa, part of the long-distance pleasure periphery, and thus a long-haul destination from the main tourist-generating markets. FIFA World Cup tournaments staged in Europe are thus much more likely to attract large numbers of tourists than a tournament staged in South Africa. In addition, sub-Saharan Africa is considered to be the poorest region in the world (UNDP 2005), further limiting the potential numbers of tourists and visitors from within the region. Although the 2010 FIFA World Cup was called a 'first for Africa', referring to South Africa as the first African country hosting the soccer World Cup and 'a soccer World Cup for the Africans', less than 5 per cent of the tickets were sold to Africans outside the borders of South Africa.

Inflated expectations: oversupply of stadiums and luxury hotel rooms

One of the current infrastructural challenges host countries face is to build ten stadiums with a minimum capacity of 70,000 each. This has placed a lot of pressure on South Africa as a developing country where the opportunity cost is considerable. South Africa does not have sufficiently large and affluent football markets in close proximity and therefore ten stadiums of this size constitute an oversupply of stadiums and some economists are already referring to some of the latter stadiums as 'white elephants' (Spronk and Fourie 2010). In this regard, the stadiums with multi-purpose capabilities (Cape Town, Durban, Ellis Park, Soccer City and Loftus) were well positioned within (or linked to) 'leisure space' and the 'luxury accommodation hubs' of their metropolitan bases. They are well integrated with efficient public transport systems, and are better off than stadiums developed in secondary cities, such as Mbombela, Polokwane, Mangaung and Rustenburg.

FIFA gave one of its official partners, 'Match', the sole right to procure graded accommodation to be part of all inclusive soccer tour packages to South Africa – a misinformed outsider (international company) with a lack of an integrated national accommodation database. It created the false impression of an undersupply of graded accommodation. As previously mentioned, South Africa had experienced an oversupply of 35 per cent in luxury hotel rooms since mid-2009. This figure excluded the 2,500 new luxury hotel beds joining the existing supply in June 2010. This situation was further exacerbated by the expectation of 750,000 international tourist arrivals. Unfortunately, the overestimation of soccer fans at the lower end of the accommodation market also trapped small, medium and micro enterprises with an oversupply of rooms. Schools and universities were also convinced that they would pocket millions of rand in housing soccer fans. Although the University of the North West, in Potchefstroom, won the bid to host the Spanish national soccer team in a new, custom-built 'sports village', Stellenbosch University lost money in redirecting annual winter holiday sports events away from Stellenbosch, banking on the idea of making more money from housing soccer fans in student accommodation facilities.

Visible or tangible benefits

Although there was no consensus on the architecture of the ten stadiums – some newly built, others upgraded and some already tagged as white elephants – there were three jewels added to the current state of contemporary architecture in South African cities. They are the 'Flying saucer' (Green Point, Cape Town), the Calabash at Soccer City (Johannesburg) and the 'Space ship' (Moses Mabhida, Durban). With its horizontal facade and expressive, curving contours, the Cape Town stadium's architectural design was intended to enhance the horizontal line of Table Mountain, and appeared as an iconic building in Cape Town. The Calabash of Soccer City resembles an African beer pot, usually made from clay. This clay pot is normally filled with homemade beer and shared with family and friends. The symbolic meaning of the Calabash in this context is the inclusiveness of the stadium and sharing generosity with other soccer family members. The newly built Moses Mabhida Stadium in Durban epitomised the architectural innovation on display in South Africa and took its design inspiration from the South African flag, with its grand arch representing the unity of this sport-loving nation. The two legs of the arch on the southern side of the stadium come together to form a single footing on the northern side, symbolising the new unity of a once-divided country.

The two upgraded airports (Oliver Tambo in Johannesburg and Cape Town International), and the newly built King Shaka in Durban, deserve their places in the visible benefits category. The Johannesburg and Cape Town airports can now be compared to some of the best in the world and, although King Shaka in Durban will struggle in its first years to be economically viable, the extra capacity will instigate marketing campaigns to grow tourist arrivals and develop Durban into a larger tourist destination. The major metropolitan cities were literally 'under construction' during the 'pregnancy phase' – preparing South Africa for the World Cup, where major road construction, a long-term necessity, was part of the development agenda and, although very uncomfortable at certain times for motorists, it is of great visible benefit and improves the flow of traffic in these highly developed urban areas.

The Gautrain rail project, although not primarily developed for the 2010 FIFA World Cup, was planned to be at least partially completed to relieve traffic congestion between Johannesburg International Airport and the high-density traffic of the Johannesburg–Pretoria freeway during the World Cup. The major legacy of the FIFA World Cup lies in the visible 'hardware' of upgraded transport infrastructure (also including the telecommunications and broadband internet connection) and, in a less important sense, the sport infrastructure, because South Africa already boasted world-class stadiums before winning the 2010 World Cup bid in 2004.

Invisible or intangible benefits

Intangible benefits of hosting the World Cup include South African forces having received training in crowd control management from the French National Police Force (Nkosi 2010). SAPS members are now well equipped to deal with violent outbreaks and the training is benefiting the people of South Africa long after the World Cup. Volunteer training is also an intangible benefit for future events. R665 million was spent on procuring special equipment, including crowd-control equipment, unmanned aircraft, helicopters, ten water cannon, 100 BMWs for highway patrol and up-to-date body armour, as well as crime scene trainers, all of which continue to assist the police in their crime-fighting initiatives long after the World Cup is over. Border security and sea and air security strategies are also in place for the future.

The FIFA World Cup 2010 was hosted with no major crime incidents; the overall safety experience of tourists during their stay in South Africa has contributed to the creation of a positive destination image for the country. In the process of preparation and getting the country in order for hosting this event, the FIFA World Cup has left a legacy of a safer South Africa for all its citizens and the birth of a positive tourism destination image for receiving future tourist arrivals. The media response to South Africa and especially Cape Town has been overwhelmingly positive. Cape Town Tourism's international representatives (based in the UK, Germany and the Netherlands) reported that there has been a complete reversal from a stance of Afro-pessimism to the overwhelmingly positive (Von Helmbold-duToit 2010).The mega event of 2010 has cemented a new image globally.

Costs: missed opportunities

Findings also indicate that the socio-economic impacts of hosting the event are somehow regressive: 'those who stand to gain the most via this international soccer event are the high income households and the benefit that is set to accrue to low households is derived from labour remuneration due to the low skills bias of the booming construction sector' (Mabugu and Mohamed 2008: 23).

Conclusion

The FIFA World Cup provided a real opportunity to give life to the ninth recommendation of the UNWTO's *Roadmap for Recovery* (2009), namely 'to improve tourism promotion and capitalize on major events'. South Africa has not been immune from the effects of the global recession and, although the World Cup has helped the South African economy to resist some of the effects of the world economic recession over the last twenty-four months, the decline in sectors such as the construction industry over the next year will remind everyone that the World Cup is well and truly over.

The eight hosting cities have benefited disproportionately more than the non-hosting cities; some areas are therefore left behind in terms of infrastructure and superstructure. And yes – the projected $6 billion impact of a proposed World Cup in South Africa in 2006, which would represent over 4 per cent of the GDP of the country in that year – was a huge overestimation.

The 'feel good factor' (which lasted for at least six weeks) positively contributed to 'nation building' and a 'yes we can' attitude in the country. According to Somerville, 'the 2010 world Cup was not a rerun of the 1995 IRB Rugby World Cup, but Zuma will be hoping that his team, his country and his ANC colleagues have helped him use South Africa's time under the floodlights of world attention to get him out of the international sin bin' (2010: 2).

As Simon Kuper and Stefan Szymanski (2009) say in their book, *Soccernomics*, 'hosting doesn't make you rich, but it does make you happy'.

Notes

1 Predictive (or *ex ante*) economic impact studies usually used by event promoters to estimate the 'direct economic impact' of the event by estimating the numbers of visitors,

the number of days each spectator is expected to stay, and the amount each visitor will spend each day. This direct impact is then subjected to a multiplier, usually around two, to account for the initial round of spending through the economy. This additional spending is known as 'indirect impact'. Thus, the total economic impact is double the size of the initial spending.

2   The term 'bread and circuses' dates from the first-century Roman empire, where extravagant games were held in conjunction with giveaways of subsidised food in order to pacify the citizenry and reduce urban unrest (Matheson 2006: 7).

3   Known as 'The Rainbow Nation', South Africa is a melting pot of ethnicities, cultures and languages.

4   At a value of $1 = R5.70 (in 2004).

5   'Meetings, Incentives, Conferences and Exhibitions'. The acronym 'MICE' is applied inconsistently with the 'E' sometimes referring to events and the 'C' sometimes referring to conventions. MICE is used to refer to a particular type of tourism in which large groups, usually planned well in advance, are brought together for some particular purpose. Recently, there has been an industry trend towards using the term 'Meetings Industry' to avoid confusion arising from the acronym (Wikipedia: MICE).

6   On 14 August 2010, $1 = R7.26.

References

Alegi, P. (2007) 'The political economy of mega-stadiums and the underdevelopment of grassroots football in South Africa', *Politikon*, 34(3): 315–31.

Azzakani, R. (2010) 'Tree op teen die wat kaartjies koop', *Die Burger*, retrieved 11 December 2010 from www.dieburger.com/.../Treeop-teen-die-wat-kaartjies-met-staatsgeld-koop-20100708.

Baxter, K. (2010) 'World Cup: want a cheap hotelroom?', *Los Angeles Times*, 23 May: 1.

Bird, R. and Donaldson, R. (2009) 'Sex, sun, soccer: stakeholder-opinions on the sex industry in Cape Town in anticipation of the 2010 FIFA Soccer World Cup', *Urban Forum*, 20: 33–46.

Cashman, R. (2005) *The Bitter-sweet Awakening: The legacy of the Sydney 2000 Olympic Games*, Sydney: Walla Walla Press.

Cornelissen, S. (2010) 'Scripting the nation: sport, mega-events, foreign policy and state-building in post-apartheid South Africa', *Sport and Society*, 11(4): 481–93.

Cornelissen, S. and Swart, K. (2006) 'The 2010 Football World Cup as a political construct: the challenge of making good on an African promise', *Sociological Review*, 54(2): 108–21.

Cottle, E. (2009) 'Profiting from 2010: bosses 10, workers 0', *Amandla!*, 9: 8–10.

Crompton, J. (2006) 'Economic impact studies: instruments for political shenanigans', *Journal of Travel Research*, 45(1): 67–82.

Deloitte (2009) 'Hotels in South Africa benefit from football and rugby event in June', press release, retrieved 10 August 2010 from www.deloitte.com/view/en_GX/global/press/global-press-releases-en/8f280c75bbaa3210VgnVCM200000bb42f00aRCRD.htm.

Deloitte (2010) *Partnering for Value: Structuring effective public-private partnerships for infrastructure*, retrieved 30 July 2010 from www.deloitte.com/view/en_US/us/Industries/usstate-government/Big-Issues-in-Government/infrastructure_renewal/5c30b9c7133 a4210VgnVCM100000ba42f00aRCRD.htm.

Department of Environmental Affairs and Tourism (DEAT) (2005) *2010 Soccer World Cup tourism organization plan: Executive summary*, Pretoria: South African Tourism.

Donaldson, S. and Ferreira, S.L.A. (2007) 'Crime, perceptions and touristic decision making: some empirical evidence and prospects for the 2010 World Cup', *Politikon*, 34(3): 353–71.

Donaldson, S. and Ferreira, S.L.A. (2009) '(Re-)creating urban destination image: opinions of foreign visitors to South Africa on safety and security?', *Urban Forum*, 20: 1–18.

Dwyer, L., Forsyth, P. and Spur, R. (2006) 'Economic impact of the sport event: a reassessment', *Tourism Review International*, 10(4): 207–16.

Faulkner, B., Chalip, L., Brown, G., Jago, L., March, R. and Woodside, A. (2000) 'Monitoring the tourism impacts of the Sydney 2000 Olympics', *Event Management*, 6(4): 231–46.

Fédération Internationale de Football Association (FIFA) (2004) *Soccer World Cup 2010: South Africa*, retrieved 1 April 2010 from www.swc2010.com/southafrica2010.php.

Fisher-French, M. (2010) 'Making sure the World Cup is money well spent', *Mail & Guardian Online*, retrieved 3 July 2010 from http://mg.co.za/article/2010-06-10-making-sure-theworld-cup-is-money-well-spent.

Fredline, E. and Faulkner, B. (2002) 'Residents' reactions to the staging of major motorsport events within their communities: a cluster analysis', *Event Management*, 7(2): 103–14.

Govender, P. (2010) 'Cash-strapped Eskom, SAA splurge on tickets', *Sunday Times*, 4 July, retrieved 7 August 2010 from www.timeslive.co.za/sundaytimes/article532107.ece/Cash-strapped-Eskom-SAA-splurge-on-tickets.

Grant Thornton (2010a) *2010 Soccer World Cup Facts You Should Know*, report by Grant Thornton's Tourism, Hospitality and Leisure Consulting Group, Johannesburg: Grant Thornton.

Grant Thornton (2010b) 'Grant Thornton says World Cup dramatically increased national brand value for South Africa', retrieved 10 November 2010 from www.gt.co.za/News/pressreleases/Strategic-solutions/2010/2010wcbrand.asp.

Hall, C.M. (2010) 'Crisis events in tourism: subjects of crises in tourism', *Current Issues in Tourism*, 13(5): 401–17.

HauBermann, H., and Simons, K. (2000) 'Die Politik der grossen Projekten – eine Politik der grossen Risiken? Zu neuen Formen der Stadtentwicklungspolitik am Beispiel des Entwicklungsgebiets Berlein-Adlershof', *Archiv für Kommunalwissenschaften*, 39(1): 56–72.

Hiller, H. (1998) 'Mega events, urban boosterism and growth strategies: an analysis of the objectives and legitimisations of the Cape Town 2004 Olympic Bid', *International Journal of Urban and Regional Research*, 24(2): 439–58.

Intelligence (2010) 'South Africa will not win from this World Cup', retrieved 10 January 2011 from www.intelligencesquared.com/controversies/south-africa-will-not-winfrom-this-world-cup/preview.

International Business Times (2010) 'World Cup 2010: only 2 pct of ticketholders are foreign African fans', retrieved 9 December 2010 from http://africa.ibtimes.com/articles/24123/20100518/world-cup-2010-only-2-pct-of-ticketholders-areforeign-african-fans.htm.

Jago, L., Dwyer, L., Lipman, G., Van Lill, D. and Voster, S. (2010) A background paper prepared for the inaugural UNWTO/South Africa International Summit on Tourism, Sport and Mega-events, Johannesburg, 24–26 February.

Jeong, G.H. and Faulkner, B. (1996) 'Resident perceptions of mega-event impacts: the Taejon international exposition case, *Festival Management & Event Tourism*, 4(1): 3–11.

Kasimati, E. (2003) 'Economic aspects and the Summer Olympics: a review of related research', *International Journal of Tourism Research*, 5: 433–44.

Kesenne, S. (2005) 'Do we need an economic impact study or a cost-benefit analysis of a sport event?', *European Sport Management Quarterly*, 5(2): 133–42.

Kim, H.J., Gursoy, D. and Lee, S. (2006) 'The impact of the 2002 World Cup on South Korea: comparisons of pre- and post-games', *Tourism Management*, 27(1): 86–96.

Kuper, S. and Szymanski, S. (2009) *Soccernomics: Why England loses, why Germany and Brazil win, and why the U.S., Japan, Australia, Turkey – and even Iraq – are destined to become the kings of the world's most popular sport*, London: Nation Books.

Lee, S. (2001) 'A review of economic impact studies on sport events', *The Sport Journal*, 4(2).

Mabugu, R. and Mohamed, A. (2008) *The Economic Impacts of Government Financing of the 2010 FIFA World Cup* (Stellenbosch Economic Working Papers 08/08), Bureau for Economic Research, retrieved 11 October 2010 from www.ekon.sun. ac.za/wpapers/2008/wp082008/wp-08-2008.pdf.

McKinley, D. (2008) '"Transformation" from above: the upside down state of the beautiful game of South Africa', *Links International Journalist of Socialist Renewal*, retrieved 9 October 2012 from http://links.org.au/node/729.

Maenning, W. and Du Plessis, S. (2007) 'World Cup 2010: South African economic perspectives and policy challenges informed by the experience of Germany 2006', *Contemporary Economic Policy*, 25(4): 578–90.

Manuel, T.A. (2006) Address to the National Assembly on tabling of the 2006 Medium-term Budget Policy Statement and the 2006 Adjustments Appropriation Bill, Cape Town, 25 October.

Matheson, V.A. (2006) *Mega-events: The effect of the world's biggest sporting events on local, regional and national economies* (Holy Cross Working Paper Series 06–10), Worcester, MA: Department of Economics, College of the Holy Cross.

Matheson, V.A., and Baade, R.A. (2004) 'Mega-sporting events developing nations: playing the way to prosperity?', *South African Journal of Economics*, 72(5): 1085–96.

MediaClubSouthAfrica (2010) '2010 FIFA World Cup stadiums', retrieved 29 July 2010 from www.mediaclubsouthafrica.com/index.php?option=com_content&view =article&id=93:world-cup-stadiums&catid=39:2010bg.

Müller, J. (2009) 'Trouble looms for SA hotels', retrieved 14 June 2011 from www.fin24.com/PersonalFinance/Property/Trouble-looms-for-SA-hotels-20091110.

Ngonyama, P. (2010) 'The 2010 FIFA World Cup: critical voices from below', *Soccer & Society*, 11(1–2): 168–80.

Nkosi, B. (2010) 'Top safety plan for World Cup', *South Africa: Future Uncertain* (blog), 23 May, retrieved from www.marvcbarr.blogspot.com/2010/05/top-safety-planfor-world-cup.html.

Oosthuizen, G.C. (2010) 'Tourism, sport and mega-events in South Africa', paper delivered at the WTO International Summit on Tourism, Sport and Mega events, Deputy Minister of Sport and Recreation, Sandton Convention Centre, Johannesburg, 25 February.

Parliamentary Monitoring Group (2009) '2010 host cities readiness: briefing by Department of Sports and Recreation and Local Organising Committee', retrieved 10 June 2011 from www.pmg.org.za/node/18801.

Phasiwe, K. (2006) 'Johannesburg airport to get R8 billion facelift', retrieved 9 May 2010 from http://allafrica.com/stories/200605240158.html.

Pillay, U. (2010) 'Attitudes to the 2010 World Cup: positive expectations', retrieved 3 February 2011 from www.hsrc.ac.za/Publication-Keyword-248.phtml.

Pressly, D. (2010) 'Treasury probes wasted money on soccer seats', *Business Report*, 14 July: 1, retrieved 20 August 2010 from www.highbeam.com/doc/1G1-231509008. html.

Preuss, H. (2000) 'Electing an Olympic city: a multidimensional decision' in K.B. Wamsley, S.G. Martyn, G.H. MacDonald, H. Gordon and R.K. Barney (eds) *Bridging Three Centuries: Intellectual crossroads and the modern Olympic movement*, London, ON: International Centre for Olympic Studies, pp. 89–104.

Preuss, H. (2007) 'The conceptualisation and measurement of mega sport event legacies', *Journal of Sport and Tourism*, 12(3–4): 207–27.

Sharife, K. (2010) 'South Africa: World Cup 2010 – FIFA's Gordian Knot', retrieved 13 March 2012 from www.allAfrica.com/stories/201006031044.html.

Smith, A. and Fox, T. (2007) 'From "event-led" to "event themed" regeneration: the 2002 Commonwealth Games legacy programme', *Urban Studies*, 44(5–6): 1125–43.

Somerville, K. (2010) 'The World Cup: big win or own goal?', retrieved 24 May 2010 from http://newafricaanalysis.co.uk/index.php/2010/05/the-world-cup-a-big-win-for-south-africa-or-an-own-goal/.

Spronk, K. and Fourie, J. (2010) 'South African mega-events and their impact on tourism', Working paper 03/2010, Stellenbosch University, Department of Economics, retrieved 21 November 2010 from www.ekon.sun.ac.za/wpapers/2010/wp0310/wp-03-2010.pdf.

Syme, G.J., Shaw, B.J., Fenton, D.M. and Mueller, W.S (eds) (1989) *The Planning and Evaluation of Hallmark Events*, Brookfield, VT: Avebury.

Szymanski, S. (2002) 'The economic impact of the World Cup', *World Economics*, 3, 169–77.

United Nations World Tourism Organization (UNWTO) (2009) *Roadmap for Recovery/ Tourism and Travel: A primary vehicle for job creation and economic recovery* (A/18/8), retrieved 19 June 2011 from www.institutodeturismo.org/ficheiros_upload/roadmap %20for%20recovery.pdf.

United Nations World Tourism Organization (UNWTO) (2010) *Tourism Outlook 2010*, retrieved 19 June 2011 from www.onecaribbean.org/.../UNWTOTOURISMOUTLOOK 2010.pdf.

United Nations Development Programme (UNDP) (2005) *The Human Development Report*, retrieved 4 January 2011 from http://hdr.undp.org/en/reports/global/hdr2005/United Nations.

Van Schalkwyk, M. (2010) 'Robust foreign arrivals to South Africa defy worldwide trend', retrieved 5 March 2010 from www.travelwires.com/wp/tag/marthinus-vanschalkwyk/.

Von Helmbold-du Toit, M. (2010) 'Impact of Lion's Tour', retrieved 17 April 2010 from www.capetown.travel/2010/blog /category/cape/P35/.

Weed, M. (2008) *Olympic Tourism*, Oxford: Elsevier.

6 Impacts of the global financial crisis on African tourism

A Tourism Confidence Index analysis

Tanja Mihalič, John Kester and
Larry Dwyer

Introduction

Tourism demand is central to tourism's economic contribution and economic impacts, as it is the associated expenditure that determines its economic effects. Research suggests that the range of factors affecting the demand for tourism is very large (Crouch 1994a; Crouch 1994b; Crouch 1995; Lim 2006; Saayman and Saayman 2008). Studies show that the purchasing power of people significantly influences their decisions to travel and helps explain tourism flows. An increase in real income provides consumers with greater spending power, resulting in the increased discretionary consumption of many types of products, including tourism. Wealthy countries and regions with strong currencies are important origin markets for international tourism.

The collapse of the real-estate market that started in the United States in 2006 expanded into a so-called global financial crisis and led to a general economic decline – the worst economic recession since the Great Depression of the 1930s (Keller 2009). Altogether, the global financial and economic crisis (GFEC)[1] has contributed to the failure of key businesses worldwide, declines in consumer wealth estimated in trillions of US dollars, substantial financial commitments incurred by governments, and a significant decline in economic activity together with business and consumer confidence (Tett 2009).

The GFEC has had an enormous impact on the business world in various sectors, with the tourism sector being no exception. Reduced wealth, slowing or falling incomes, rising unemployment and low consumer and business confidence have negatively influenced tourist expenditure across the world. Tourism spending in many countries, as part of discretionary consumer spending, has typically fallen even more than other consumer spending. Generally, the price effects in destination markets have not overcome the income effects or exchange rate falls. As a result, major origin markets have delivered fewer tourists to the world and destinations worldwide have experienced reduced tourist numbers and associated loss of expenditure. The GFEC has reduced international tourism growth rates on all continents. International tourist arrivals declined by 4.2 per cent in 2009 and international tourism receipts by 5.7 per cent in real terms (by comparison world gross domestic product (GDP) growth was –0.6 per cent purchasing power parity weighted and –2 per cent market exchange rate weighted, and overall exports declined by 11 per cent). To illustrate this, taking the achieved growth rate in international tourist arrivals in 2008 as a standard, the world tourism growth rate for 2007/2008 dropped by 4.2 per cent (in Europe by 5.7 per cent, Asia and the Pacific 1.3 per cent, America 4.6 per cent and the Middle East 4.9 per cent). Africa faced an increase of 2.9 per cent and is the only world region that reported a positive, yet for Africa a relatively low, growth rate value (UNWTO 2010a).

The ability to predict future demand and business confidence helps managers and policy makers see the threats or opportunities facing their organisations. In the circumstances of worsening economic conditions, a tool to predict future business confidence helps managers and policy makers adapt and react. Further, to monitor this reaction, managers need a tool to help them evaluate past performance and the efficiency and success of the mitigation, adaptation and other actions they might have taken (Mihalič and Kuščer 2007).

A possible source of information on consumer and investor behaviour is contained in the various types of confidence indices that can be constructed. Confidence indices can act as 'leading', 'coincident' or 'lagging' indicators of economic activity. Leading indicators precede business cycles' turning points (i.e. peaks and troughs) and can be used as a barometer to predict that activity. Coincident indicators move in step with business cycles, while lagging indicators follow or lag turning points in business cycles.

Confidence indices can provide valuable knowledge regarding the intentions of both consumers and businesses in times of financial and economic crisis. Tourism forecasting tends to concentrate on the projection of absolute numbers (arrivals, expenditure etc.), rather than on the discovery of turning points in the data or changes in the growth rate of the data (Song and Li 2008; Dwyer *et al.* 2010). Yet, these latter variables may be more appropriate for the development of risk management strategies by destination managers and tourism businesses. It may be of particular interest to the various tourism industry sectors to know whether a change in the demand trend for their products is likely. For certain strategic business decisions, it may be more important to correctly forecast the direction of change in either tourism demand (i.e. whether tourism demand is likely to increase or decrease over a particular time period) or the rate of growth of tourism demand, rather than to minimise error magnitude using sophisticated forecasting techniques.

In order to follow global and regional business tourism confidence, the United Nations World Tourism Organization (UNWTO) introduced a panel of tourism experts, currently consisting of some 350 active members in over 100 countries around the world, who three times a year report their opinions on the sector's future and past developments. This provides the basis for the UNWTO Tourism Confidence Index (TCI) survey, which calculates global and regional TCIs and has been conducted since 2003 (UNWTO 2010b).

This chapter has several objectives. The first one is to explore the importance of measuring the confidence of tourism stakeholders, the method used to construct the TCI and the role the TCI can play in determining levels of confidence among tourism stakeholders. The type of data provided by this index are extremely important for providing information about strategies on the supply side affecting tourism investment and infrastructure development as well as future tourism flows and associated expenditure. What is the potential of the TCI to forecast tourism demand? The second objective is to assess the relevance of the TCI in the context of the GFEC's effect on a relatively neglected area of research – African tourism. In particular, measurements based on the TCI will help us assess the extent to which confidence levels globally and within Africa itself have impacted upon tourist numbers and expenditure and hence their economic impacts on destinations. How reliable are the calculated TCI prospects and evaluations for the African region? Have the calculations efficiently predicted and evaluated the impact of the financial crisis on African inbound tourism? These are important questions that tourism stakeholders in Africa need to have answered. The third objective of the chapter is to discuss the implications of the findings. Considering the enormous consequences of various crises and events for tourism business, it is crucial for tourism stakeholders to implement tools and methods that can accommodate unexpected events and predict possible impacts. What is the TCI's potential to assist scenario analysis of the tourism public and private managers and which requirements have to be met?

The UNWTO Tourism Confidence Index and the global financial and economic crisis

Confidence measurements help tourism business respond to the new opportunities or threats arising from changes in the industry or remote environment. They identify business circumstances that are away from 'business as usual' and inform managers of expected future developments in tourism markets.

Several different confidence indices have been developed to measure various aspects of business performance or to help improve such performance and management. Within the category of indices that measure customer or business confidence, the American Consumer Confidence Index from The Conference Board (2009) has been in operation since 1967. Within the category of tourism confidence studies the American Customer Satisfaction Index (ACSI) covers forty-four different American industries, including hotels, restaurants and the airline industry, and has been in operation since 1994 (ACSI 2010). The ACSI is the standardised tool that measures performance via customer satisfaction and is also used outside the United States in six other countries worldwide and will be launched in another three countries, including South Africa, in 2010. Next in the category of tourism confidence studies is the Country Land & Business Association (CLA 2006) Rural Tourism Confidence Index (RTCI), which has been produced annually since 2005 to provide a picture of business confidence in the rural tourism sector in England and Wales. In addition, the aforementioned UNWTO TCI has been in operation since 2003 (UNWTO 2010a). The TCI has been developed and carried out by the UNWTO to predict future tourism developments and evaluate the past performance of tourism regions and destinations globally. The TCI is calculated for the world and five world regions. Since 2008 it has also been used to measure tourism confidence at the country level in Slovenia (STO 2008).

As indicated above, the kind of business information provided by confidence measurements may, in certain circumstances, replace more demanding modelling that strongly depends on the accuracy of the assumptions and still give reliable information on future business and consumption developments to the business world, as proven in the literature (Backman *et al.* 1992; Batchelor and Dua 1998; Eppright *et al.* 1998).

The UNWTO TCI survey asks respondents to assess the past tourism performance and then give their opinion on the future development of tourism business. It distinguishes a panel assessment of a destination's tourism performance (evaluation) and predictions about future tourism performance (prospects). Both types of index are calculated yearly and every four months. Both are based on the opinions of a world panel of tourism experts who cover five UNWTO world regions: Europe, Asia and Pacific, the Americas, Africa and the Middle East. Of the 300 tourism experts from more than one hundred countries, 47 per cent are European, 28 per cent American, 8 per cent African and 13 per cent Asian and Pacific experts. The remainder are experts from the Middle East region.

In addition to regional TCIs, world TCIs are also calculated based on a sample of tourism experts from different world regions. The experts or members of the panel come from the public and private sectors and different groups such as destination management and accommodation sectors through to tour operators, transport and the media. The pre-set rating scale uses a five-step 0 to 200 scale – from much worse to much better. The panel of tourism experts is also asked what were/will be the most important determinants contributing to tourism growth in the previous/coming four months (Table 6.1).

It is imperative to understand what kinds of impacts different events have on tourism demand and business revenues and profits. Actual hard data have sufficed to some extent in the past, but the bottom line of a TCI is that it taps into stakeholders' sentiments to give information about the near future that is not readily available in hard data and can be used as an input for forecasting, in combination with extrapolation and structural modelling. One reason to calculate the TCI is that it provides such information. In addition, there are many other good features of the TCI. It evaluates tourism performance on both the demand and supply side, creating an international benchmark allowing a direct comparison among world regions and with global tourism confidence. A comparison of data broken down by sector enables the study and analysis of the views of different stakeholders in tourism. A comparison of TCI predictions and evaluations enables a comparison of expected tourism results (prospects) with actual ones (evaluation). The analysis of qualitative questions or factors of tourism demand enables analysts to highlight the positive and negative impact factors and the strategic responses needed by stakeholders. This can potentially stimulate companies and organisations to react aptly and swiftly to identified environmental changes. The UNWTO TCI can be

Table 6.1 TCI methodology

Panel of tourism experts by sector	Rating scale	TCI	Question – rating	Question – determinants
1	2	3	4	5
• Destinations	Much worse (0)	Evaluation	What is your assessment of the tourism performance in your destination/business in the period* just ended as compared to the previous period*?	What have been the main determinants . . .
• Transport	Worse (50)			
• Accommodation and Catering				
• Tour Operators and Travel Agencies	Equal (100)	Prospects	What are your prospects for tourism performance in your destination/business in the coming period* compared to the period* just finished?	What will be the main determinants . . .
• General Industry and Other	Better (150)			
• Consultancy, Research and Media	Much better (200)			

Source: Mihalič (2010).

Note: * The term period refers to 'year' (January–December) and to 'four-month periods' (January–April, May–August and September–December).

a tool to measure the future and past effects of events on tourism such as financial crises, terrorism, political events and sport events such as the Olympic Games, the 2010 FIFA World Cup in South Africa and other mega events. It provides business users with updated information that can be used as a leading indicator of crises. It can also help inform policy and mitigation measures that can be put in place before, during and after an event. Last but not least, the TCI also promotes the image of tourism among all tourism and non-tourism stakeholders since the tourism industry is, like other economic activities such as real estate or finance, measured by its economic performance and confidence (Mihalič and Kuščer 2007).

As indicated above, economic conditions are regarded as one of the main factors influencing tourism demand. Yet other types of crises such as terrorist attacks or natural catastrophes, deadly diseases or volcanic eruptions also affect demand with an immediate and immense impact on international tourism, since tourists are risk averse and highly sensitive to such adverse events. On the other hand, the influence of an economic crisis or decreasing life standard on the number of tourists and their associated expenditure is much slower (Wang 2009). However, while in this case the drop might be slower and less deep, it may last longer. We also know from economic theory that, with increasing income, consumers become less sensitive to changes in income and prices as the price and income elasticity of tourism demand decreases and the need to travel becomes stronger.

The study of economic conditions as one of the main factors influencing tourism demand dates back at least to 1959. Menges (1959) studied the interaction between tourism spending and income for Germany and Switzerland and found strong and significant connections. Many scholars have studied the effects of income, prices, exchange rates and other variables on tourism demand. Crouch (1995) analysed eighty and Song and Li (2008) 121 such studies of international tourism demand. Among newer studies, Lim and McAleer (2005) examined the impact of the Asian financial crisis in 1997 and its impact on Japanese travel to Australia in the 1976–2000 period. Okumus and Karamustafa (2005) evaluated the impacts of the 2001 economic crisis on the tourism industry in Turkey. They identified negative and also positive impacts of the crisis, although its potential benefits are often overlooked. On the one hand, a crisis has negative consequences such as a fall in demand and consequently in revenues, profits and salaries, along with rising costs, investment and staff reductions, and even the closure of organisations. On the other hand, such an event may also offer opportunities to introduce new and innovative tourism products and new management programmes, access new markets and find new ways to reduce costs. Papatheodorou *et al.* (2010) claim that reduced tourist numbers can expedite the introduction of e-commerce practices in tourism, resulting in a substantial reduction in transaction costs. Many expect that the GFEC will bring positive developments in service quality and green initiatives as destinations will seek to improve their competitiveness and avoid significant price reductions (Kester 2010; Papatheodorou *et al.* 2010; UNWTO 2010a).

Wang (2009) studied the impact of crisis events and macro-economic activity on Taiwan's international inbound tourism demand. In terms of losses incurred, the number of inbound tourism arrivals suffered the greatest decline during the outbreak of SARS, followed by the 21 September 1999 earthquake and the 11 September 2001 terrorist attacks. He found that, compared to these special events, the impact of the Asian financial crisis on Taiwan's tourism, which occurred some years earlier, was relatively mild.

At present, only a few empirical studies of tourism confidence or forecasts on the impact of the GFEC on inbound tourism have been published. In one study on tourism confidence Mihalič (2010) studied the connections between TCI, inbound tourism and GDP. She found statistically significant correlations among world data for three out of five UNWTO regions: Europe, America and the Middle East.

In mid-2009, some way into the GFEC, the International Academy for the Study of Tourism discussed its impact on world tourism. The Academy concluded that the GFEC had strongly lowered tourism confidence. Tourism spending has experienced greater falls than other consumer spending and has reduced the economic contribution of tourism to destinations worldwide. Consequently, tourism investment has been reduced, with consequent impacts on employment in the industry. At the same time, the GFEC is also considered to present opportunities for tourism operators and destination managers to enhance their competitive advantage in the longer term. Tourism stakeholders need to cut their operating costs, improve productivity, implement innovations and adapt the tourism product to access existing and future markets in the light of changing consumer values and needs (Sheldon and Dwyer 2010).

In the context of the GFEC's impact on inbound tourism, Smeral (2010) studied the demand for international travel in the United States, Canada, Australia and Japan. According to his study, the negative economic and social consequences of the crisis will affect the tourism industry for many years. In the medium term, only moderate growth rates in global tourism demand are expected. Internationally, the tourism industry may be faced with massive structural change as a 'new' consumer with more limited financial and economic means might emerge from the crisis. Song and Lin (2010) forecasted the GFEC's impacts on inbound tourism to Asia and outbound tourism from Asia. They expect a significantly negative impact on tourist arrivals to Asia and tourist expenditure by Asian tourists outside Asia. In particular, the long-haul markets for arrivals to Asia, such as Europe and North America, will decline significantly. Ritchie *et al.* (2010) studied the GFEC's impact on tourism in Canada, the United States and Mexico. They confirmed the GFEC's impact in the case of Canada and America. In contrast, tourism in Mexico has been affected more directly and to a much greater extent by the swine flu pandemic, exchange rates and weather conditions than by the economic crisis itself.

No study investigating the impacts of the GFEC on tourism demand for Africa has been published so far. While Africa is an important and attractive continent with a growing tourism industry, it is reasonable to expect that African tourism has suffered from the same decline as tourism on other continents. The question remains of whether the intensity, pace and time span of the impact has been the same, given that Africa is very diverse, less developed and still an emerging tourism region.

Since the onset of the GFEC, the tourism industry around the world has been 'in crying need of information and knowledge for decision making and for strategies to effectively respond to the current situation' (Papatheodorou *et al.* 2010: 39). Private and public decision makers have been looking for reliable information on future economic confidence in order to protect their businesses and set an appropriate course of action. Although in 2010 there had been a gradual recovery of the world economy, it remains unclear as to when confidence levels and market activity will return to normal. At the present time, some years after the beginning of the GFEC, our understanding of the changed circumstances may not be very much greater than it was during the 2007–9 period. While private and public decision makers have looked for reliable predictions of future economic confidence in order to protect their businesses and set an appropriate course of action, such predictions are fraught with difficulties. Consider just some of the possible types of consumer responses to the GFEC: While some people will travel less or not at all, what will they do with the money they save? Will some instead travel to closer destinations, purchase other products, reduce their debts or add to their savings? Will some instead travel to closer destinations? Is there some shifting to domestic tourism or some 'trading down' (e.g. towards low-cost carriers, lower standard hotels, business class to economy class etc.)? Does the crisis imply that potential travellers become more sensitive to price signals and differentials and, if so, for how long will this last? And how much tourism-related investment is 'in the pipeline' as opposed to being shelved permanently? There are many similar questions that tourism stakeholders would like answers to. However, we simply do not know enough about consumer travel behaviour or investor behaviour to provide definite answers to such questions.

The GFEC has highlighted the inadequacies of many research findings to explain consumer behaviour, since estimates of demand elasticities have generally been based on data accumulated over long periods of time that have tended to 'smooth out' income variability and price shocks in time-series analysis. Consumer responses to a short, sharp shock in income remains a relatively neglected area of research. This is where the TCI can play an important role. This chapter discusses this role in the context of African tourism as affected by the GFEC.

Methodology

Data

Data on the TCI, real GDP, an indicator of the GFEC and international tourism arrivals from the 2002–10 period were used. The selected data periods were adjusted to the availability of TCI measurements, which started in 2003 and produce yearly and four-monthly data. The latest updated data were collected from

IMF financial statistics and UNWTO databases available in July 2010 (UNWTO 2010c; IMF 2010). In addition to data for Africa, data on the world level were used as a standard for benchmarking.

Study specification

The study model for Africa assumes that international tourism arrivals as a measure of African tourism demand were, among other determinants, influenced by economic conditions, particularly by the GFEC of 2007–10. Some previous studies for other world regions, as discussed above, have already confirmed the dependence of international tourism and tourism confidence on the cycle of the GFEC. Therefore, this chapter hypothesises that the African TCI also reflects tourism confidence and that its fluctuations follow the pattern of GDP – an indicator of the GFEC. Consequently, African inbound tourism numbers, GDP and TCI prospects and evaluations were expected to be significantly interdependent and to follow the same pattern, which was expected to be in line with the same pattern of world tourism. Due to the cyclical character of the financial and economic crisis, a U-shape cycle form is expected.

Limitations of the study

Due to difficulties with the availability and accuracy of statistical data for African countries, this study has several limitations. The methodology and coverage varies among African states and regions, as differences occur in the categories of visitors covered. Some countries follow international visitor arrivals that include same-day visitors, instead of international tourism arrivals. Further, a number of countries only report arrivals by air. Some countries need more time for reporting and therefore the UNWTO data are partly based on projections and constantly updated as the actual data arrive. At the time of preparing this chapter, substantial additional data were still expected.

Although it would be more logical to measure tourism demand with financial indicators, we were unable to do so as it is much harder to obtain and analyse such data due to exchange rate fluctuations and inflation. Instead, this analysis uses the number of inbound tourists as an indicator because such statistics are more reliable (Dritsakis 2004; Song and Witt 2006).

Another limitation of the study is the small sample size involved in the statistical analysis. As data on tourism TCI evaluations start in 2002 and data on tourism prospects in 2003, we were only able to use data series starting from 2002 and 2003.

Due to the seasonal character of tourism, scholars in the field recommend the use of monthly or quarterly data when forecasting tourism demand (Witt and Witt 1995). Fortunately, the TCI data are available for four-month periods that correspond to tourism seasons and our analysis is based on these data to the greatest possible extent. Unfortunately, we were unable to obtain data on real GDP growth for the same period. Instead, this chapter analyses some GFEC impacts on African inbound tourism on a sample of yearly data.

Africa as a tourist destination

As one of the UNWTO's largest regions, Africa comprises over fifty very different countries and territories. According to the World Economic Forum (WEF 2008), its many natural and cultural attributes make Africa attractive as a potential tourist destination and can help establish Africa as a leading tourism force in the future. On the one hand, some African countries already rank highly on the world tourism competitiveness list as they have good transport and tourism infrastructure and responsible governments that prioritise the development of tourism. For example, South Africa ranks 61 out of 133 countries. On the other hand, many countries from sub-Saharan Africa have not yet found a way to appear on the tourist map. Ivory Coast, Burundi, Lesotho and Chad are the lowest-ranked destinations on the list. In most cases African destinations have underdeveloped transportation and tourism infrastructure and security and health problems that make them less attractive to international tourism. On top of that, the policy environment in these countries is not very supportive of tourism development, even though it is probably the key to starting the tourism cycle. According to Kester (2003), the insufficiency of air transport between the African regions and the rest of the world, and between African countries themselves, continues to pose a major obstacle to tourism development. Another key challenge African destinations face is to improve their weak or negative image. Too often a negative perception prevails of Africa being a continent of poverty, disease and conflict (Kester 2003). As a result, Africa's market share is still fairly low – 5.2 per cent in 2009 (UNWTO 2010a). In spite of the tremendous challenges, conditions are gradually improving. Africa has shown consistent growth in the past decade, increasing its international tourist arrivals from 26.5 million in 2000 to 45.6 million in 2009, and increasing its international tourism receipts from USD 10.4 billion to USD 28.7 billion in the same time span.

Taking the UNWTO data for 2008 into account, 42 per cent of all travel in Africa was from within the African continent, whereas visitors from the European region represented 32 per cent, from the Americas 4 per cent, from the Middle East 5 per cent and from the Asia and Pacific region 4 per cent, with the origin of the remaining 13 per cent not specified (Kester 2010). However, according to 2009 data (Table 6.2), Africa only attracted 45.6 million tourists or 5 per cent of the international world tourism market (UNWTO 2010a), with 2 per cent travelling to North African countries, mainly Morocco and Tunisia, and the remaining 3 per cent to sub-Saharan Africa, where the strongest tourism-receiving country is South Africa, having received about seven million international visitors in 2009 (UNWTO 2010a). It was expected that the FIFA World Cup 2010 would have both a short- and long-lasting positive tourism effect on both South African and African inbound tourism.

The impact of the GFEC on African inbound tourism

As already explained, it is expected that the GFEC has lowered destination tourism performance indicators and, given the GFEC's size, it is reasonably expected that

Table 6.2 African and world tourism; yearly data 1990–2009

Destination	International tourist arrivals (m)							Average annual growth	Market share (%)	Change (%)		
	1990	1995	2000	2005	2007	2008	2009	2000/8	2009	2007/6	2008/7	2009/8
Africa	15.1	20.0	27.9	37.3	43.2	44.3	45.6	6.7	5.18	8.4	2.4	2.9
North Africa*	8.4	7.3	10.2	13.9	16.3	17.1	17.6	6.7	2.00	8.5	4.8	2.5
Sub-Saharan Africa**	6.7	12.7	17.6	23.4	26.8	27.1	27.9	6.7	3.17	8.3	1.0	3.1
World	438	534	689	804	904	919	880	3.8	100	6.1	2.0	−4.2

Source: UNWTO (2010a).

Notes: * North Africa includes Algeria, Morocco, Sudan and Tunisia. (NB: Egypt and Libya are in the UNWTO region of the Middle East.) ** Sub-Saharan Africa includes all other countries of the continent (and some in the Indian ocean).

many have dropped into negative values. The latter is certainly true for the world economy and world tourism, but not for Africa. Contrary to the world GDP real growth rate of –0.6 per cent, according to 2010 IMF data the African figures remained positive (Table 6.3). The same pattern can be seen if we compare the world international tourism arrivals growth rate of a highly negative value of –4.2 per cent in 2009 with the corresponding African figures that, again, dropped but remained positive, at around 3 per cent (Table 6.2). In line with our expectations, world tourism arrivals significantly correlate to the movement of world GDP (thus following the pattern of the financial crisis), yet we cannot claim the same for African inbound tourism (see Table 6.4).

Table 6.4 shows calculations for yearly data that do not take account of the seasonal character of tourism demand, with its obvious high and low seasons. Therefore, it is preferable to use monthly or several-month data, aggregated by

Table 6.3 GDP annual percentage change and TCIs for the world and Africa, 2003–10

Country group name	2003	2004	2005	2006	2007	2008	2009	2010
GDP growth rate, constant prices (ppp weighted)								
World	3.6	4.9	4.5	5.08	5.2	3.0	–0.6	4.2
Middle East and North Africa	6.9	5.8	5.4	5.68	5.6	5.1	2.4	4.5
Sub-Saharan Africa	5.0	7.1	6.3	6.45	6.9	5.5	2.1	4.7
TCI prospects								
World	n.a.	150.0	143.6	139.71	137.1	132.4	7 1.2	131.0
Africa	n.a.	142.3	144.1	160.0	160.0	143.2	100.0	142.9
TCI evaluations								
World	119.0	144.3	140.3	135.52	142.9	98.1	71.5	n.a.
Africa	125.0	144.1	165.0	145.24	156.8	118.2	111.9	n.a.

Source: IMF (2010); UNWTO (2010c).

Table 6.4 Pearson's correlations among world TCI prospects, evaluations and GDP growth; yearly data 2003–10

Variable	World		Africa	
	Prospects	GDP growth	Prospects	GDP growth
GDP growth	0.728*		0.875*	
Int. arrivals growth	0.695*	0.716*	0.528	0.542

Source: Mihalič (2010).

Notes: * Correlation is significant at the 0.01 level.

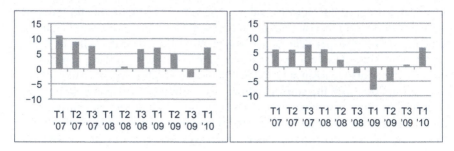

Figure 6.1 International tourism arrivals growth rates, Africa (left) and the world (right)
in percentages; four-month data 2007–10.

Source: UNWTO (2010c).

tourism seasons (Witt and Witt 1995), to gain a better insight into the reaction of
tourism to the GFEC. Figure 6.1 takes into account four-month data that better
follow the tourism seasons. Again, it is obvious that African inbound tourism
development during the GFEC shows no expected cycle pattern in the form of
the letter 'U' (Figure 6.1, left). This is very different from the world tourism pattern
that follows the development of the financial crisis' 'U' cycle quite closely (Figure
6.1, right). Other determinants apart from the GFEC must have influenced inbound
tourism in different African countries.

Nevertheless, both TCIs on prospects and evaluations for the world and Africa
show a much more similar cycle (Figure 6.2, Table 6.5). Yet TCI analysis confirmed that the African tourism expert panel was more optimistic during the GFEC
than the world tourism experts panel (see Table 6.A1 in the Appendix to this
chapter). They have also been more pleased with tourism development in the past
as the TCI values on their evaluations are significantly higher for Africa compared
to the world average.

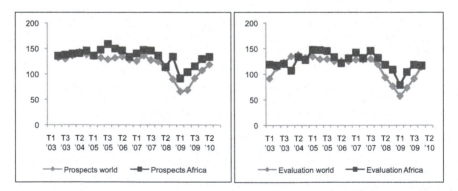

Figure 6.2 TCI prospects (left) and evaluations (right) for the world and the Africa region;
four-month data 2003–10.

Source: UNWTO (2010c).

Table 6.5 Pearson's correlations among world TCI prospects, evaluations and international tourist arrivals growth; four-month data 2003–10

World/Region	Variable	World			Africa	
		Evaluations	Prospects	Int. arrivals growth	Evaluations	Prospects
World	Evaluations					
	Prospects	0.954**				
	Int. arrivals growth	0.873**	0.779**			
Africa	Evaluations	0.776**				
	Prospects		0.854**		0.761**	
	Int. arrivals growth			0.243	0.270	0.439*

Source: UNWTO (2010c).

Notes: * Correlation is significant at the 0.05 level. ** Correlation is significant at the 0.01 level.

However, we have failed to prove the usefulness of the African TCI on prospects for forecasting tourism demand. There is no significant correlation at the regional level between African inbound tourism and the TCI in respect of prospects (Table 6.2). Such a regional analysis, based on aggregate data from very different countries that have faced very different positive and negative growth rates in inbound tourism during the GFEC, was unable to confirm a common pattern. During the period of the GFEC, African inbound tourism at the country level reveals very different growth rates in inbound tourism, with some being positive and some negative. For example, in 2009 in Kenya, Swaziland, Algeria, Morocco, Botswana and South Africa, inbound tourism grew, whereas Mozambique, Senegal, Mauritius, Sudan, Rwanda and Tunisia experienced negative tourism growth rates (Kester 2010). The monthly evolution of tourism demand at the regional level is strongly driven by a relatively small number of destinations with large numbers of tourists that all had their own dynamic independent of the GFEC. These include South Africa in the run up to the FIFA World Cup, Kenya rebounding from its post-election troubles, and Morocco continuing its strong momentum and gaining a share in the Mediterranean.

African tourism has obviously been influenced by the GFEC, as periods of tourism decline in terms of international tourism arrivals growth rates, as well as tourism prospects and evaluations, are clearly seen. At the same time it has done relatively well during the crisis with growth rates above the world average. The TCIs reveal a clear pattern that follows the economic (and other) circumstances and shows that tourism confidence in Africa during the GFEC was on average at a higher level than worldwide. This is justified as African GDP growth rates have not dropped into the red. Indeed, the UNWTO tourism business-cycle clock shows that African tourism skipped the recession quadrant for a short time when moving from a down- to an upswing quadrant and then recovered to the boom

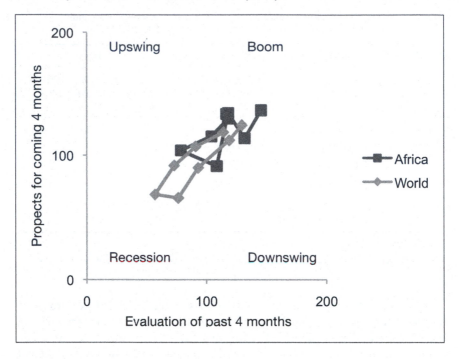

Figure 6.3 UNWTO tourism business-cycle clock for the world and Africa; four-month
        data 2008–10.

Source: UNWTO (2010c).

section, with prospects and evaluation above the business as usual value. By
contrast, world tourism stayed in recession for more than a year – from September
2008 to December 2009 (Figure 6.3).

Despite the relatively optimistic picture for African tourism shown in Figure
6.3, the present analysis has pointed to the TCI's limited potential for forecasting
tourism demand at the aggregated, regional level. Africa consists of many very
different tourism country destinations that have reacted differently to the GFEC.
Thus, such regional forecasts of tourism confidence and demand might be of
limited value for these countries; country/destination-specific analysis would be
more useful for public and private tourism stakeholders who, at the single-
destination level, manage tourism business and thus have to predict, plan and react
to an ever changing business environment.

Discussion and conclusions

This chapter has confirmed that the GFEC has not had the same impact on all
continents and their tourism industries. Africa's real GDP has fallen by less than
the average drop in world GDP. The same is true for African inbound tourism in
general. Yet we know that inbound tourism in different African countries has been

differently affected by the crisis. In 2009, some countries, including Mozambique, Senegal, Mauritius and Sudan, experienced negative growth rates in both inbound tourism numbers and expenditures. In contrast, Kenya, Swaziland, Algeria, Morocco, South Africa and Botswana recorded positive growth rates compared to 2008. In such circumstances, when different regions and countries are differently affected by a given event, world regional TCI calculations may help us understand the role that changes in tourism confidence may play in determining tourism flows to different regions. At the same time, tourism policy resides at the country or destination level rather than the level of world regions. Given this, tourism policy makers and private managers need more accurate information at the country or single destination level, making the estimation of country/destination- and also sector-level TCIs even more meaningful. At present, to our knowledge, as mentioned above, there are only two such destination-level tourism confidence surveys in place: the RTCI for England and Wales and the Slovenian TCI for the needs of its tourism decision makers. During the GFEC, tourism demand in Slovenia has encountered the expected cycle, but the economic and tourism downtrends for this destination started later and were less deep, and the recovery in tourism confidence has been slower compared to that at the European level (STO 2008).

Another issue in need of discussion is the relationship between domestic and foreign tourism and TCI calculations. In our research, we used only inbound tourism data and thus domestic tourism demand has been neglected. Another outcome of the GFEC for many countries has been the recognition of the importance of domestic tourism as a substitute, given the constraints on international and long-haul travel and possible reductions in the time people have to travel and the money they have to spend. Domestic tourism as a substitute for outbound travel reduces the expenditure leakages that occur and has the potential to create income and employment in the home economy. While increased marketing efforts in respect of domestic tourism markets will have no expansive effects on foreign exchange earnings, they can, however, serve to enhance the viability of home tourism products through crises such as the GFEC, providing a basis for future recovery. This old trick of the tourism industry – to attract domestic tourism in times of falling foreign visitor numbers – has been seen in periods of economic crisis in many European countries in the past and also in 2009, when many countries tried to focus their promotion efforts on domestic and neighbouring countries. It has often been observed that, in times of economic crisis, consumers tend to travel closer to home or stay in their home country. In the 2009 financial crisis, several destinations, such as China, Brazil and Spain, saw domestic tourism replace the fall in foreign tourism (UNWTO 2010b). In general, as the TCI reflects future and past tourism development, which includes both foreign and domestic visitations and thus relates to total tourism development in a country, it might not be an accurate tool for predicting/evaluating each of these kinds of tourism independently. Certainly, the TCI correspondents take account of the overall picture in their destination that includes the potential of domestic tourism when they give their opinions for predicting future tourism and evaluating past results. A more detailed analysis of the association between the TCI and tourism demand would consider total tourism demand. Yet, due to the unavailability of such and timely data at the world and regional levels, this would be more feasible at the individual country level.

In sum, tourism is a volatile industry. When general conditions are good, it can perform strongly. When conditions are bad and expected to become worse, it is likely to perform well below average. The tourism industry should plan on the basis that it will be disproportionately affected by financial and economic crises. The industry needs to develop more tools such as the TCI and more methods to provide accurate and timely information on future tourism demand. Such information at the world or world regional level is welcome for international and global organisations active in the field of tourism, and can provide a benchmark for individual countries that use this information to shape their tourism policy. At the same time, such information is needed even more at the destination level, as well as at the level of different tourism sectors, in order to help tourism stakeholders take advantage of the business opportunities and avoid the threats emerging from the ever changing conditions that shape target tourism markets. In comparison to traditional demand forecasting methods, confidence indices have many strengths. They do not require any data that are often not easily accessible and comparable or even not available in time. Further, they are based on tourism experts' opinions and at the same time take into account many demand determinants as seen by those experts. By comparison, the other methods available may only take a limited or selected number of demand factors into account if not corrected in line with expert opinions. In general, the TCI has the potential to provide effective and useful information to public and private stakeholders and it will be a challenge for tourism managers to implement and use it more broadly in the future.

Note

1   Authors often refer to the 2007–10 financial and economic event as the global financial crisis (GFC), as the economic crisis started with the turbulence and crisis in the financial markets.

References

ACSI (2010) 'The American customer satisfaction index', retrieved 17 July 2010 from www.theacsi.org.

Backman, K.F., Uysal, M. and Backman, S.J. (1992) 'Index Number: a tourism managerial and policy-making tool', *Journal of Applied Recreation Research*, 17: 158–77.

Batchelor, R. and Dua, P. (1998) 'Improving macro-economic forecasts: the role of consumer confidence', *International Journal of Forecasting*, 14: 71–81.

Conference Board, The (2009) *Consumer Confidence Index*, retrieved 7 January 2012 from www.conference-board.org.

Country Land & Business Association (CLA) (2006) *Business Confidence in Rural Tourism 2005*, London: Country Land and Business Association, retrieved 14 August 2012 from www.cla.org.uk/policy_docs/business_confidence_in_rural_tourism_2006.pdf.

Crouch, G.I. (1994a) 'The study of international tourism demand: a review of findings', *Journal of Travel Research*, 33: 12–23.

Crouch, G.I. (1994b) 'The study of international tourism demand: a review of practice', *Journal of Travel Research*, 33: 41–54.

Crouch, G.I. (1995) 'A meta-analysis of tourism demand', *Annals of Tourism Research*, 2: 103–18.

Dritsakis, N. (2004) 'Cointegration analysis of German and British tourism demand for Greece', *Tourism Management*, 2: 111–19.

Dwyer L., Forsyth, P. and Dwyer, W. (2010) *Tourism Economics and Policy*, Bristol, UK: Channel View Publications.

Eppright, D.R., Arguea, N.M. and Huth, W.L. (1998) 'Aggregate consumer expectation indices as indicators of future consumer expenditures', *Journal of Economic Psychology*, 19: 215–35.

International Monetary Fund (IMF) (2010) International Monetary Fund, retrieved 14 July 2010 from the World Economic Outlook Database (WEO) database.

Keller, P. (2009) *Global Financial and Economic Crisis: What are the implications for world tourism?*, Madrid: United Nations World Tourism Organization.

Kester, J.G.C. (2003) 'International tourism in Africa', *Tourism Economics*, 9: 203–21.

Kester, J.G.C. (2010) 'Short- and long-term trends in tourism to African destinations', paper presented at the meeting Routes Africa, Swaziland, May–June.

Lim, C. (2006) 'A survey of tourism demand modelling practice: issues and implications', in L. Dwyer and P. Forsyth (eds) *International Handbook on the Economics of Tourism*, London: Edward Elgar, pp. 45–72.

Lim, C. and McAleer, M. (2005) 'Analyzing the behavioral trends in tourist arrivals from Japan to Australia', *Journal of Travel Research*, 43: 414–21.

Menges, G. (1959) *Die touristische Konsumfunktion Deutschlands 1924–1957*, Bern: Schweizerischer Fremdenverkehrsverband.

Mihalič, T. (2010) 'Potential of the Tourism Confidence Index in the circumstances of economic crisis', paper presented at the AIEST conference, Potchefstroom, South Africa, September.

Mihalič, T. and Kuščer, K. (2007) *Indeks turističnega zaupanja* (Tourism Confidence Index), Ljubljana: Inštitut za turizem Ekonomske fakultete, Univerza v Ljubljani.

Okumus, F. and Karamustafa, K. (2005) 'Impact of an economic crisis: evidence from Turkey', *Annals of Tourism Research*, 32: 942–61.

Papatheodorou, A., Rosselló, J. and Xiao, H. (2010) 'Global economic crisis and tourism: consequences and perspectives', *Journal of Travel Research*, 49: 39–45.

Ritchie, J.R.B., Molinar, C.M.A. and Frechtling, D.C. (2010) 'Impacts of the world recession and economic crisis on tourism: North America', *Journal of Travel Research*, 49: 5–15.

Saayman, A. and Saayman, A. (2008) 'The determinants of inbound tourism to South Africa', *Tourism Economics*, 14: 81–96.

Sheldon, P. and Dwyer, L. (2010) 'The global financial crisis and tourism: perspectives of the academy', *Journal of Travel Research*, 49: 3–4.

Smeral, E. (2010) 'Impacts of the world recession and economic crisis on tourism: forecasts and potential risks', *Journal of Travel Research*, 49: 31–8.

Song, H. and Li, G. (2008) 'Tourism demand modelling and forecasting: a review of recent research', *Tourism Management*, 29: 203–20.

Song, H. and Lin, S. (2010) 'Impacts of the financial and economic crisis on tourism in Asia', *Journal of Travel Research*, 49(1): 16–30.

Song, H. and Witt, S.F. (2006) 'Forecasting international tourist flows to Macau', *Tourism Management*, 27: 214–24.

Slovenska turistična organizacija (STO) (2008) *Tourism Confidence Index Survey: Economic performance and opportunities of Slovenian tourism*, Ljubljana: Slovenska turistična organizacija.

Tett, G. (2009) *Fool's Gold: How unrestrained greed corrupted a dream, shattered global markets and unleashed a catastrophe*, London: Little, Brown, Simon and Schuster.

United Nations World Tourism Organization (UNWTO) (2010a) *World Tourism Barometer*, vol. 8, June, Madrid: UNWTO.

United Nations World Tourism Organization (UNWTO) (2010b) *World Tourism Barometer*, vol. 8, January, Madrid: UNWTO.

United Nations World Tourism Organization (UNWTO) (2010c) *UNWTO Data*, July, Madrid: UNWTO.

Wang, Y. (2009) 'The impact of crisis events and macroeconomic activity on Taiwan's international inbound tourism demand', *Tourism Management*, 30: 75–82.

Witt, S.F. and Witt, C.A. (1995) 'Forecasting tourism demand: a review of empirical research', *International Journal of Forecasting*, 11: 447–75.

World Economic Forum (WEF) (2008) *Travel and Tourism Competitiveness Report*, Geneva: WEF.

Appendix

Table 6.A1 Paired samples test; four-month data 2003–10

Pair	Paired differences							
	Mean	*Standard deviation*	*Standard error mean*	*95% confidence interval of the difference*		*t*	*df*	*Significance (1-tailed)*
				Lower	Upper			
Prospects world – Prospects Africa	−14.864	11.647	2.483	−20.028	−9.700	−5.986	21	0.000*
Evaluation world – Evaluation Africa	−10.773	14.547	3.101	−17.222	−4.323	−3.473	21	0.001*
International tourist arrivals growth rate world – International tourist arrivals growth rate Africa	−3.43636	5.77932	1.23215	−5.99877	−0.8739	−2.789	21	0.001*

Source: UNWTO (2010c).

Note: * Correlation is significant at the 0.01 level (1-tailed).

7 Hibernating economic decline?

Tourism and labour market change in Europe's northern periphery

Dieter K. Müller

Introduction

As a literature review by Hall (2010) indicates, the interrelationship between crisis and tourism is poorly understood thus far. Although there is substantial research on the impact of economic and financial downturns on tourism, it seems that there is a lack of understanding regarding what could be considered crisis and a normal state. Still, it can be argued that the interrelationship between crisis, particularly in the economic sector, and tourism is not unidirectional. Instead, tourism is often forwarded as a solution to economic crisis, not least in peripheral areas (Baum 1999; Hall and Boyd 2005; Hall 2007; Jóhannesson and Huijbens 2010). Hall (2007) points out that this idea is not by any means new, but that tourism has often failed to deliver what has been promised. Moreover, even when tourism development is successful, there are warnings that it is just another staple industry in peripheral economies based on resource extraction and, thus, a dependency on extractive industries is simply exchanged for a dependency on tourism (Schmallegger and Carson 2010).

A common problem in this context is that research seldom acknowledges the long-term dynamics of industrial development. Instead, it focuses on crisis and its immediate impacts on communities, economy and other industries. This notion coincides with, and is reminiscent of, Hall's (2010) comment on the 'normal state' of things. For example, in economic history and economic geography, cyclical development is assumed to be the most common development of economies (Kondratieff 1984; Knox *et al.* 2008). Accordingly, a 'normal state' never occurs.

Particularly with reference to peripheral economies dependent on the extraction of natural resources, boom and bust cycles have been recorded (Clapp 1998). Consecutively, periods of crisis and economic decline are frequently followed by periods of recovery or economic growth. Globalisation implies that peripheral economies are tied into complex global markets and networks with specific sets of rules and preconditions for different industries, hence causing different preconditions for innovation (Hayter *et al.* 2003; Malerba 2005). Thus, a decline in one industry does not necessarily imply a decline in all others.

Peripheral economies are traditionally based on the extraction of natural resources, such as forest timber or minerals. This chapter therefore addresses the interrelationship between these industries and tourism from a labour market perspective. This is achieved by analysing labour market changes in northern Sweden during the period 1990–2007. The chapter continues with a review of the literature, followed by a presentation of data and methodology. Then, the research area is briefly presented. Finally, the chapter ends with the Results and Conclusion sections.

Staple economies and resource peripheries

Tourism has often been considered a tool for regional development. However, many studies in tourism have only marginally taken advantage of research within economic geography and regional science. Hence, tourism has been considered in isolation as one industry without a sufficient acknowledgement of its inter-relations with other sectors of the economy. Saarinen (2007) points out this problem with regard to approaches to regional planning in tourism destinations. Accordingly, tourism-centred approaches that fail to acknowledge alternative development options compete with development-centred approaches that acknow-ledge tourism as just one possible option. Particularly, the aspiration for sustainable development is put at stake when the 'tourism first' (Burns 1999) solution is chosen, since linkages to other local or regional industries are usually weak, which limits the potential indirect and induced impacts of tourism development.

Early on, resource peripheries caught the interest of nation states for their ability to provide important resources for domestic production and further trade on a global market. This is also true for northern Europe, where not least forest and mineral resources entailed large-scale colonisation programmes to facilitate the extraction of these resources (Sörlin 1988). Similar situations are recorded in Canada, where forest resources have also been regarded as a tool for regional development. Innis (1930/1956) and Mackintosh (1939/1964) argued that access to abundant natural resources, the so-called staples, is a path to export-led growth. In short, capital, entrepreneurs and demand are imported from the outside to facilitate the extraction of the resource. Processing prior to transportation from the area creates additional positive local and regional impacts and enables a diversification of the regional economy. Obviously, reality often turned out to be not that simple and thus diversification never took place, since linkages to regional industries remained underdeveloped, entailing a 'truncated economy' (Gunton 2003: 69). Instead, because of the high capital input, extraction companies were large scale and located outside the periphery. Research and development, as well as other knowledge-intensive stages of the production process, remained outside the area, too, in summary causing a leakage of capital from the periphery. Moreover, an effective staple production became the predominant focus of government and industry, while regional development ideas tended to fade away, at least as long as employment in the staple industries was guaranteed (Innis

1930/1956; Markey *et al.* 2006). For the Swedish case, Westin (2006) argued that investments in welfare were seen as compensation for the stagnating development and life in less attractive and remote areas.

Variations in the global economy contributed to shifting prices as well as downturns and upswings in demand for the staple. Then, many resource peripheries were caught in a staple trap. However, following the arguments of Mackintosh (1939/1964), Gunton (2003) noted that staple traps are not inevitably the outcome of each staple-based economy. Instead, he argued, a focus on the dependency pattern potentially created in staple economies shadows the latent comparative advantages related to access to staple resources. For example, Hayter (2003) and Clapp (1998) did not see the situation as positive and pointed rather at the dependency patterns and the resulting marginality created by staple economies. The shift from Fordist to post-Fordist production, in particular, created problems. Hayter *et al.* (2003) argued that Fordism in resource peripheries was always a bastardised form, as levels of export and external control always remained high. The urge for cheap resources entailed the extraction of the most financially promising resources first, causing increasing costs over time and eventually crisis, not least in a situation of rising globalisation and international competition from areas recently integrated into the world economy (Clapp 1998; Hayter 2003; Hayter *et al.* 2003). However, changes in the global economy can also lead to a revival of resource demand and a new cycle of extraction.

Peripheral resource extraction is usually a capital-intensive undertaking. Post-Fordist demand for flexible production can, however, be met with strategies such as disintegration, outsourcing and fly-in/fly-out strategies for labour on demand, likely to further limit positive impacts on local and regional economies (Storey 2001, 2010; Hayter 2003). However, the globalisation of resource peripheries also entailed the advent of new stakeholders that value resources differently than the extracting companies do (Hayter *et al.* 2003). Most prominently, environmental non-governmental organisations (ENGOs) accuse staple economies of destroying ecological values. Sometimes this implies that global ENGOs impose on peripheries ideas and values that are alien to local traditions and desires (Hayter 2003). In many cases, however, ENGO resistance is exercised globally, while locally it combines global environmental values with a local democratic desire to influence the future development of community (Hayter and Soyez 1996). Alliances with indigenous peoples occur in this context, since they realise the opportunity to lift their issues to a global scene and thus increase pressure on governments (Barker and Soyez 1994; Green 2009).

In summary, resource peripheries can be described as strained by resource cycles and an increasing global interest in various aspects of the resources (Hayter *et al.* 2003). The ongoing changes, particularly the shift from a Fordist to post-Fordist production regime, entailed a number of consequences on the local labour markets of the resource periphery, usually implying a decline in employment in the local sectors of the staple economy. This is of course a problem for policy makers and development officers, who have to look for alternative livelihood opportunities to sustain peripheral communities.

The role of tourism in restructuring northern staple economies

In peripheral areas, tourism was already seen as a source of livelihood prior to the shift to post-Fordist production regimes (Lundgren 2001; Hall 2007). Indeed, in an attempt to define the role of peripheries in Europe, Christaller (already in 1964) pointed at tourism and its ability to attract capital to remote places. At any rate, the interest in tourism certainly stepped up due to declining or non-existent employment in traditional staple industries (Baum 1999; Saarinen 2005; Müller and Jansson 2007; Hall *et al.* 2009). Time series clearly indicate a growth in tourism numbers in polar and sub-polar areas at least since the 1980s, but particularly during the early twenty-first century (Hall and Johnston 1995; Hall and Saarinen 2010).

Tourism is thus expected to create new employment opportunities in peripheries (Townsend 1997; Jenkins *et al.* 1998). A restructuring of the regional economy from resource to service industries is not a smooth process, however (Lundmark 2006; Müller and Jansson 2007). This is partly because restructuring should not simply be seen as a shift from one industry to another, but also as including qualitative changes (Hoggart and Paniagua 2001). Path dependency and 'lock-in' effects, however, have been identified as constraining such a development (Martin and Sunley 2006). This seems to be particularly valid for truncated economies (Gunton 2003; Markey *et al.* 2006). In the context of the European Union (EU), attempts to facilitate restructuring are heavily supported by regional policy schemes and funds injecting enormous capital into peripheral areas, and 'new' industrial sectors such as tourism have been set up (Saarinen 2005). A basic aspiration of this policy is to discontinue the dependency on exogenous development by utilising local resources (Ray 2000). Thus, tourism development in peripheral areas is often small-scale and is organised and financed locally or regionally, and products are based on nature. However, as has been shown by Müller and Kouljok Huuva (2009), for example, there are institutional barriers to tourism development. This has also been highlighted by Amin (1999) and other followers of the institutionalist turn in economic geography (Martin 2000), calling for greater attention to institutional factors related to networks, trust, cooperation and mutuality in regional development policies.

The declining importance of staple industries in northern locations, at least in the European case, has implied a greater turn to nature preservation often being promoted as a way to stimulate tourism development (Wall Reinius and Fredman 2007; Lundmark and Stjernström 2009). It is contested, however, whether this is in fact an asset or a burden to local communities. Regarding Sweden, Lundmark and Stjernström (2009) point at consequences regarding land use. Accordingly, the designation of national parks and nature reserves transfers control over land use from local municipalities to regional and national authorities. Moreover, as Lundmark (2006) demonstrated, the assumed positive relationships between national parks and tourism development turned out to be unstable. In fact, resorts relying on outside capital entailed far greater local economic benefits than small-scale nature-based tourism. Thus, Schmallegger and Carson (2010) wonder whether a shift towards tourism in fact only causes dependency on just another staple industry.

Müller (2011) thus argues that some stakeholders regard tourism as only a temporary solution. Path dependence, not least manifested in educational profiles among the local labour force, makes a return to previous staple industries attractive. Thus, in northern Sweden nature protection does not hinder the issuance of new exploration permits for minerals. Instead, current practice seems to open opportunities for a return to the traditional staple. From a perspective focusing on GDP contribution, this makes great sense since tourism income can hardly substitute for incomes from staple industries (Lundgren 2004). However, from a community perspective, tourism is still able to contribute to local employment and in-migration (Müller 2006) and to a re-imaging of peripheral areas (Butler and Hall 1998).

It can be argued that public efforts to develop tourism are sometimes lip service rather than serious attempts to change labour market structures. Müller and Jansson (2007) in fact speculate that tourism is forwarded as a tool for development due to a lack of alternatives and suboptimal knowledge of the preconditions and impacts of tourism development, and because tourism investment is rather cheap compared to investments in other sectors of the economy. Although this is difficult to confirm empirically, it is still possible to check whether tourism solutions are viable even in times of recovery within traditional industries.

Methodology

To reveal the relationship between tourism and staple economies, labour market statistics from 1990 to 2007 were reviewed. The focus is on the province of Lapland, comprising the interior parts of Sweden's two northernmost counties, Norrbotten and Västerbotten. The area is sparsely populated with a density of about one inhabitant per square kilometre. The data for the area come from Astrid, a comprehensive database on individuals in Sweden, compiled by Statistics Sweden and based at the Department of Social and Economic Geography, Umeå University.

For the analysis, all individuals working in one of the twelve municipalities in the area were selected. Furthermore, the standard industrial classification (SIC) code for each individual in employment was retrieved to enable a classification of industries. Since SIC does not classify tourism as a distinct industry, estimates from the domestic tourism satellite account (TSA) were used to calculate the annual employment in tourism. The TSA estimates mirror the economic transactions related to tourism for various industries in the national economy (Meis 2001). Applied to labour market statistics the results are tourism job equivalents, in fact implying that the actual number of jobs dependent on tourism income is far greater.

Although the TSA varies over the years, changes are minor and thus the figures from 2007 were used to estimate the amount of tourism-induced employment

Table 7.1 Tourism share in various industries in Sweden in 2007 according to the Tourist Satellite Account

SIC code	Branch	Share of tourism (%) for total value
55	Hotel and restaurant	60
60.1	Railroad transportation	15
60.21–23	Other land transportation	17
61	Shipping	6
62	Aviation	89
63.3	Travel agencies	100
70.2	Services for houses	8
92	Culture, recreation, sports	14
50–52	Retail trade	5
71	Leasing	10
74.8	Other services	7

Source: Nutek (2008).

(Table 7.1). This methodology can be criticised for being based on a national average rather than regional preconditions. However, since the labour market in the area is highly dependent on tourism (Müller and Ulrich 2007), using the TSA implies a conservative estimate, underrating the actual importance of tourism. Similar problems do not occur for other industries at stake since these are classified thoroughly within the SIC. Another shortcoming of the analysis is the treatment of seasonal and part-time employment. In the available data, only the greatest source of work income is registered. However, in a previous study it was shown that tourism-related work in Sweden increasingly shared characteristics with other industries in terms of working periods and, thus, that differences should not be too great – not least when considering that even forestry entails seasonal employment (Müller and Ulrich 2007).

The manipulated data were then transferred into a geographical information system, where further analysis was conducted. The analysis is at the municipal level, which roughly corresponds to labour market regions.

A background

Northern Sweden has traditionally been Sami land. The indigenous population and their reindeer herding industry still exist, however today the Sami comprise only a weak stakeholder in northern development. Instead, the north has been colonised and developed owing to its resources, primarily from the seventeeth century onward (Arell 1979). Particularly during the nineteenth century, interest in northern resources increased (Sörlin 1988). Besides forests, mineral resources such as gold, silver, iron and copper became main staples to be exported from northern Sweden. The establishment of a railway network facilitated transportation to the Baltic Sea port of Luleå and later also to the Atlantic port of Narvik. At the same time populations grew, mainly owing to natural population increase, and

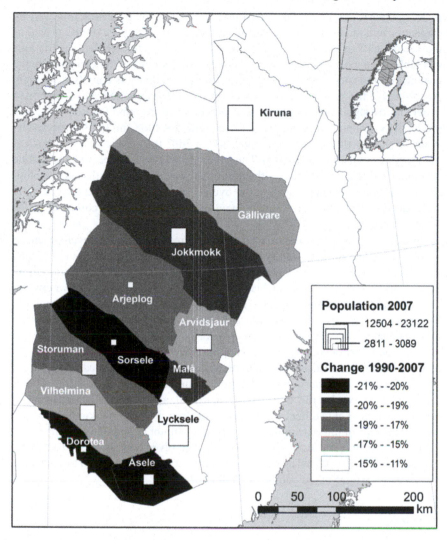

Figure 7.1 Population change in Swedish Lapland, 1990–2007.

provided the labour force necessary to exploit the resources (Håkansson 2000). Technological shifts during the 1950s, such as the introduction of the chainsaw and tractor, caused a decline in labour demand that led to out-migration from the area (Westin 2006). The population decline continued until the end of the research period in 2007 (Figure 7.1). Thus, while the population was 113,118 in 1990, it had dropped by 15 per cent to 95,741 in 2007.

At any rate, a general economic growth also meant an increase in the gross regional product (GRP) in northern Sweden (Olsson Spjut 2010). However, the development has not been linear and is characterised by significant setbacks.

In Norrbotten County, a drop caused by the oil crisis in 1972 was followed by stagnation and moderate decline during the late 1980s and early 1990s, as well as the second half of the 1990s. Unfortunately, there are no detailed calculations available, but a look at per capita productivity reveals some of the variations in the mining and industry sectors where per capita productivity is usually very high. Accordingly, the two northernmost counties of Västerbotten and Norrbotten experienced a significant decline in per capita productivity from 1995 onward, with productivity dropping to values previously recorded in 1968 and 1978, respectively. After 1999, growth was again recorded, and in 2007 the productivity was back at the 1995 level (Olsson Spjut 2010). Thus, these periods seem to be times of decline in mining and related industries – the traditional staples in the north. The development in northern Sweden mirrored the overall situation in the country generally well but, after 1995, the development in northern Sweden lagged compared to the national average.

This time period corresponds well to the increasing tourism development in northern Sweden. Sweden's entry into the EU in 1995 provided access to regional funds, and a paradigm of endogenous development also gained acceptance. However, tourism has a substantial history within the area. The railway network, already established around 1900, was a way not only of exporting natural resources from the area but also of bringing tourists to the north (Lundgren 1995). Europe's first national parks were established in 1908, close to the railway lines (Wall Reinius 2009). Subsequently, a wide-ranging system of national parks and nature reserves has been established in the north recently, not least justified by its impact on employment and tourism development (Lundmark and Stjernström 2009). For tourism in Sweden the area remains marginal, although it is attractive on an international market (Müller 2011). Moreover, from a labour market perspective, tourism became of ultimate importance for many minor communities in the north. Up to 30 per cent of the local labour market has involved tourism-related activities (Müller and Ulrich 2007). The dominating products are nature-based tourism and, increasingly, winter-based activities (Hall *et al.* 2009).

Results

The regional level

During the research period, the working population in Lapland declined from 61,505 to 53,683 – a drop of 13 per cent.

Within the study area, employment in the dominating staple industries of forestry and mining dropped significantly between 1990 and 2003 (Figure 7.2). In the case of forestry, this indeed meant a cut of almost 50 per cent while employment in mining declined by about 25 per cent. It is first in 2004 (and onward) that improving employment can be registered. The development of tourism-induced employment, however, provides a mirror picture of development in the staple industries. An almost constant increase since 1990 turned downward in 2004, the year the staple industries start to improve again. In absolute figures,

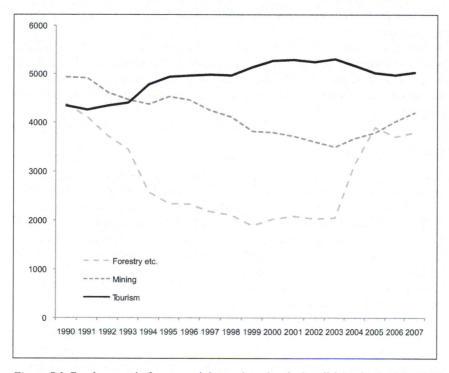

Figure 7.2 Employment in forestry, mining and tourism in Swedish Lapland, 1990–2007.
Source: Astrid Research database.

at the end of the research period the staple sector offered fewer than 8,000 jobs compared to more than 9,300 jobs in 1990. The minimum was reached in 2003, when only slightly more than 5,500 people were employed there.

It can be noted that tourism-induced employment indeed passed mining in its importance for the regional labour market in 1994/95. Also, during the recovery of the staple industries, tourism more or less maintained its quantitative importance for the labour market. In absolute figures, tourism-induced employment grew from about 4,300 job equivalents to more than 5,300 in 2003.

It should be noted that other sectors besides those discussed above declined during the study period to the same extent as mining and forestry did. However, the decline in these sectors was more or less linear, mirroring the general population loss, and thus does not correlate with the variations shown in tourism-induced employment. Moreover, based on the staple theory, the staple industries are basic industries that have indirect and induced effects on other industries and services.

Since even the population declined during the research period, the relative importance of the sectors for local employment did not change as dramatically. On average, staple industries employed between 11 and 15 per cent of the labour force, with peaks at the beginning and end of the study period and the lowest rates between 1999 and 2003. In contrast, tourism-induced employment increased from

7 per cent in 1990 to 11 per cent in 2003. Afterwards, in 2007, it again declined to 9 per cent.

However, Lapland is a vast area and the mining industry is dominant mainly in the two northernmost municipalities of Kiruna and Gällivare, which also have the greatest population in the area. Thus, to further confirm the relationship between staple industries and tourism, it is necessary to shift to another geographical level.

The municipal level

The amount of tourism-induced employment in fact increased, despite declining population figures in all municipalities but Gällivare (Table 7.2). In contrast, all municipalities except Dorotea, Sorsele and Malå lost jobs in mining and forestry.

The relative development in the municipalities differs, however. Gällivare and Kiruna, the major mining municipalities in Sweden, show a steady dominance of staple industries over tourism during the entire research period (Figure 7.3). Even Lycksele shows the same development, although here the major staple sector is forestry. Another common characteristic of these three municipalities is that they are the largest in population within the area.

In most municipalities, however, tourism-induced jobs outnumbered those in the staple industries. This is particularly applicable to the time from 1993/94 onward, although the recovery of the staple industries towards the end of the research period meant that several municipalities reached a situation in which the sectors provided similar numbers of jobs.

Some municipalities deviate dramatically from the others. Arjeplog, which had a clear majority of its labour force in staple industries, lost its mine and thus became a municipality where tourism-induced employment dominates over staple-sector employment. In contrast, in Sorsele new mines were opened and caused the

Table 7.2 Absolute employment change in tourism, mining and forestry, 1990–2007

	Tourism	Staple industries	Mining	Forestry etc.
Kiruna	203	−286	−240	−46
Gällivare	−35	−59	−81	22
Jokkmokk	35	−28	−18	−10
Arjeplog	68	−295	−283	−12
Arvidsjaur	19	−50	−33	−17
Lycksele	87	−611	−211	−400
Åsele	19	−21	−2	−19
Vilhelmina	90	−86	15	−101
Dorotea	41	21	−2	23
Sorsele	30	67	86	−19
Storuman	92	−27	11	−38
Malå	40	52	22	30
Total Lapland	689	−1,323	−736	−587

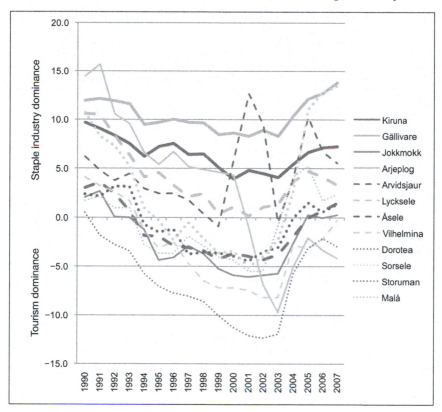

Figure 7.3 Differences in the roles of staple industries and tourism for local labour markets, 1990–2007.

opposite development (Knobblock and Pettersson 2010). Finally, Åsele underwent the greatest changes, but these are related to variations in the forestry sector.

As discussed earlier, development since 1990 can be divided into three phases. A first phase of relative stability with a moderate decline in the staple sector and a small increase in tourism until 1995 is followed by a time of moderate increase in tourism and strong decline in the staple sector. From 2003 onward, employment in the staple industries has increased steadily while tourism employment is declining and stagnating. Not all municipalities follow these exact patterns, however. During the first phase, the development can be registered in all municipalities (Table 7.3). Tourism gained relative importance for the local labour market at the same time as staple industries lost importance. During the second phase, development differs. A relative decline in staple industries can be noted in six municipalities. In four municipalities the staple industries maintained their relative importance for the labour market while in two, Dorotea and Malå, staple industries in fact increased their relative share regarding local employment. At the same time, the importance of tourism-induced employment increased in all

Table 7.3 Changing labour market importance (per cent) of staple industries and tourism, 1990–2007

	1990–1995		1995–2003		2003–2007	
	Staple	Tourism	Staple	Tourism	Staple	Tourism
Kiruna	−1.0	1.5	−2.0	1.2	2.8	−0.3
Gällivare	−1.1	1.2	0.2	1.6	3.5	−2.0
Jokkmokk	−3.7	2.7	−0.1	1.3	4.1	−1.9
Arjeplog	−5.5	3.6	−13.4	1.7	4.6	−0.9
Arvidsjaur	−3.5	1.4	−1.2	0.7	4.6	−0.7
Lycksele	−4.4	1.6	−1.7	1.5	1.3	−0.6
Åsele	−3.3	0.4	0.4	3.4	5.5	−0.6
Vilhelmina	−4.5	2.8	−1.4	3.6	5.2	−2.7
Dorotea	−2.8	1.1	2.3	3.8	3.0	−1.4
Sorsele	−9.4	1.6	0.1	2.1	14.2	−1.5
Storuman	−3.8	3.7	−0.7	4.2	5.1	−3.9
Malå	−3.3	2.1	4.0	1.2	2.3	−1.0
Total Lapland	−2.5	1.8	−1.2	1.8	3.7	−1.3

municipalities. During the third phase the share of tourism-induced employment decreased in all municipalities except Kiruna, the major city in terms of overnight tourism stays in the area (Müller 2011), while the staple industries more or less regained their previously lost role on the local labour market. Particularly in Sorsele, the establishment of a new mine created a significant increase in employment.

Conclusions

The obvious relationship between tourism-induced employment and employment in the staple industries cannot automatically be interpreted as a causal relationship. A decline in the traditional staple industries, here mainly mining and forestry, indeed occurred at the same time as an increase in tourism-induced employment. However, as previous studies have already indicated, restructuring cannot be understood as a simple shift of labour from one sector to another (Lundmark 2006). This appears to be particularly true for a shift between male-dominated sectors such as mining and forestry and service sectors such as tourism. Thus, employees in tourism are hardly those previously employed in the staple sector. Instead, it can be argued that tourism development is a reaction to crisis in other sectors, probably born out of an insight that new ways of sustaining communities are needed.

This development has certainly been supported by government initiatives and regional policy schemes aiming at creating new livelihoods and alternative development options in the periphery (Jenkins *et al.* 1998). However, this chapter has argued and showed that crisis in staple economies is a cyclical event (Clapp 1998). This means that the need for public response to crisis risks becoming cyclical as well. Although political initiatives to counteract crisis should usually be expected to aim at a diversification of peripheral economies, it seems to be a difficult thing to achieve. Instead, truncated economies originally created by the desire of southern authorities to maximise income from natural resource extraction appear thorny to overcome, as has been shown in this study.

Tourism is only slightly related to the basic industries in place. Although its roots can be traced back more than one hundred years, it is often seen as having been brought in from the outside and is seldom deeply embedded in place. Moreover, although tourism development creates significant numbers of employment opportunities (Müller and Ulrich 2007), it fails to create the economic values and salaries associated with staple industries (Lundgren 2004). Thus, in the case of a passed crisis, returning to a previous development path makes perfect sense, if economic concerns are allowed to dominate. Certainly, depending on the taxation system in place, this is true for local and regional government in many countries. Hence, path dependency is institutionalised, that is, institutions – like taxation systems but also school curricula and traditions – favour a return to the extracting industries.

This creates a gloomy situation for tourism developers. Although tourism development is preached by politics, there is little incentive to actually put effort into it. Particularly under periods of population decline, the need to sustain public households implies local profit-maximising strategies. In this context, efforts for tourism development may appear less valuable regarding their outcomes and, thus, tourism is at risk of being a secondary topic on local agendas. However, development differs between places. Although declining in importance, tourism development is not wiped out, but rather continues on a slightly lower level. This indicates that tourism-induced labour markets and employment in staple industries are only loosely interlinked, and that in fact tourism development has actually led to a diversification of local labour markets. Thus, in fact, crisis may be an opportunity to develop alternative options. In this context, tourism development may be one of these options. Examining the details of this process was outside the focus of this chapter, but should be studied in the future.

Acknowledgement

The research for this chapter was conducted with the financial support of the Swedish Research Council (VR) and the Swedish Foundation for Strategic Environmental Research (MISTRA), which are hereby gratefully acknowledged.

References

Amin, A. (1999) 'An institutionalist perspective on regional economic development', *International Journal of Urban and Regional Research*, 23(2): 365–78.

Arell, N. (1979) *Kolonisationen i lappmarken*, Lund: Esselte Studium.

Astrid Research database, Department of Social and Economic Geography, Umeå University.

Barker, M.L. and Soyez, D. (1994) 'Think locally, act globally? The transnationalization of Canadian resource-use conflicts', *Environment*, 36(6): 12–20.

Baum, T. (1999) 'The decline of the traditional North Atlantic Fisheries and tourism's response: the cases of Iceland and Newfoundland', *Current Issues in Tourism*, 2(1): 68–81.

Burns, P. (1999) 'Paradoxes in planning: tourism elitism or brutalism?', *Annals of Tourism Research*, 26: 329–48.

Butler, R.W. and Hall, C.M. (1998) 'Image and reimaging of rural areas', in R. Butler, C.M. Hall and J. Jenkins (eds) *Tourism and Recreation in Rural Areas*, Chichester, UK: Wiley, pp. 115–22.

Christaller, W. (1964) 'Some considerations of tourism location in Europe: the peripheral regions – underdeveloped countries – recreation areas', *Papers in Regional Science*, 12(1): 95–105.

Clapp, R.A. (1998) 'The resource cycle in forestry and fishing', *The Canadian Geographer*, 42(2): 129–44.

Green, C. (2009) *Managing Laponia: A world heritage as arena for Sami ethno-politics in Sweden*, Uppsala, Sweden: Cultural Anthropology.

Gunton, T. (2003) 'Natural resources and regional development: an assessment of dependency and comparative advantage paradigms', *Economic Geography*, 79(1): 67–94.

Hall, C.M. (2007) 'North–South perspectives on tourism, regional development and peripheral areas', in D.K. Müller and B. Jansson (eds) *Tourism in Peripheries: Perspectives from the far North and South*, Wallingford, UK: CABI: pp. 19–37.

Hall, C.M. (2010) 'Crisis events in tourism: subjects of crisis in tourism', *Current Issues in Tourism*, 13(5): 401–17.

Hall, C.M. and Boyd, S. (2005) 'Introduction: nature-based tourism in peripheral areas', in C.M. Hall and S. Boyd (eds) *Nature-based Tourism in Peripheral Areas: Development or disaster?*, Clevedon, UK: Channel View, pp. 3–17.

Hall, C.M. and Johnston, M.E. (1995) 'Introduction: pole to pole: tourism issues, impacts and the search for management regime in polar regions', in C.M. Hall and M.E. Johnston (eds) *Polar Tourism: Tourism in the Arctic and Antarctic regions*, Chichester, UK: Wiley, pp. 1–26.

Hall, C.M. and Saarinen, J. (2010) 'Tourism and change in polar regions: introduction – definitions, locations, places and dimensions', in C.M. Hall and J. Saarinen (eds) *Tourism and Change in Polar Regions*, London: Routledge: 1–41.

Hall, C.M., Müller, D.K. and Saarinen, J. (2009) *Nordic Tourism: Issues and cases*, Bristol, UK: Channel View.

Håkansson, J. (2000) *Changing Population Distribution in Sweden: Long term trends and contemporary tendencies*, Umeå, Sweden: Department of Social and Economic Geography.

Hayter, R. (2003) '"The war in the woods": post-Fordist restructuring, globalization, and the contested remapping of British Columbia's forest economy', *Annals of the American Association of Geographers*, 93(3): 706–29.

Hayter, R. and Soyez, D. (1996) 'Clearcut issues: German environmental pressure and the British Columbia forest sector', *Geographische Zeitschrift*, 84: 143–56.

Hayter, R., Barnes, T.J. and Bradshaw, M.J. (2003) 'Relocating resource peripheries to the core of economic geography's theorizing: rationale and agenda', *Area*, 35(1): 15–23.

Hoggart, K. and Paniagua, A. (2001) 'What rural restructuring?', *Journal of Rural Studies*, 17(1): 41–62.

Innis, H.A. (1930/1956) *The Fur Trade in Canada: An introduction to Canadian economic history*, Toronto: University of Toronto Press.

Jenkins, J.M., Hall, C.M. and Troughton, M. (1998) 'The restructuring of rural economies: rural tourism and recreation as a government response', in R. Butler, C.M. Hall and J. Jenkins (eds) *Tourism and Recreation in Rural Areas*, Chichester, UK: Wiley, pp. 43–68.

Jóhannesson, G.T. and Huijbens, E.H. (2010) 'Tourism in times of crisis: exploring the discourse of tourism development in Iceland', *Current Issues in Tourism*, 13(5): 419–34.

Knobblock, E. and Pettersson, Ö. (2010) 'Restructuring and risk-reduction in mining: employment implications for northern Sweden', *Fennia*, 188(1): 61–75.

Knox, P., Agnew, J. and McCarthy, L. (2008) *The Geography of the World Economy*, London: Hodder.

Kondratieff, N. (1984) *The Long-Wave Cycle*, New York: Richardson and Snyder.

Lundgren, J.O.J. (1995) 'The tourism space penetration processes in northern Canada and Scandinavia', in C.M. Hall and M.E. Johnston (eds) *Polar Tourism: Tourism in the Arctic and Antarctic regions*, Chichester, UK: Wiley, pp. 43–62.

Lundgren, J.O.J. (2001) 'Canadian tourism going north: an overview with comparative Scandinavian perspectives', in B. Sahlberg (ed.) *Going North: Peripheral tourism in Canada and Sweden*, Östersund, Sweden: Etour, pp. 13–46.

Lundgren, T. (2004) 'The determinants of economic growth in the Swedish Mountain Region: the role of the forest industry, the tourism sector, and protected land', *FjällMistra-report*, 8, Umeå, Sweden: FjällMistra.

Lundmark, L. (2006) *Restructuring and Employment Change in Sparsely Populated Areas: Examples from northern Sweden and Finland*, Umeå, Sweden: Department of Social and Economic Geography.

Lundmark, L. and Stjernström, O. (2009) 'Environmental protection: an instrument for regional development? National ambitions versus local realities in the case of tourism', *Scandinavian Journal of Hospitality and Tourism*, 9(4): 387–405.

Mackintosh, W.A. (1939/1964) *The Economic Background of Dominion–Provincial Relations*, Toronto: McClelland and Stewart.

Malerba, F. (2005) 'Sectoral systems of innovation: basic concepts', in F. Malerba (ed.) *Sectoral Systems of Innovation: Concepts, issues and analyses of six major sectors in Europe*, Cambridge: Cambridge University Press, pp. 9–41.

Markey, S., Halseth, G. and Manson, D. (2006) 'The struggle to compete: from comparative to competitive advantage in northern British Columbia', *International Planning Studies*, 11(1): 19–39.

Martin, R. (2000) 'Institutional approaches in economic geography', in E. Sheppard and T.J. Barnes (eds) *A Companion to Economic Geography*, Oxford: Blackwell, pp. 77–94.

Martin, R. and Sunley, P. (2006) 'Path dependence and regional economic evolution', *Journal of Economic Geography*, 6: 395–437.

Meis, S. (2001) 'Towards comparative studies in Tourism Satellite Accounts', in J.J. Lennon (ed.) *Tourism Statistics: International perspectives and current issues*, London: Continuum, pp. 14–23.

Müller, D.K. (2006) 'Amenity migration and tourism development in the Tärna Mountains', in L.A.G. Moss (ed.) *The Amenity Migrants: Seeking and sustaining mountains and their cultures*, Wallingford, UK: CABI, pp. 245–58.

Müller, D.K. (2011) 'Tourism development in Europe's "last wilderness": an assessment of nature-based tourism in Swedish Lapland', in A. Grenier and D.K. Müller (eds) *Polar Tourism and Regional Development*, Montreal: UQAM.

Müller, D.K. and Jansson, B. (2007) 'The difficult business of making pleasure peripheries prosperous: perspectives on space, place and environment', in D.K. Müller and B. Jansson (eds) *Tourism in Peripheries: Perspectives from the far North and South*, Wallingford, UK: CABI, pp. 3–18.

Müller, D.K. and Kouljok Huuva, S. (2009) 'Limits to Sami tourism development: the case of Jokkmokk, Sweden', *Journal of Ecotourism*, 8(2): 115–27.

Müller, D.K. and Ulrich, P. (2007) 'Tourism development and the rural labour market in Sweden, 1960–1999', in D.K. Müller and B. Jansson (eds) *Tourism in Peripheries: Perspectives from the far North and South*, Wallingford, UK: CABI, pp. 85–105.

Nutek (2008) 'Fakta om svensk turism och turistnäring', Stockholm.

Olsson Spjut, F. (2010) *BRP i Norr – utveckling och trender: bruttoregionproduktens utveckling i Norrlandslänen 1968–2007*, Umeå, Sweden: CERUM.

Ray, C. (2000) 'Endogenous socio-economic development in the European Union: issues of evaluation', *Journal of Rural Studies*, 16(4): 447–58.

Saarinen, J. (2005) 'The regional economics of tourism in northern Finland: the socio-economic implications of recent tourism development and future possibilities for regional development', *Scandinavian Journal of Hospitality and Tourism*, 3(2): 91–113.

Saarinen, J. (2007) 'Tourism in peripheries: the role of tourism in regional development in northern Finland', in D.K. Müller and B. Jansson (eds) *Tourism in Peripheries: Perspectives from the far North and South*, Wallingford, UK: CABI, pp. 41–53.

Schmallegger, D. and Carson, D. (2010) 'Is tourism just another staple? A new perspective on tourism in remote regions', *Current Issues in Tourism*, 13(3): 201–21.

Sörlin, S. (1988) *Framtidslandet: debatten om Norrland och naturresurserna under det industriella genombrottet*, Stockholm: Carlssons.

Storey, K. (2001) 'Fly-in/fly-out and fly-over: mining and regional development in Western Australia', *Australian Geographer*, 32(2): 133–48.

Storey, K. (2010) 'Fly-in/fly-out: implications for community sustainability', *Sustainability*, 2010(2): 1161–81.

Townsend, A.R. (1997) *Making a Living in Europe: Human geographies of economic change*, London: Routledge.

Wall Reinius, S. (2009) 'A ticket to national parks? Tourism, railways, and the establishment of national parks in Sweden', in W. Frost and C.M. Hall (eds) *Tourism and National Parks: International perspectives on development, histories and change*, London: Routledge, pp. 184–96.

Wall Reinius, S. and Fredman, P. (2007) 'Protected areas as attractions', *Annals of Tourism Research*, 34(4): 839–54.

Westin, L. (2006) 'Trading natural resources for public grants: development rhetoric, image, and social capital in north Sweden', in I. Kasuhisa, H. Westlund, K. Kobayashi and T. Hatori (eds) *Social Capital and Development Trends in Rural Areas*, 2, Kyoto: Kyoto University, pp. 71–84.

8 The crisis of induced uneven development through South African tourism marketing strategies

Gustav Visser

Introduction

In many regions around the world, tourism is viewed as providing a means for the United Nations Millennium Project's various development objectives to be achieved (Rogerson and Visser 2011; Saarinen *et al.* 2011; Visser and Hoogendoorn 2011). Similarly, in South Africa, tourism has received significant prominence as a development agent in post-apartheid policy discourse (Department of Tourism 2011). Recently, the national government has effected significant changes in its ministries, including the creation of a separate Ministry of Tourism, thereby indicating that the South African tourism industry has grown in stature in its importance to the state (Visser and Hoogendoorn 2011). In addition, tourism was specifically highlighted in the 2011 State of the Nation address for the first time; some analysts suggest it is 'encouraging to see that the expectations which were formulated in the New Economic Growth Path are continuing with the tourism sector highlighted as a priority' (Saunders 2011). The most recent indication of the central role government affords tourism as a developmental tool is seen in the new *Rural Tourism Strategy* (Department of Tourism 2012).

Since 1996 when the first tourism White Paper was published, a number of additional policy documents and frameworks have been promulgated – not least among them, the new directives contained in the aforementioned *Rural Tourism Strategy* (Department of Tourism 2012: 8). Whereas no direct project planning stemming from this latter document has materialised, there have been numerous attempts arising from previous policy documents and frameworks. In the main, four principle concerns have regularly been highlighted as urgent: (1) the limited involvement of previously disadvantaged individuals in the South African tourism system; (2) uneven investment in the country's tourism industry across all regions, particularly in light of the fact that there are limited investment incentives; (3) the highly uneven tourism space economy, which has limited the impact of those tourism investments that have been made; and (4) the slow pace at which the tourism system is transforming in terms of pro-poor development (SAT 2011).

In order to help confront these challenges, the national government created a parastatal: South African Tourism (SAT). SAT is tasked with developing both the domestic and international tourism markets by increasing tourist arrivals, increasing the total expenditure of tourists in South Africa, optimising the length of stays, improving the distribution of tourists throughout the country and during the year, and improving activity and spending patterns to enable development through tourism (Visser 2003). Since 2000, SAT has been active in marketing South Africa both locally and abroad, with a range of successful and imaginative campaigns. From a policy perspective, SAT has also conducted research into various market segments with the Tourism Growth Strategy (SAT 2002) – an excellent example of what concrete steps it has taken to fulfil its mandate.

A decade ago, an analysis of SAT's first Tourism Growth Strategy was undertaken (Visser 2003). The focus was on one aspect of SAT's mandate: improving the regional distribution of tourists through the country. It was concluded that, ironically, SAT's marketing strategy risked perpetuating South Africa's uneven tourism space economy, rather than changing it. It was argued that, should well-intentioned government interventions not be put into practice with due care, they could perpetuate a crisis within the geographical distribution of tourists in the South African tourism system. Ten years on, it seems that analysis was correct. Indeed, the latest South African national tourism policy document, *Rural Tourism Strategy*, indicates that its central concern is 'to enhance the growth and development of tourism in rural communities particularly in less visited provinces' because a number of 'key tourist attractions are located in rural areas and are not receiving the benefits stemming from the tourism industry' (Department of Tourism 2012: 8).

Recently, a revised version of the *Marketing Tourism Growth Strategy for South Africa 2011–2013* was published (SAT 2011). The task of this investigation is to assess the degree to which the marketing strategy has changed and its potential to address a tourism space economy, which is still as uneven as when SAT penned its first marketing strategy (Cornelissen 2005). It is suggested that, a decade after SAT's commitment to a more even distribution of tourists across the region, there remains a significant schism between the marketing strategies and information presented by SAT relative to the stated objectives and mandate of the organisation. In particular, SAT is still not encouraging the redress of the uneven South African tourism space economy through its current marketing material. In fact, the spatial implications of the contents of their web-based marketing initiatives could potentially aggravate (rather than address) the development of an already uneven tourism space economy.

The South African tourism space economy and international tourism marketing

Over the past fifteen years, a key challenge to tourism policy development in South Africa has been the need to distribute the potential benefits of tourism expansion more evenly across the country and indeed the whole of the southern African region. This objective was and still is formulated in terms of the highly uneven and polarised tourism space economy of South Africa. The dimensions of the uneven tourism space economy have been discussed at length in the research of Scarlett Cornelissen (2005) and Christian Rogerson (2002, 2011). The most recent research by Jayne Rogerson (2010, 2011a, 2011b) on hotel accommodation in South Africa provides a useful proxy variable in which it is clearly demonstrated that the post-apartheid tourism boom has resulted in a very significant expansion of formal hotel accommodation across South Africa, but with the main expansion to be found in very particular locations. In fact, she observes that 'geographically, the hotel sector became more concentrated upon four key urban tourism nodes and in certain cities the over-production of hotel accommodation is an emerging problem' (Rogerson 2012; see also Rogerson and Kotze 2011). Her analysis also highlights that there are major nodes of 'tourism spend' concentrated in the Johannesburg and Pretoria area, Cape Town and Durban.

Suffice to say that the Gauteng tourism node is mainly led by different forms of business tourism (Visser 2003), whereas the Durban and Cape Town nodes are primarily based in international (and domestic) leisure tourism. International leisure tourism is of particular importance in Cape Town and its environs, although conference tourism is also an important and growing niche market. Outside these urban centres, the only significant nodes of tourism development are in Mpumalanga and parts of Limpopo – the host provinces of many of South Africa's game parks and lodges – and along the Garden Route in the Western Cape. These geographically polarised patterns of tourism development result in the benefits of tourism being distributed in a spatially uneven manner with few benefits and opportunities flowing outside these major tourism areas. At issue is that this pattern of tourism development is no different from that which SAT aimed to change in their first marketing strategy.

In 2002, SAT developed an international marketing strategy, which focused on a core set of markets that together could deliver the highest yield against their stated strategic objectives. The strategy development process sought the identification of target markets and followed a two-stage procedure. First, choices were made about the countries and 'purpose markets' that needed to be defended, or that presented the greatest opportunities for growth. Second, choices were made about which market segments required defensive or growth actions that were internal to those countries identified (SAT 2011).

In the development of SAT's strategic focus, Africa was dealt with as a separate market from the outset. Given its importance in terms of visitor volumes and extremely high market share, this was not surprising. Evidently, the strategic focus in respect of this market means that enhancing the extraction of further value, rather than volume growth, was essential to developing the South African tourism market. Generally, a means of extracting more value implied up-selling and cross-selling into other product areas.

The main thrust of the strategy development process, however, was the analysis of the international overseas visitors market to South Africa. In terms of the country-level choice process, SAT first set out to establish where the greatest opportunities for growth existed. This was achieved by identifying those markets that generated more than a million long-haul holiday trips. This listing included many European countries, North America and markets such as China, Japan and South Korea. Primarily because of limited resources, SAT argued that, in the context of the overall set of actions required within the portfolio, it could not realistically afford to develop all these markets. As a result, a further level of elimination was required, deploying further criteria (Visser 2003). In the end, SAT identified eleven markets, which in turn framed the nature of its efforts in the short to medium term along the following lines:

- In the UK and Germany, where South Africa already has an established market presence, SAT decided to defend its market position and aggressively focus on growth.
- In the Netherlands, where South Africa has a comparatively strong presence together with enabling conditions such as language affinity, the relative gain was interpreted as being less than in other markets. Consequently, SAT aimed to focus on defending its existing position while building growth.
- The USA and Japan represented markets where gain is at its greatest, but where the required effort would be significant. Both markets were seen to represent investment targets for SAT, with the USA being the first country where SAT would be entering to build long-term growth. Japan would follow over the medium to longer term.
- Other countries, such as Australia, Canada, China, France, Italy and Sweden, were to be the focus of targeted efforts by SAT with a view to 'picking off' key valuable segments through very focused efforts in the short term (SAT 2002, 2011).

With respect to purpose markets, various purpose-driven travel markets were evaluated, including Meetings, Incentives, Conferences and Exhibitions (MICE) as well as shopping and medical tourism. In the main, it was argued that SAT should leave these markets to industry, and rather provide ongoing support and market intelligence to aid these efforts.

Whereas SAT identified source markets in terms of countries, the success of a marketing strategy was also dependent upon the targeting of specific segments internal to these markets. These segments were distinguished by analysing buying processes and buying criteria characteristics in each country. In the end, a range of target groups was identified.

Given the dramatic expansion in tourism volumes to South Africa across all tourism markets and segments, the marketing strategy has been highly effective against such criteria. However, as already suggested, the uneven development of the South African tourism system has remained. Consequently, the initial strategy has recently been revisited. It is acknowledged that, 'While SA Tourism has made progress in growing the markets in its portfolio, there is still significant opportunity in (above mentioned) target markets' (SAT 2011: 8). It is noted that 72 per cent of South Africa's arrivals are from its neighbouring six states, but given 'the high market share already in SADC and the absence of any true competition, the strategy for SADC shifts to one of "defend" and the extraction of additional value outside of neighbouring SADC' (SAT 2011). There is also emphasis on exploiting new source markets, particularly 'smaller high-end leisure volumes which in the long term may provide growth in markets in East and West Africa' (SAT 2011: 37). In terms of consumer segments, it is acknowledged that business and events tourism offers the most realistic high-growth opportunities. In addition, it is noted that, in terms of overseas markets, South Africa is probably over-reliant on European source markets and the USA, and needs to focus increasing attention on the Far East.

The spatial implications of South African Tourism's current web-based marketing efforts

SAT acknowledges that, despite their previous strategies, the distribution of international (particularly overseas) tourists remains a major challenge. It notes, 'if tourism is to impact significantly on poverty and unemployment, then tourism must develop in areas beyond the traditional tourism routes and nodes currently used'. In their view, 'the challenge ... was to seek opportunities to extend the access to markets for less-developed provinces ... In part, this would include developing products to encourage international tourists to increase the average number of provinces visited on a trip' (Visser and Kotze 2006).

However, in terms of the spatial distribution of tourists in South Africa, an analysis of the current travel suggestions published by SAT does not go far enough in achieving its marketing strategy objectives. The link to the above discussion is that, although a range of tourist markets and specific tourist profiles might be identified and marketing efforts made in particular regions, these market segments require information for planning their travel programmes in South Africa, not least the official tourism website of the country. As a consequence, this investigation analyses the SAT website and scrutinises the online marketing material presented to potential tourists. SAT's web pages are arranged around a number of different themes. These include a suite of so-called Top 10 'attractions, trips, cities, towns and regions' to visit. In addition, there are other categories such as Top 10 'experiences, events and activities' in South Africa. On the whole, these web pages are informative and attractive to potential tourists. However, as the following analysis aims to demonstrate, this does very little to address the issue of the uneven distribution of overseas tourists in South Africa.

A starting point is to first consider the Top 10 attractions that SAT suggests tourists visit in South Africa. The analysis has set out to visualise the information contained in SAT's marketing material. As seen in Figure 8.1, the Top 10 suggested attractions in South Africa present a very specific tourism geography.

The first consideration is that the top three 'attractions' and 'trips' in South Africa are all centred on Cape Town and the Western Cape region more generally: Cape Town and the Peninsula, the Garden Route and the Cape Winelands are promoted. The majority of the remaining key attractions are concentrated in Gauteng and Mpumalanga with some suggestions focused on KwaZulu-Natal. For example, Johannesburg, Soweto and Durban are suggested as key destinations.

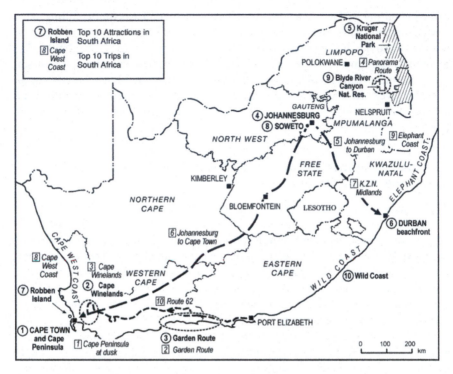

Figure 8.1 Top 10 attractions and trips for tourists in South Africa.

Source: South African Tourism (2012).

Similarly, the Kruger National Park and a range of destinations in Mpumalanga are also highlighted.

As seen in Figure 8.2, the same pattern is repeated in terms of the Top 10 'cities, towns and regions' to visit in South Africa. In the western part of South Africa, Cape Town, Stellenbosch, Franschhoek and Knysna are suggested as specific urban places to visit. In addition, four of the ten regions to visit – the Cape Winelands, Garden Route, Cape Peninsula and Cape West Coast – are promoted by SAT.

The spatial analysis of these suggested attractions, trips, cities, towns and regions to visit reveals much. The most important is that, despite the stated objective of SAT to aim towards greater evenness in the distribution of overseas tourism across South Africa, their marketing efforts are in fact, concentrating visitors in very specific parts of the country. Some provinces are essentially totally ignored in this promotional material. For example, the Eastern Cape, Free State, Northern Cape and North West provinces are largely overlooked (SAT 2012).

In addition, as demonstrated in Table 8.1, the main suggested experiences, events and activities to be undertaken during a visit to South Africa overlap in the main with locations found in the Western Cape, KwaZulu-Natal, Mpumalanga and Gauteng. The so-called Top 10 experiences have sub-categories around which travel programmes can be developed. These experiences include natural scenic

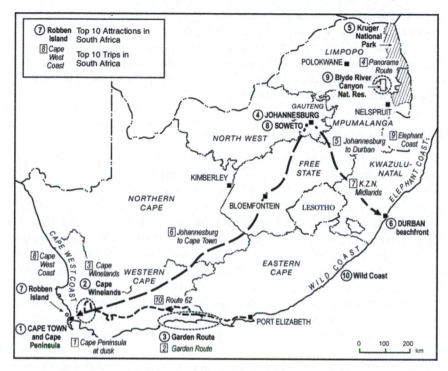

Figure 8.2 Top 10 cities, towns and regions for tourists in South Africa.
Source: South African Tourism (2012).

Table 8.1 Top 10 experiences, events and activities promoted by South African Tourism

Top 10 experiences	Top 10 events	Top 10 activities
Scenic splendour and serenity	KaapseKlopse, Cape Town	Game viewing and safari
Wine tasting	Namaqualand Daisies in Springtime	Nightlife
Five-star safari	Comrades Marathon	Shopping
Struggle sites	Grahamstown National Arts Festival	Beaches
Magnificent marine		Township tours
Cultural encounters	Argus Cycle Tour	Adventure
Outdoor rush	Sardine Run	Theme parks
Urban rhythm	Johannesburg Easter Festival	Casinos
Your South African feast		Ostrich farms
Indulge your senses	Soweto Derby	Be a sport
	Klein Karoo Nasionale Kunstefees	
	Knysna Oyster Festival	

sites, wine tastings, safaris and struggle sites. The central observation is that these experiences are nearly all located in or along existing tourism nodes and routes. Similarly, the Top 10 events and activities promoted in the marketing material do precisely the same. On the whole, the conclusion that can be drawn is that it is evident that there is a major schism between roughly speaking the east and west of South Africa versus the rest of the country.

Implications of current SAT marketing

South African Tourism has a number of objectives that it is mandated to achieve. As already stated, these include increasing foreign tourist arrivals, increasing their total expenditure in South Africa, optimising the length of stays, improving the regional distribution of tourists through the country and throughout the year, and improving activity and spending patterns to enable transformation and promote black economic empowerment. It would appear that, despite those ambitions, the current marketing material presents a disappointing spatial outcome. As matters stand, SAT has identified a number of market segments that can increase tourist flows to South Africa. This action may be successful in increasing the length of stay and the general expenditure of tourists. Although the suggested destinations are in some cases spread out across the country, it still does not challenge, or demonstrate the potential to change, the general tourism space economy of the country. As seen, the travel and destination suggestions fail to reach out to those regions most in need of the development opportunities associated with tourism expansion. However, there is also a related set of issues: the increased emphasis on other source markets; the type of tourists; and the types of product offerings that challenge the potential of SAT to distribute tourists more evenly across South Africa.

In terms of shifting the regional focus of marketing efforts to include the Far East relative to SAT's ambitions to distribute tourists, some issues need to be highlighted. Focusing on the Chinese, Indian and Japanese markets is a sound strategic ambition, particularly in light of China's and India's massive economic expansion. However, these tourist markets are not familiar with South Africa – and in the case of China, tourists are not likely to be independent travellers (the very type of tourist needed to explore South Africa beyond the current tourist routes and nodes). Until now, tourists from China have tended to explore South Africa in structured formats and to visit those regions in South Africa that are 'characteristic' of Africa, namely game parks, and cities that are perceived to represent urban South Africa (Rogerson and Visser 2007). The current marketing material only serves to reinforce this travel behaviour. This should also be linked to the fact that, for the foreseeable future, the language barrier will limit how independently Chinese tourists engage with South Africa. In addition, even if one could redirect these tourist flows, the formal travel format is not likely to lead to tourists supporting small, medium and micro enterprises (SMMEs) but rather corporate tourism service providers in and along well-established tourism nodes and routes. While Indian tourists are not presented with the language barrier to the same extent and could potentially travel more independently, it is again important to realise that what wealthy Indian tourists would seek in South Africa is probably luxury wildlife experiences and products of superior quality and novelty – something the SAT marketing material reinforces. These products are not evenly distributed across South Africa but are clustered to the east and west of the country.

The East and West African tourist markets present opportunities for growing the national tourism system and expanding the South African presence in these markets is certainly also a sound strategy. However, it is doubtful that exploiting these markets will lead to a better distribution of tourists across South Africa. A wealthy Kenyan or Tanzanian tourist does not visit South Africa to view wildlife, nor are our cultural tourism products likely to be a drawcard – they have enough of these products on their doorsteps. These tourists, at least till now, have sought out urban-based products comprising business, shopping and healthcare tourism (Rogerson and Visser 2007). There seems to be no reason why this would change in the future. Similarly, focusing on a rapidly growing Nigerian market is prudent, but these tourists are unlikely to explore far-flung regions of South Africa – again, they are far more likely to engage South Africa for products either not available at home or that are of a lower standard or priced higher in their home country.

In terms of the focus on tourist categories such as the broader business tourism segment, challenges to the geographic spread of tourists are also presented. The focus on business tourists is sound; however, perhaps SAT is overplaying the ability to direct these tourists to remote rural areas and provinces. Business tourists can and do add leisure components to their travel itineraries, but are guided by similar concerns of what 'represents' a South African experience and are framed by where they conduct their business. Business tourists based in Johannesburg might add both urban-based and wildlife components to a tour programme, but these are most likely to be in destination areas that are relatively accessible from where they have conducted their business. For example, a tour of the main sites in Johannesburg and Pretoria and/or a few days at a safari lodge in Mpumalanga or even a trip to Cape Town might be undertaken, but road trips to remote locations they do not know or care for are unlikely. The range of what constitutes events tourism is vast, but in order to present events that have international (or even national) appeal, appropriate organisational and physical infrastructure are required. These types of resources are either absent or in short supply in most of the provinces SAT aims to direct international tourists towards.

There is an important point of practicality, policy ambitions and marketing tourism growth strategies for South Africa that requires consideration. SAT is tasked with very ambitious objectives. However, in terms of aiming to distribute international tourists more evenly across South Africa, they might be aiming for a goal that requires a range of different types of resources that are simply not available. In addition, these resources, both actual and required, are located in, and associated with, a range of different institutions and actors, including local, provincial and national governments, as well as private, human and social capital. These resources are not evenly distributed, nor investment in them necessarily justified.

Finally, it might need to be acknowledged that some regions of South Africa simply have very limited or extremely specific tourism potential. The attempt to include all of these in the tourism system, which is a laudable ambition, might not be practical or necessarily justifiable. Just as SAT acknowledges that it is not possible and practical to market South Africa in all source markets, it has to face the real possibility that it might not be possible to present all regions in South Africa as holding tourism potential. In the end, tourism is not a viable development strategy for all regions, locations and communities.

Conclusion

Tourism systems are faced by all manner of crises that can be (and are) generated by both external and internal crisis events. One of the factors influencing the development trajectory of national, but also regional, tourism systems is that of internal policy frameworks and directives, in addition to the manner in which they are put into effect. In many parts of the world, there is recognition that one of the crises in tourism can be the distribution of tourists over a tourism space economy. Merely being able to draw tourists to a particular country does not mean that tourism is a necessarily successful route by which to address developmental challenges in a whole region. Not everyone will benefit from increased tourism receipts if they are unevenly distributed over a tourism space economy, and those that are generally excluded from access to tourists and its associated economies and benefits are very often those in greatest need of them.

Perhaps a central crisis for the tourism and development nexus discourse is tourist distribution. What policy makers and governments might need to face is the proposition that tourism simply is not a cure-all and that some communities will never benefit from tourism expansion or policy frameworks aimed at this goal, because they are simply not easily accessible. Unless very serious efforts are made to address the spatial distribution of tourists, uneven tourism development will remain. The crisis is that those countries and regions most in need of distributing the benefits of tourism expansion across their national and regional tourism space economies are the very ones that do not have the resources to do so.

Acknowledgements

Wendy Job at the University of Johannesburg is gratefully acknowledged for the preparation of the maps. Valuable comments by reviewers are appreciated.

References

Cornelissen, S. (2005) 'Producing and imaging "place" and "people": the political economy of South African international tourist representation', *Review of International Political Economy*, 12(4): 674–99.

Department of Tourism (2011) *National Tourism Sector Strategy*, Pretoria: Department of Tourism.

Department of Tourism (2012) *Rural Tourism Strategy*, Pretoria: Department of Tourism, retrieved 10 September 2012 from www.info.gov.za/view/DownloadFileAction? id=163828.

Rogerson, C.M. (2002) 'Driving developmental tourism in South Africa', *Africa Insight*, 32(3).

Rogerson, C.M. (2011) 'Urban tourism and regional tourists: shopping in Johannesburg', *Tijdschrift voor Economische en Sociale Geografie*, 102(3): 316–30.

Rogerson, C.M. and Visser, G. (2007) *Urban Tourism in the Developing World: The South Africa experience*, New Brunswick, NJ: Transaction Press.

Rogerson, C.M. and Visser, G. (2011) 'African tourism geographies: existing paths and new directions', *Tijdschrift voor Economische en Sociale Geografie*, 102(3): 251–9.

Rogerson, J.M. (2010) 'The boutique hotel industry in South Africa: definition, scope and organization', *Urban Forum*, 21: 425–39.

Rogerson, J.M. (2011a) 'The limited services hotel in South Africa: the growth of City Lodge', *Urban Forum*, 22: 343–61.

Rogerson, J.M. (2011b) 'The changing all suite hotel in South Africa: from "extended stay" to African "condo hotel"', *Tourism Review International*, 15: 107–21.

Rogerson, J.M. (2012) 'Reconfiguring South Africa's hotel industry 1990–2010: structure, segmentation, and spatial transformation', *Journal of Applied Geography*, in press.

Rogerson, J.M. and Kotze, N. (2011) 'Market segmentation and the changing South African hotel industry 1990 to 2010', *African Journal of Business Management*, 5: 13523–33.

Saarinen, J., Becker, F., Manwa, H. and Wilson, D. (eds) (2011) *Sustainable Tourism in Southern Africa: Local communities and natural resources in transition*, Bristol, UK: Channel View.

Saunders, N. (2011) Tourism bigger than ever: Minister, *The Sunday Times*, retrieved 26 May 2011 from www.timeslive.co.za/local/2011/05/26/tourism-bigger-thanever-minister.

South African Tourism (SAT) (2002) *Tourism Growth Strategy*, Pretoria: South African Tourism.

South African Tourism (SAT) (2011) *The Marketing Tourism Growth Strategy for South Africa 2011–2013*, Pretoria: South African Tourism.

South African Tourism (SAT) (2012) South African Tourism.net, retrieved 16 May 2012 from www.southafrica.net/sat/content/en/za/home.

Visser, G. (2003) 'South African Tourism and its role in the perpetuation of an uneven tourism space economy', *Africa Insight*, 33(1): 116–23.

Visser, G. and Hoogendoorn, G. (2011) 'Current paths in South African tourism research', *Tourism Review International*, 15(1/2): 5–20.

Visser, G. and Kotze, K. (2006) 'The Free State tourism economy: current dynamics, immediate challenges and future prospects', *South African Geographical Journal*, 88(1): 88–101.

9 Responses to climate change mitigation during recessionary times

Perspectives from accommodation providers in the Southwest of England

Tim Coles and Anne-Kathrin Zschiegner

Introduction

In times of recession, investment in innovation, research and development, human resources and training are reduced by many businesses – irrespective of their size and operating characteristics. For many commentators, this type of organisational behaviour is argued to be somewhat irrational; in other words, at a time when it is most needed to enhance competitiveness or readiness for commercial uplift, businesses contract, suspend or withdraw their plans for investment (Hatch 2006; Wilson 2010). From an environmental perspective, this behaviour is also a lost opportunity. As Stern has noted, 'the climate is already changing. To act as if the future will be like the past is simply foolish' (2009: 56). Inaction is inadequate and it presents 'large probabilities of enormous changes' (Stern 2009: 26) to the climate and way of life. Significant behaviour change is required to stabilise greenhouse gas (GHG) emissions at relatively stable levels of 500–550 ppm CO_2 and the cost of action is equivalent to a reduction of around 1 per cent in global gross domestic product (GDP) (Stern 2007). Of greater concern, the scale of the problem (and hence the cost of solutions) will become much larger in the future if there is no immediate action to abate climate change. Delays in response only serve to exacerbate matters, not postpone current problems, and in this regard the tourism sector can – and indeed should – be a significant part of the solution (Gössling and Hall 2006a; Becken and Hay 2007; Scott *et al.* 2010). The tourism sector is vulnerable to global environmental changes to which its current carbon dependency contributes (Hall and Higham 2005; Gössling and Hall 2006b).

Climate change is a major global issue. It is a current concern and it will be a continuing one for decades to come. It is also one that connects economic and environmental discourse. Economic arguments and the business case are vital to encouraging more sustainable behaviours and the uptake of environmental measures in enterprises of all sizes and in all sectors (Stern 2007; Giddens 2009).

Mitigation requires innovation (Mowery *et al.* 2009; Pinske and Kolk 2009; Stern 2009); that is, changes to products, processes, producers, premises and organisation. Innovations can be ambitious in scope and radical in nature or they can also be quite modest and incremental (Tidd 2006; Tidd and Bessant 2009). Innovation may require investment and/or an adjustment to business plans. Notable 'win-win' scenarios are possible (see Boiral 2006; Llewelyn 2007; Stern 2009). Low(er) carbon or cleaner technologies can deliver significant environmental gains, for instance, in the reduction of emissions while contributing to increased profitability through significant cost savings.

Nevertheless, despite the potential for such apparently virtuous circles of action, the role of the recent global economic downturn as an important potential modifying factor in the response to climate change has been overlooked. Recent global macro-economic conditions since the 'credit crunch' have been accompanied by rising (energy, utilities, interest etc.) costs and a contraction in the availability of investment capital, especially to the small and medium-sized enterprises (Cummaford 2010) that dominate the tourism sector (numerically at least). Payback periods on investments (such as renewable technologies) alter as a result, and what were once viable investments before the downturn may appear altogether less attractive when reappraised in a new light. Thus, the economic also has the potential to frustrate the environmental. This raises important questions of whether the recent economic downturn has impacted on efforts to mitigate climate change in the tourism sector and, if so, how. Put another way, has recession delayed the response to another major global crisis in a sector that some commentators allege already has a patchy record in setting and achieving targets for emissions reductions (Scott *et al.* 2010)?

This chapter examines these questions in the context of a study of climate change mitigation and business innovation among accommodation providers in the Southwest of England. Through the Stern Report, the United Kingdom has occupied a prominent position in global discourse on climate change, and it has set itself targets for emissions that are more ambitious than its obligations under the Kyoto Protocol (Giddens 2009). The Southwest is one of the leading domestic and in-bound destinations in the UK (after London); more importantly though, the principles of sustainable development have been long embedded in tourism management and governance in the region (SWT 2005), it has led on the policy agenda on tourism and climate change in the UK (Coles 2008), and well over a third of all members (38 per cent) of the UK-wide Green Tourism Business Scheme – one of the principal accreditation and benchmarking schemes for sustainable tourism – are located in the region (SWT 2007; GTBS 2010).

Tourism, climate change and mitigation

While there are still some dissenting voices, there is now a widespread consensus around the world that global climate patterns are shifting and this is inducing a series of connected environmental changes (Giddens 2009; Stern 2009). As a form of production and consumption, tourism is notable insofar as it is simultaneously impacted by, and contributes to, climate change as a carbon-intensive activity (Gössling and Peeters 2007). For instance, the recent emphasis among consumers and policy makers on improving the quality of tourism services and experiences is inherently dependent on the use of resources such as fossil fuels, electricity and water; that is, the same resources that need to be used far more wisely in order to reduce emissions from tourism. In fact, the United Nations World Tourism Organization, which confidently predicts major growth in international tourism in the coming decades, has estimated that tourism is currently responsible globally for 5 per cent of CO_2 emissions (UNWTO 2007), and is much higher in the developed world. Tourism contributes other GHG emissions that contribute to global warming, such that the sector is likely to contribute 5–14 per cent of the overall human-induced warming (Simpson *et al.* 2008: 15).

The precise array and magnitude of human-induced climate and environmental changes continue to be debated. However, there is general consensus that there needs to be a timely and major response from the tourism sector. As Gössling and Hall (2006c: 305) put it (somewhat prosaically), now is the time to 'wake up . . . this is serious'. Reponses to this rallying call have been too numerous to review here in any great depth (see Hamilton *et al.* 2005; Dubois and Ceron 2006a; Gössling and Peeters 2007; Hall 2008; Gössling 2009; Scott and Becken 2010). While this level of recent attention is encouraging on one level, on another it is somewhat disappointing that adaptation has featured far more prominently than mitigation as a behavioural response to climate change in the tourism sector (see Scott and Becken 2010). Adaptation refers to the ability of individuals, businesses and organisations to modify their activities to the predicted and actual magnitude and impacts of climate change in the future. Mitigation, in contrast, recognises that GHG emissions are necessary and unavoidable outcomes of processes of production and consumption, but seeks to identify means by which to reduce them and their contribution to global warming.

Three connected limitations are associated with the current imbalance of attention. First and practically, adaptation deals with possible responses over much longer timeframes (in terms of potential future scenarios), although there is a strong case for more immediate action (Stern 2007). In a whole raft of international agreements including and since the Kyoto Protocol (see Pinske and Kolk 2009), the reduction of GHG emissions has been central to delivering a more sustainable future. However, adaptation and mitigation should not be perceived as alternatives but complementary. According to Stern, 'adaptation is essential, but it is making the best of a bad job' (2009: 58). In these terms, mitigation is arguably more important because it is about ensuring the 'job' is not as 'bad' as it could have been by limiting the most severe impacts before they occur.

Stern (2007, 2009) advocates Pacala and Socolow's (2004) 'stabilisation wedges' as one of the more elegant and compelling approaches to reducing emissions (see WWF 2007). Delivered by emissions-avoiding technologies, each wedge contributes progressively more over time to stabilising the problem. 'Wedges' are also an important metaphor for wider action. For greater emissions reductions to be achieved, collective changes over time are required in all aspects of life and sectors of business. The biggest difference will be when behaviour change is not the responsibility of the few, but as many individuals, businesses and organisations as possible increasingly take action as time passes. As a second limitation then, a more complete understanding of mitigation and the prospects moving forward is vital to informing more accurate and appropriate policy and planning responses in the future. Both better- and worse-than-expected reductions in emissions in the short term necessitate revisions to potential adaptation scenarios over the medium to long term. Developing such understanding is especially necessary in the case of the business response to climate change – not just in the developing world (Gössling and Schuhmacher 2010) but also in the developed world where emissions are disproportionately concentrated. Conditions in the macro-business environment are, though, yet to be fully acknowledged in this discussion (Hall and Coles 2008), despite their significance to the impact on mitigation. Proposals for adaptation are routinely informed by the latest climate forecasting and modelling (Viner and Agnew 1999; Gössling 2002; Lise and Tol 2002; Dubois and Ceron 2006b). However, as advanced as these may be, their ability to predict is a function of the assumptions they make and the accuracy of the data they utilise at the time that they are run. In many cases, steady state macro-economic conditions are assumed, as is a level of willingness among businesses and individuals to respond to new operating environments and proposed policy interventions (Gössling and Schuhmacher 2010). Even the briefest of scans of macro-business environments reveals that economic conditions do not remain steady over time: individual business cycles are linked to economic cycles, and economic cycles are connected to electoral cycles and the fortunes of governments.

Finally, there has been a relative lack of interest in how mitigation features in business plans in the tourism sector currently and moving forward. Energy and water use in tourism businesses has been investigated (Deng 2003; Warnken *et al.* 2005; Byrnes and Warnken 2006; Bohdanowicz and Martinac 2007; Kelly and Williams 2007; Chan *et al.* 2008), but importantly not as part of whole-business approaches to climate change. Perceptions of climate change among small groups of tourism entrepreneurs have been explored (Hall 2006; Saarinen and Tervo 2006). Sensitivity to environmental concerns and climate change are reported as secondary to economic considerations in the management of the business. Although these perspectives are instructive, it is through business administration and operations that tourism enterprises will contribute directly to mitigation. If tourism businesses, like those in other sectors, are to contribute to emissions reductions (and increasingly over time) they will have to introduce management and process innovations (Hjalager 2002: 465); that is, changes in the approach to running the business, and changes to particular practices and features. Entrepreneurs and managers in the tourism sector are – perhaps unfairly (Shaw and Williams 2009) – not always recognised as being among the most innovative (Hjalager 2002; Hall and Williams 2008). The great majority of enterprises are micro (0–10 employees) and small scale (11–50 employees) in nature; they lack formal business plans, and they lack long-term perspectives on business development (Shaw 2004; Shaw and Williams 2004). Perhaps most importantly, they lack access to development capital and specialist expertise, in particular in the area of environmental management (Vernon *et al.* 2003; Tzschentke *et al.* 2008). Depending on the (renewable) technology being adopted, process innovations can require significant investment in the context of an SME. In the current economic circumstances capital is at a premium and, where credit can be obtained, it is becoming extremely costly from ever more risk-averse lenders (Hopkins 2010). Thus, this raises the prospect that conditions during an economic downturn can frustrate efforts to mitigate in the tourism sector.

Methods

These issues were addressed in a programme of research on accommodation providers in the Southwest of England. From November 2009 to February 2010, a comprehensive questionnaire survey was conducted in conjunction with a series of semi-structured interviews. The aim of this research was to examine and situate current practices in, and future plans for, climate change mitigation among tourism businesses. It explored the attitudes and motivations towards, and measures taken to mitigate, climate change among accommodation providers from the Southwest of England. In this context, and in view of the period of the research, two questions were included in both survey instruments on the effects of the recession on the business and, in the case of interviews, directly on mitigation activities and plans. These formed the foundations for the analysis presented below. The full questionnaire comprised thirty-one questions in three sections: the first explored general attitudes in business towards the environment; the second interrogated the environmental practices in each business; and basic operating characteristics were surveyed in the final section in order to provide a series of explanatory variables. Southwest Tourism, the regional tourism board, mailed the questionnaire to over 5,000 regional accommodation providers, with a nominal response rate of 8.9 per cent. The 417 usable responses compared to an estimated total of 14,790 accommodation providers in the region (not all of whom have usable or current email addresses in databases). Hence the sample represents around 2.8 per cent of the background population. Eighteen follow-up interviews were conducted with managers who had completed the questionnaire and these lasted between 40 and 127 minutes. Extensive analysis of the empirical data is not possible in the context of this chapter (see Coles *et al.* 2010), which instead concentrates on answering the questions posed above by means of relevant quantitative and qualitative data from the questionnaire and interviews.

Climate change mitigation and business innovation in the Southwest

Businesses that participated in this survey were typically micro- and small-sized tourism enterprises, as the average number of employees and average turnover in 2009 indicate (Table 9.1). Businesses had been in their current ownership for 10.4 years on average, and in existence for three decades. In the context of this research, this is important. In many cases, current ownership pre-dated the great surge in

Table 9.1 Selected characteristics of tourism businesses in the survey

Business attribute	Value
Average number of employees (full-time equivalents)	3.2
Average turnover in 2009 (£k)	60
Percentage for whom turnover decreased in last 12 months	20.3
Average occupancy in 2009 (%)	53.4
Average number of bed spaces*	15.9
Accommodation graded 3-star (%)	21.3
Accommodation graded 4-star (%)	55.7
Accommodation graded 5-star (%)	10.1
Average date business established (year)	*1980*
Percentage of businesses operating before 1980	34.9
Average length of business in current ownership (years)	10.4
Average date premises first built (year)	*1919*
Premises built after 1980 (%)	11
Average number of innovations made in last 10 years	8.2
Average number of planned innovations in next year	3.2
Average total investment over past 10 years (£k)*	12.6
Average proportion of costs as energy bills (%)	14.8
Average proportion of costs as water bills (%)	6.8

Note: * 5 per cent trimmed mean.

public interest and debate on climate change in the UK after 2005. Moreover, many owners and/or operators had had ample time to implement mitigation measures. Based on these average figures for turnover and length of ownership, the average total investment in six typical areas of mitigation (see the notes below Table 9.4 for a description) represented a (re)investment into the business by the current owners of around 2 per cent of total revenue over the previous decade.

A range of accommodation providers was evident from full-service hotels (3.6 per cent) to farmhouses (3.4 per cent), general self-catering (27.6 per cent), bed-and-breakfast establishments (B&Bs, 14.1 per cent) and guest accommodation (28.3 per cent) according to Southwest Tourism's categories. Under the terms of the National Quality Assurance Scheme (NQAS), around 40 per cent of the sample comprised B&Bs and guest houses. Nearly two-thirds of the accommodation was graded four-star or above. From the quality of experience offered to their guests, this would indicate that around two-thirds of the businesses were well run.

Recession and business

The recession does not appear to have impacted negatively on the majority of accommodation businesses in the Southwest. Quite the contrary: only 20.3 per cent had experienced a decrease in their turnover in the last twelve months, whereas for nearly three-quarters of businesses it had either remained the same (29.3 per cent) or (more pointedly) had grown in the previous year (2008–9). Nearly half of all businesses (48.4 per cent) reported an increase in their turnover since the recession elsewhere in the UK economy had started. Increases in both domestic and international demand were identified as the reasons and likely causes of the increases by the interviewees. Pound sterling exchange rates had weakened, in particular against the euro, and this mediated against competitor destinations in short-haul European markets, as one interviewee noted:

> The cost of going on holiday to Germany or France is, like, an extra 50% compared to what it was two years ago so they've [the customers] stayed in the UK. It's been like an inverse recession for our industry really – to us it has been a boom.

There was clear evidence of the so-called 'staycation' effect that was widely reported in the UK media in the summer of 2009 (Grove 2009; Walker 2009; Olive Insight 2010); more precisely, that is, domestic visitors chose to holiday at home rather than travel abroad. As one of the leading destination regions in the UK, the Southwest had clearly benefitted. As one farm stay operator noted, 'People who used to go to Spain . . . are now coming to the UK.' While the majority of businesses had not been adversely affected, it is useful to note that the (positive) effects of the recession were not felt evenly across the sector. For some businesses, turnover had declined. Some interviewees pointed to a more competitive operating environment and suggested that lower-quality establishments were more likely to suffer, and first of all: 'I think good places are not suffering as much as sort of the tatty and tired places'; and 'The recession will affect bad businesses before it affects good businesses.'

This broad trend is evident in Table 9.2, which demonstrates that greater proportions of businesses in higher grades experienced increases in turnover. The cross-tabulation is not statistically significant ($x^2 = 4.949$, df = 6, p = 0.550), which may be for reasons of sampling, table structure or, more likely, the variability and complexity of other background effects. For instance, other interviewees noted a reduction in the winter off-season, reduced business travel throughout the year, and the loss of some of their regular, repeat visitors. In the case of the latter, these were soon replaced by new visitors to the establishment. Some reported that more bookings and higher occupancy were necessary because many of their visitors booked shorter stays and ancillary revenues were down. Visitors spent less on food and beverages, in particular. The more robust businesses cited their product and positioning as reasons why their businesses were succeeding in such testing times: 'Our business is fairly recession proof because of the quality of the offer, . . . so we are busier than we've ever been and we have more bookings going further into the future than ever before.'

Perhaps the biggest challenge presented by the recession, which was articulated by the majority of interviewees, was uncertainty. On the demand side, this manifested itself in late or last-minute bookings from which successful businesses

Table 9.2 The relationship between quality grading and turnover in the previous twelve
months

| Quality grading | In the past twelve months, turnover had . . . | | | |
	Increased	Stayed the same	Decreased	Total
1–2-star	10	10	4	24
Percentage	*41.7*	*41.7*	*16.7*	*100*
3-star	37	20	18	75
Percentage	*49.3*	*26.7*	*24.0*	*100*
4-star	96	55	39	190
Percentage	*50.5*	*28.9*	*20.5*	*100*
5-star	20	12	3	35
Percentage	*57.1*	*34.3*	*8.6*	*100*
Mixed grades*	15	4	2	21
Percentage	*71.4*	*19.0*	*9.5*	*100*
Total	**178**	**101**	**66**	**345**
Percentage	*51.6*	*29.3*	*19.1*	*100*

Note: * Premises with mixed accommodation rating, i.e. 2–3-star, e.g. holiday cottage complexes.

had benefitted. So, even those businesses that had weathered the storm and seen
their turnover rise had not necessarily been absolutely certain throughout the entire
year that the recession would not actually affect them. More troubling still was
what the future held (i.e. the 2010 season). Some businesses noted that there may
be a delayed reaction: 'I think the recession is going to hurt people more this year
[2010] even though they say it's over.'

One interviewee confidently predicted (in January 2010) that his business was
'recession proof' because its customers are mainly 'government employees, you
know they have fixed salaries, they've got pensions, cheap mortgages . . .'. In the
June 2010 Emergency Budget, the new coalition government announced that they
aimed to cut public sector spending by 25 per cent across the board (Curtis 2010),
with the precise allocations to be announced in October 2010. Thus, the summer
season and important September 'shoulder months' of the tourism market in the
Southwest were framed by uncertainty in a market segment that had been relied
upon previously as a cornerstone of demand.

Recession and investment in environmental measures

Nearly a half of businesses (48.1 per cent) reported that they had not suspended
their investment in environmental measures to tackle climate change because of
the recession. Well under a fifth of businesses (13.9 per cent) had deferred their
plans because of the less favourable conditions and 38.0 per cent were uncertain
of the situation. This is encouraging because, as Table 9.1 and Figure 9.1
demonstrate, a range of process innovations had been introduced. Practically all

businesses (99.5 per cent) had introduced one or more measures to mitigate the effects of climate change. On average, 8.2 measures had been taken and the average total investment (not indexed) was £12,623 across six typical mitigation technologies. Furthermore, businesses planned to make 3.2 innovations in the coming year. The average maximum acceptable payback period for an investment in energy- or water-saving equipment was 5.2 years. Measures to tackle climate change featured in the future investment plans of 45 per cent of businesses.

Beyond recycling, which was very widespread, the most popular innovations were installing loft insulation, more efficient boilers, A-rated appliances, water-saving measures (i.e. dual flush toilets, 'Hippo' water savers), towel (i.e. refresh) agreements, and efficient shower heads and taps (Figure 9.1). These had been implemented by over half of all businesses. In contrast, more advanced (and/or more expensive) renewable technologies such as solar panels and water-heating systems, as well as wood-chip boilers and smart metering, had been introduced by less than 15 per cent of businesses. Formalisation of environmental management in the form of an appointed manager or agreed plan had taken place in less than 25 per cent of businesses. The relatively high average number of investments may reflect some advance towards more sustainable operating practices but progress should not be over-valorised. These data suggest that 'quick wins' were prioritised first of all. In contrast, there were much lower levels of take-up for more advanced renewable technologies; that is, innovations that are most likely to lead to the biggest reductions in emissions.

The relationship between reported turnover in the previous year and investment in environmental measures was examined by chi-square test and found to be statistically significant ($\chi^2 = 18.514$, df = 4, p = 0.001). In general, this test of association suggested that those businesses that enjoyed an increase in turnover were also those that continued with their investment plans; those businesses where turnover had remained the same were comparatively more uncertain about their investment plans; and investment plans had been suspended (in relative terms) most of all where turnover had reduced (Table 9.3). Table 9.4 added to the emerging view that the recession did not have an adverse effect on investment plans in environmental measures. There was no statistically significant difference in the planned number of innovations to be introduced in the next year. Those businesses in which turnover had increased had introduced significantly more innovations than businesses where turnover had declined or stayed the same. The magnitude of the difference among groups was low.

Alongside sales performance and cash flow, the timing of investments and the (currently) short-run nature of the present recession were the other main reasons why investment plans had not been abated by nearly a half of businesses. The collapse of the bank, Northern Rock, in autumn 2007 is commonly regarded as heralding the start of the worst of the recent downturn in the UK (BBC 2009), with the economy in the deepest recession since the 1930s during 2008 and 2009 (Gilmore and Lindsay 2010). As Figure 9.1 demonstrates, many of the current measures were taken before that time, when working capital was more cheaply and readily available, and banks were more willing to lend to SMEs. Other

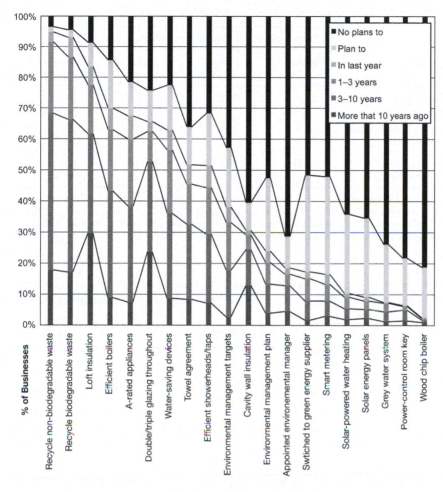

Figure 9.1 Specific environmental practices implemented by tourism businesses and their implementation dates.

Table 9.3 The relationship between turnover in the last twelve months and investment in environmental measures to tackle climate change

We have suspended our investment in environmental measures to tackle climate change because of the recession:	In the past twelve months, turnover had . . .		
	Increased	Stayed the same	Decreased
Disagreed	109	59	27
Neither agreed nor disagreed	68	49	35
Agreed	22	13	22
Total	**199**	**121**	**84**

Table 9.4 The relationship between turnover and mitigation activity

	In the past twelve months, turnover had . . .			
Variable	*Increased*	*Stayed the same*	*Decreased*	*Test statistics***
Total number of innovations	8.59	7.71	8.01	$\chi^2 = 7.635$ $p = 0.022$
Innovations planned in next year	3.41	2.80	3.19	$\chi^2 = 3.639$ $p = 0.169$
Average total investment (£)*	**14,716**	**10,397**	**14,067**	$\mathbf{\chi^2 = 5.147}$ $\mathbf{p = 0.076}$

Notes: * In six typical areas of mitigation activity to reduce emissions within a business, including: roof insulation; wall insulation; efficient heating systems (water, central heating); renewable energy technologies (solar, wind, water); deliberate purchasing of more efficient (i.e. A-rated) appliances; and double glazing. Five per cent trimmed mean calculated. ** Degrees of freedom = 2.

measures were introduced in the period 2006–9 as the new economic conditions unfolded; that is, while it was unknown precisely how bad conditions would eventually become. Counter-cyclical investment plans were not, though, always inadvertent. In some isolated instances, interviewees argued that they were in business for the long term, that the current operating circumstances were temporary, and that the overriding trend continues to be towards growth:

> [W]e've been here 20 years. When we came here at the end of the 80s, there was another recession then, you see, and that was far worse for Weymouth [a resort town in Dorset, host for the 2012 Olympic Regatta] . . . we had to struggle for two or three years in that recession. This recession is not too bad.

Towards the political economy of tourism and climate change

This was certainly not a common perspective and it is important to note that, on average, businesses had been in their current ownership for around ten years. Put another way, under their present owners, most businesses had only previously operated in favourable macro-economic conditions in the UK. However, it reminds us that this empirical work was politically situated. It was conducted towards the end of the third term of what turned out to be a thirteen-year Labour government. It was also economically situated. Technically, the UK emerged from recession (after two years) in the fourth quarter of 2009 (Gilmore and Lindsay 2010). The previous administration saw signs of growth and upturn, which is one set of reasons why it called a general election for May 2010, practically at the last possible moment. Budget figures published in March 2010 suggested that the then (Labour) government had borrowed £163.4 billion in the financial year 2009, and total government debt was £893.4 billion or equivalent to 62.1 per cent of GDP (BBC 2010). In its emergency budget of June 2010, the new Conservative-Liberal

Democrat coalition set out plans to make £90 billion of savings up to 2014–15, by which time borrowing of £37 billion would be half of that planned by the previous administration (Inman 2010). Its critics argued that an austerity budget may plunge the UK into a second bout of recession in a so-called 'double-dip' (Elliot and Allen 2010).

Climate change was an imperative of the previous Labour administration, which legislated three times from 2008 and 2010 in the area (Giddens 2009), and it features in the new government's agenda (Cabinet Office 2010). The Department for Energy and Climate Change (DECC) was established in October 2008 to bring together two mutually reinforcing areas of policy: energy and climate change. The DECC assumed responsibility and ownership in government for delivering the UK's target to reduce UK GHG emissions by 80 per cent from 1990 levels by the year 2050 and to ensure 15 per cent energy generation by renewable and low-carbon energy sources by 2020 (DECC 2010a, 2010b). In order to address these targets, several policy instruments were introduced with differing potential to impact on the tourism sector (see Coles *et al.* 2010). Most importantly here, the Energy Act of 2008 included provision for a 'Feed-in Tariff' (FiT) and Renewable Heat Incentive (RHI).

Both set out to stimulate demand and supply, especially among smaller-scale energy users (households and SMEs) for alternative sources of energy production and consumption (DECC 2010c). The FiT started in April 2010. It enables private individuals and businesses to be paid for the energy they produce from clean sources, in turn assisting the licensed electricity supplier to meet their annually increasing obligations to source their supplies from renewable or low-carbon sources. Guaranteed minimum payments are made for all the electricity generated by this system, and there is an additional contribution for any excess that is exported to the national grid. Similar in concept to the FiT, the RHI will support a range of new, more efficient technologies used in a variety of contexts (i.e. households, businesses, offices etc.). At the time of the research, the RHI was under consultation with a view to its introduction in April 2011 (DECC 2010d).

In terms of their design, both the FiT and the RHI were designed to address negative preconceptions of extended and hence infeasible payback periods among SMEs on what are, after all, technologies that are most likely to deliver the greater reductions in emissions in sectors such as tourism. For example, electricity generation under the current FiT regulations rewards businesses for all energy generated, with a supplement based on that exported to the national grid. With the cost savings from sourcing fewer (even no) energy supplies from the market, there are three potential contributions to the bottom line after the initial investment in micro-generation. Nevertheless, as Figure 9.1 and our interview data reveal, these messages have not been received and/or – in some cases – decoded as government may have anticipated or desired. Typical of comments in this regard, one interviewee put it:

> [People] are right to be sceptical if they are doing it [installing renewables] for financial reasons because they will never pay back ... [We] generated

1200 KWh but it's about £300 in oil so not a great deal. So by the time they pay themselves back, you probably have to replace them – [they're] financially viable only if you get them for free.

Conflicting information was cited as a potential disincentive to action because it too added to the uncertainty:

I don't know what the payback period for these [solar thermals] will be [but] with rising prices it will be less. [The] Internet provides different estimates of payback period, 10 years, 15 years, depending on the way it is calculated.

For the majority of respondents, payback periods represented a major barrier (62.8 per cent) to further action on climate change as did their premises (67.1 per cent) and planning regulations (55.7 per cent). Payback periods were commonly perceived as being too long, despite the government incentives that had been communicated for some time (and that were clearly not fully understood or factored into cost-benefit equations). A long-term investment that had yet to pay itself back was considered a major liability on the balance sheet in a sector where margins are typically tight and which commonly experiences high levels of business turnover. So too was an investment for which the payback period could not be accurately determined, not least because (as several interviewees argued) it is unclear whether incentives would be maintained at the relatively generous levels set by the previous administration or cut as part of the current coalition government's drive to reduce public spending.

Somewhat perversely then, the main impact of recent government policy interventions was, according to our interview data, to prompt accommodation providers in the Southwest to review their costs and to consider how they could make savings in their utility bills. This has not resulted in greater take-up of renewables, as indeed is necessary to meet the UK's climate change commitments. However, it has raised awareness of a key source of costs, how little measurement and monitoring was being conducted in the sector, and the need to be more proactive in order to address a current business vulnerability (Figure 9.2; see Coles *et al.* 2010 for a fuller discussion). Finally, some of the apparently less positive features of the market had acted as a clear stimulus to action for some of the more entrepreneurial owners and managers. For instance, interest rates were so low that there was an opportunity cost associated with saving their surpluses. Rather, it was perceived that there was a better return on investment in the long term by spending on environmental measures that could yield significant costs savings on utility bills, which comprise around a fifth of all costs and which were rising for the majority of businesses (see Table 9.1): 'Interest rates are so low at the bank that you may as well put it to work . . . that has definitely made us get on with it and do it now rather than wait a year.'

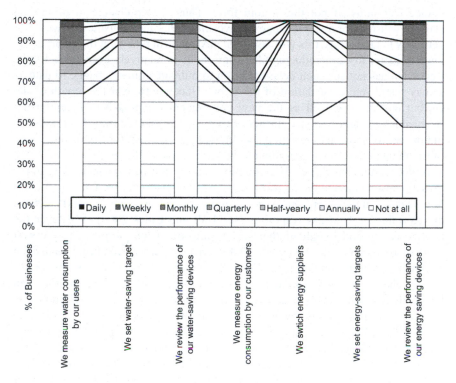

Figure 9.2 Approaches to managing water and energy.

Conclusion

To return to the questions posed in the introduction, the recent economic downturn has impacted on the efforts of some businesses to mitigate climate change. However, just 20 per cent of the businesses recorded a decrease in turnover on the previous year, and less than 20 per cent claimed that they had suspended investment to tackle climate change because of the recession. Many of the businesses had started to implement measures ahead of the onset of recession in 2007 and were already locked into change. Far from a 'perfect storm', the levels and types of mitigation activity in the Southwest in 2010 suggest that the tourism sector still has significant progress to make if, as policy makers and academics are determined, it should deliver a significant contribution to reducing CO_2 emissions. Starkly put, one of the most extensive surveys of mitigation behaviours among tourism businesses has revealed that accommodation providers in the Southwest could contribute far more towards meeting the UK government's targets for emissions reductions and renewables. Relatively easy 'quick wins' requiring lower capital investment were more popular than more advanced renewable energy technologies, which, although they are relatively more expensive and require more radical transformation of operations, have more potential to reduce emissions (if not the bottom line). Thus, a step-change in mitigation activity will require a step-change in investment that most businesses were not yet ready to take. Thus, this will be a vital next stage in renewing the effort in the tourism sector towards reducing GHG emissions to relatively acceptable levels. Recession has not so much delayed action to mitigate climate change to date as it may retard future escalation of the effort. Uncertainty over the length of the current downturn as well as the new government's approach to incentivising renewables mediate against further activity in the short term. This delay is important. As noted above, action should not be postponed if the scale and scope of the mitigation effort is not going to become worse in the future.

A deeper understanding of mitigation among tourism businesses requires greater consideration of the political economy of climate change, and in particular how features in the macro-business environment such as economic and electoral cycles influence business responses (see Hall and Coles 2008). Whatever the precise nature and length of the current episode, a long-term environmental (arguably economic – see Stern 2007, 2009) crisis, apparently requiring immediate response, has been running in parallel with a much shorter-term economic crisis. As this chapter has demonstrated, crises do not occur in isolation, and they can be subtly and intricately connected. They can compound or ameliorate one another, resulting in outcomes that are not always obvious or predictable (Coles 2003). Economic cycles in coming decades will influence the ability and willingness among businesses (and citizens) to respond to climate change, to meet the targets set by scientists and politicians, and hence to adapt to future change as it unfolds. Mitigation may have been the poor relation of adaptation so far in tourism studies; however, current speculation on the long-term effects of climate change may be nothing more than that without a clearer understanding of the unfolding response from businesses in the tourism sector, both currently and moving forward.

References

Becken, S. and Hay, D. (2007) *Tourism and Climate Change: Risks and opportunities*, Clevedon, UK: Channel View Publications.

Bohdanowicz, P. and Martinac, I. (2007) 'Determinants and benchmarking of resource consumption in hotels: case study of Hilton International and Scandic in Europe', *Energy and Buildings*, 39(1): 82–95.

Boiral, O. (2006) 'Global warming: should companies adopt a proactive strategy?', *Long Range Planning*, 39: 315–30.

British Broadcasting Corporation (BBC) (2009) 'Timeline: credit crunch to downturn', 7 August, retrieved 23 July 2010 from http://news.bbc.co.uk/1/hi/business/7521250.stm.

British Broadcasting Corporation (BBC) (2010) 'UK budget deficit revised lower by ONS', 21 May, retrieved 23 July 2010 from www.bbc.co.uk/news/10136055.

Byrnes, T.A. and Warnken, J. (2006) 'Greenhouse gas emissions from marine tours: a case study of Australian tour boat operators', *Journal of Sustainable Tourism*, 14(3): 255–70.

Cabinet Office (2010) *The Coalition: Our programme for government*, London: Cabinet Office.

Chan, W.W., Mak, L.M., Chen, Y.M., Wang, Y.H., Xie, H.R., Hou, G.Q. and Li, D. (2008) 'Energy saving and tourism sustainability: solar control window film in hotel rooms', *Journal of Sustainable Tourism*, 16(5): 563–74.

Coles, T.E. (2003) 'A local reading of a global disaster: some lessons on tourism management from an annus horribilis in Southwest England', *Journal of Travel and Tourism Marketing*, 15(2/3): 173–97.

Coles, T.E. (2008) 'The implementation of sustainable tourism: a project-based perspective', in S. Gössling, D. Weaver and C.M. Hall (eds) *Sustainable Tourism Futures: Perspectives on innovation, scale and restructuring*, London: Routledge, pp. 204–21.

Coles, T.E., Zschiegner, A.-K. and Dinan, C.R. (2010) *The Future's Bright, The Future's Greener: Climate change mitigation and business innovation in the tourism sector in the South West of England*, Exeter, UK: University of Exeter Business School.

Cummaford, D. (2010) 'Small business on bank lending', BBC News online, 2 August, retrieved 3 August 2010 from www.bbc.co.uk/news/business-10841243.

Curtis, P. (2010) 'Budget 2010: public sector faces deepest ever spending cuts', *The Guardian*, 22 June, retrieved 23 July 2010 from www.guardian.co.uk/uk/2010/jun/22/2010-budget-public-sector-cuts.

Deng, S. M. (2003) 'Energy and water uses and their performance explanatory indicators in hotels in Hong Kong', Energy and Buildings, 35(8): 775–784.

Department for Energy and Climate Change (DECC) (2010a) *Climate Change Act 2008*, retrieved 8 July 2010 from www.decc.gov.uk/en/content/cms/legislation/cc_act_08/cc_act_08.aspx.

Department for Energy and Climate Change (DECC) (2010b) *Renewables Obligation*, retrieved 8 July 2010 from www.decc.gov.uk/en/content/cms/what_we_do/uk_supply/energy_mix/renewable/policy/renew_obs/renew_obs.aspx.

Department for Energy and Climate Change (DECC) (2010c) *Energy Act 2008*, retrieved 8 July 2010 from www.decc.gov.uk/en/content/cms/legislation/energy_act_08/energy_act_08.aspx.

Department for Energy and Climate Change (DECC) (2010d) *Consultation on the Renewable Heat Incentive (RHI)*, retrieved 8 July 2010 from www.decc.gov.uk/en/content/cms/consultations/rhi/rhi.aspx.

Dubois, G. and Ceron J.-P. (2006a) 'Tourism and climate change: proposals for a research agenda', *Journal of Sustainable Tourism*, 14(4): 399–415.

Dubois, G. and Ceron, J.-P. (2006b) 'Tourism/leisure greenhouse gas emissions forecasts for 2050: factors for changes in France', *Journal of Sustainable Tourism*, 14(2): 172–91.

Elliot, L. and Allen, K. (2010) 'Budget risks return to recession, warns Treasury select committee', *The Guardian*, 20 July, retrieved 23 July 2010 from www.guardian.co.uk/business/2010/jul/20/budget-risks-recession-treasury-select.

Giddens, A. (2009) *The Politics of Climate Change*, Cambridge: Polity Press.

Gilmore, G. and Lindsay, R. (2010) 'Britain exits longest recession on record – just', *The Times*, 26 January, retrieved 23 July 2010 from http://business.timesonline.co.uk/tol/business/economics/article7002715.ece.

Gössling, S. (2002) 'Global environmental consequences of tourism', *Global Environmental Change*, 12: 283–302.

Gössling, S. (2009) 'Carbon neutral destinations: a conceptual analysis', *Journal of Sustainable Tourism*, 17(1): 17–37.

Gössling, S. and Hall, C.M. (2006a) *Tourism and Global Environmental Change: Ecological, social, economic and political interrelationships*, London: Routledge.

Gössling, S. and Hall, C.M. (2006b) 'Introduction to tourism and global environmental change', in S. Gössling and C.M. Hall (eds) *Tourism and Global Environmental Change*, London: Routledge, pp. 1–34.

Gössling, S. and Hall, C.M. (2006c) 'Conclusion: wake up-this is serious', in S. Gössling and C.M. Hall (eds) *Tourism and Global Environmental Change*, London: Routledge, pp. 305–20.

Gössling, S. and Peters, P. (2007) '"It does not harm the environment!" An analysis of industry discourses on tourism, air travel and the environment', *Journal of Sustainable Tourism*, 15(4): 402–17.

Gössling, S. and Schuhmacher, K.P. (2010) 'Implementing carbon neutral destination policies: issues from the Seychelles', Journal of Sustainable Tourism, 18(3): 377–392.

Green Tourism Business Scheme (GTBS) (2010) 'The Green Tourism Business Scheme', retrieved 16 February 2010 from www.green-business.co.uk/.

Grove, S. (2009) 'Staying home for the holidays: strapped vacationers are discovering the attractions in their own backyards: bad news for the global economy', *Newsweek*, 2 May, retrieved 8 June 2010 from www.newsweek.com/id/195707.

Hall, C.M. (2006) 'New Zealand tourism entrepreneur attitudes and behaviours with respect to climate change adaptation and mitigation', *International Journal of Innovation and Sustainable Development*, 1(3): 229–37.

Hall, C.M. (2008) 'Tourism and climate change: knowledge gaps and issues', in J. Saarinen and K. Tervo (eds) *Tourism and Climate Change in Polar Regions*, Finland: Oulu University Press, pp. 6–17.

Hall, C.M. and Coles, T.E. (2008) 'Introduction: tourism and international business – tourism as international business', in T.E. Coles and C.M. Hall (eds) *International Business and Tourism: Global issues, contemporary interactions*, London: Routledge, pp. 1–26.

Hall, C.M. and Higham, J. (eds) (2005) *Tourism, Recreation and Climate Change*, Clevedon, UK: Channel View Publications.

Hall, C.M. and Williams, A.M. (2008) *Tourism and Innovation*, London: Routledge.

Hamilton, J.M., Maddison, D.J. and Tol, R.S.J. (2005) 'Climate change and international tourism: a simulation study', *Global Environmental Change*, 15: 253–66.

Hatch, M.J. (2006) *Organization Theory: Modern symbolic and postmodern perspectives*, Oxford: Oxford University Press.

Hjalager, A.-M. (2002) 'Repairing innovation defectiveness in tourism', *Tourism Management*, 23: 465–74.

Hopkins, K. (2010) 'Banks fail to meet targets to increase lending to small business', *The Guardian*, 1 April, retrieved 23 July 2010 from www.guardian.co.uk/business/2010/apr/01/banks-fail-lending-business-targets.

Inman, P. (2010) 'Budget 2010: plans to turn record debt into surplus cheers City', *The Guardian*, 22 June, retrieved 23 July 2010 from www.guardian.co.uk/uk/2010/jun/22/budget-2010-public-sector-cuts.

Kelly, J. and Williams, P.W. (2007) 'Modelling tourism destination energy consumption and greenhouse gas emissions: Whistler, British Columbia, Canada', *Journal of Sustainable Tourism*, 15(1): 67–89.

Lise, W. and Tol, R.S.J. (2002) 'Impact of climate on tourist demand', *Climatic Change*, 55(4): 429–49.

Llewelyn, J. (2007) *The Business of Climate Change: Challenges and opportunities*, New York: Lehmann Brothers.

Mowery, D.C., Nelson, R.F. and Martin, B. (2009) *Technology Policy and Global Warming: Why new policy models are needed*, London: NESTA.

Olive Insight (2010) 'The future of staycation: research report on behalf of VisitEngland', retrieved 4 August 2010 from www.enjoyengland.com/Images/Staycation%202010%20Internet%20Version%20(NXPowerLite)_tcm21-189855.pdf.

Pacala, S. and Socolow, R. (2004) 'Stabilization wedges: solving the climate problem of the next 50 years with current technologies', *Science*, 305(5686): 968–97.

Pinske, J. and Kolk, A. (2009) *International Business and Global Climate Change*, London: Routledge.

Saarinen, J. and Tervo, K. (2006) 'Perceptions and adaptation strategies of the tourism industry to climate change: the case of Finnish nature-based tourism entrepreneurs', *International Journal of Innovation and Sustainable Development*, 1(3): 214–28.

Scott, D. and Becken, S. (2010) 'Adapting to climate change and climate policy: progress, problems and potentials', *Journal of Sustainable Tourism*, 18(3): 283–94.

Scott, D., Peeters, P. and Gössling, S. (2010) 'Can tourism deliver its "aspirational" greenhouse gas emission reduction targets?', *Journal of Sustainable Tourism*, 18(3): 393–408.

Shaw, G. (2004) 'Entrepreneurial cultures and small business enterprises in tourism', in A.A. Lew, C.M. Hall and A.M. Williams (eds) *Companion to Tourism*, Oxford: Blackwell, pp. 122–34.

Shaw, G. and Williams, A.M. (2004) 'From lifestyle consumption to lifestyle production: changing patterns of tourism entrepreneurship', in R. Thomas (ed.) *Small Firms in Tourism: International perspective*, Oxford: Elsevier.

Shaw, G. and Williams, A.M. (2009) 'Knowledge transfer and management in tourism: an emerging research agenda', *Tourism Management*, 30: 325–35.

Simpson, M.C., Gössling, S., Scoot, D., Hall, C.M. and Gladin, E. (2008) *Climate Change Adaptation and Mitigation in the Tourism Sector: Frameworks, tools and practices*, Paris: UNEP, University of Oxford, UNWTO, WMO.

Southwest Tourism (SWT) (2005) *Towards 2015: Shaping tomorrow's tourism*, Exeter: Southwest Tourism.

Southwest Tourism (SWT) (2007) 'Over 300 tourism pioneers', retrieved 29 February 2008 from www.swtourism.co.uk/content/news/over-300-tourism-pioneers.ashx.

Stern, N. (2007) *The Economics of Climate Change: The Stern Review*, Cambridge: Cambridge University Press.

Stern, N. (2009) *A Blueprint for a Safer Planet: How to manage climate change and create a new era of progress and prosperity*, London: The Bodley Head (Random House).

Tidd, J. (2006) *A Review of Innovation Models*, Discussion Paper 1, retrieved 14 January 2009 from www3.imperial.ac.uk/portal/pls/portallive/docs/1/7290726.pdf.

Tidd, J. and Bessant, J. (2009) *Managing Innovation: Integrating technological, market and organizational change*, Chichester, UK: Wiley.

Tzschentke, N.A., Kirk, D. and Lynch, P.A. (2008) 'Going green: decisional factors in small hospitality operations', *International Journal of Hospitality Management*, 27(1): 126–33.

United Nations World Tourism Organization (UNWTO) (2007) *Climate Change and Tourism: Responding to global changes: advanced summary*, Madrid: UNWTO.

Vernon, J., Essex, S., Pinder, D. and Curry, K. (2003) 'The "greening" of tourism micro-businesses: outcomes of focus group investigations in South East Cornwall', *Business Strategy and the Environment*, 12(1): 49–69.

Viner, D. and Agnew, M. (1999) *Climate Change and its Impact on Tourism*, report prepared for WWF-UK, Godalming, UK.

Walker, P. (2009) 'Recession-hit Britons abandon foreign holidays in favour of "staycations": big drop in trips abroad by UK residents this year', *The Guardian*, 13 August, retrieved 8 June 2010 from www.guardian.co.uk/.

Warnken, J., Bradley, M. and Guilding, C. (2005) 'Eco-resorts vs. mainstream accommodation providers: an investigation of the viability of benchmarking environmental performance', *Tourism Management*, 26: 367–79.

Wilson, F. (2010) *Organizational Behaviour: A critical introduction*, Oxford: Oxford University Press.

World Wild Fund for Nature (WWF) (2007) *Climate Solutions: WWF's vision for 2050*, Gland: WWF International.

10 Tourism-led development and backward linkages

Evidence from the agriculture–tourism nexus in southern Africa

Holly Hunt and Christian M. Rogerson

Introduction

In what is recognised as a seminal article in tourism scholarship relating to the Global South, sixteen years ago, Brohman (1996) highlighted a suite of emerging problems surrounding the adoption of outward-oriented neoliberal development strategies. The appearance of this analysis was timely as in the context of existing development discourse tourism was increasingly touted as an important source of outward-oriented growth in many parts of developing Africa, Asia and Latin America (Telfer 2002). During the 1990s, international tourism garnered widespread currency in development literature as one of an array of new 'growth sectors' believed to exhibit much promise in developing countries based upon their so-termed 'comparative advantages' (Telfer and Sharpley 2008). Nevertheless, the development literature pointed also to several inherent dangers that accompanied the embrace of neoliberal planning strategies. Past export-oriented development models had often been associated with vicious cycles of polarisation and repression. During the 1980s, dependency theories showed the existence of high rates of leakage associated with international tourism in developing countries (Britton 1982). The appearance of such dangers highlights that national governments and policy makers must proceed cautiously with tourism-led development strategies, more especially if growth in the volume of international tourism is 'not to be accompanied by many of the problems historically linked with outward-oriented development strategies' (Brohman 1996: 50).

Mitchell and Ashley point to the unexploited potential of linkages and suggest national tourism policies should focus 'more attention on how to promote linkages in tourism' (2006: 4). Arguably, a critical need exists for policy makers to prioritise the creation (or expansion) of local linkages so as to spread more widely the benefits of growth in social, sectoral and spatial terms and, in so doing, to avert crises relating to the dangers of unfolding pathways of tourism-led economic development (Lacher and Nepal 2010). Brohman stresses 'in the absence of well-developed linkages between the external sectors and the rest of the economy, a limited and polarised form of development takes place that cannot act as a stimulus for broadly-based development' (1996: 50). Establishing and consolidating economic linkages is viewed necessary to maximising tourism's potential for more broadly based patterns of economic and social development (Lejarraja and Walkenhurst 2007; Sandbrook 2010). Indeed, if tourism is to contribute to the well-being of destinations 'it is important that careful consideration be given to enhancing backward economic linkages' (Telfer and Wall 1996: 300). Spenceley and Meyer (2012: 302) identify research questions around intersectoral linkages as critical for tourism and poverty reduction. Tourism planners acknowledge, however, that intersectoral linkages between tourism and other economic sectors are often weak in developing countries. In particular, Sandbrook points out that leakages are considered strong 'in the case of luxury tourism where accommodation and service providers tend to be owned by non-local actors' (2010: 22). Nonetheless, the evidence is mixed and 'the density of poverty-reducing local linkages is variable' (Mitchell and Ashley 2010: 3).

One challenge for tourism-led development strategies clearly is to enhance the density of both intersectoral and local linkages by integrating tourism more closely into local, regional and national economic development (Lacher and Nepal 2010). Jenkins and Henry suggest strong government actions may be required in order to 'devise and implement policies to secure the most benefits from potential intersectoral linkages' (1982: 509). Against this backdrop, the aim in this chapter is to examine aspects of this important challenge and to present findings from recent empirical research concerning the extent and depth of linkages between the tourism and agriculture sectors in rural southern Africa. The particular relevance of investigating agriculture/tourism linkages in sub-Saharan Africa was identified by Seif and Rivett-Carnac (2010) in their introduction to a special collection of articles on African tourism for *Development Southern Africa*. This collection is of interest as it appears in what is the most important journal outlet for research on the tourism and development nexus in contemporary Africa (Rogerson and Rogerson 2011). In several articles, the question of closer linkages between tourism and small-scale agriculture was raised.

Here, specific attention is upon the luxury safari lodge sector, one of the main assets for contemporary tourism-led economic development for several African countries (Spenceley 2010a, 2010b). Among others Koelble (2011) shows that in parts of eastern and southern Africa there evolved an extensive luxury game lodge or safari lodge industry, the foundation for tourism to be a vehicle for outward-looking economic development. Our three country case studies are Botswana, South Africa and Zambia, all leading developing tourism economies in the southern African region (Rogerson 2009). In South Africa, a game lodge is defined officially as 'an accommodation facility located in natural surroundings', where rates charged are usually inclusive of game drives as well as food and beverage services (Meintjes *et al.* 2011: 234). Across the southern African region, safari lodges are marketed as 'eco-tourism destinations' where wildlife protection, the maintenance of biodiversity and community development are espoused as central values of the business model. The question of developing local linkages is particularly relevant in an environment, such as exists with the safari lodge industry, where these high-cost luxury tourism establishments operate in remote peripheral rural areas in close proximity to marginalised and poor (mainly) farming communities (Massyn and Koch 2004).

Agriculture–tourism linkages in developing countries

Considerable changes have occurred recently in 'attitudes concerning the linkages between tourism and agriculture' (Richardson-Ngwenya and Momsen 2011: 141). During the 1960s and 1970s a stream of writings claimed that tourism threatened agriculture by competing for labour, water and land resources through increasing their reserve prices (Latimer 1985). This 'anti-tourism' literature is now largely discredited, viewed by Latimer (1985: 42) as positively mischievous. Other simplistic relationships have also come under critical scrutiny. In particular, the assumption that tourism revenues automatically 'trickle down' to other sectors, including agriculture, is widely challenged (Rueegg 2009: 9). Trends in contemporary scholarship highlight that tourism is considered to offer the potential to galvanise local agricultural development through establishing backward linkages and to allow local farmers to supply the food needs of tourism establishments (Torres and Momsen 2004; Rogerson 2012). In a recent analysis of Samoa and Tonga, the Food and Agriculture Organization (FAO) asserts that fomenting linkages and creating synergies between tourism and agriculture 'should help harness the tourism dollar to achieve the objectives of sustained growth' (2012: 7).

Strengthening the linkages between agriculture and tourism is central to promoting symbiosis rather than conflict between the two sectors. Currently, it is argued that scope exists for policy innovation and intervention to boost the agricultural supply chain and foster greater linkages between agriculture and tourism, a relationship that potentially could have pro-poor benefits (Torres and Momsen 2004, 2011). The results from a number of recent value chain and economic mapping exercises disclose the significance of agricultural supply chains as a crucial vehicle for poor people to secure meaningful benefits from a developing tourism sector (Mitchell and Ashley 2010). Pro-poor tourism writings highlight why local farmers in developing countries might supply tourism enterprises with food products (Meyer 2007). In many developing countries tourism projects are situated in regions where the livelihoods of the poor are dominated by food production (FAO 2012). It is therefore emphasised that, by supplying formal tourism establishments with food products, the poor can build upon their existing skills without changing their livelihood strategies (Torres and Momsen 2004: 302). In addition, the provision of food products involves utilising the productive assets of the poor in terms of land and labour. New skills learned in the production of food for tourism establishments might potentially also allow farmers to transfer such skills to other food supply chains. Finally, pro-poor tourism proponents suggest that an untapped potential exists for poor people to furnish 'authentic' locally produced food for which there is growing demand in several destinations (Meyer 2007).

Across much of the developing world, however, the tourism industry, such as in the Caribbean, evolved 'largely apart from other sectors such as agriculture' (McBain 2007: 5). In the Pacific Islands the growth and development of the agriculture and tourism sectors 'have been pursued separately and policy and institutions have not been geared toward fostering positive linkages' (FAO 2012: 5). In what are sometimes described as 'disarticulated' local economies agriculture evolved mainly to satisfy export markets, with the result that domestic agriculture was undeveloped and, to a large extent, displaced by food imports (Belisle 1983; Timms and Neill 2011). As a consequence, in the US Virgin Islands, for example, the local agriculture sector fails to capture backward linkages from an expanding tourism and hospitality sector (Mwaijande 2007). Among others, McBain argues that in the 'sea, sun and sand' resorts of the Caribbean, most tourism leakage is attributed to the procurement arrangements of large international hotel chains because of a 'need to maintain the same standard throughout the chain' (2007: 27). Here a high level of food imports has been observed by several investigations and considered as negatively affecting local agricultural production possibilities (Belisle 1983; Rueegg 2009). Foreign-owned accommodation establishments and large resorts tend to import most food supplies in part 'due to the focus of their chefs on international cuisine and the reluctance of their purchase managers to deal directly with local farmers' (McBain 2007: 27). The preferred channel for food sourcing has been through agents or middlemen who procure through imports (Belisle 1983). It is argued that the high price of local produce (due in part to the small scale of production), inconsistency of supply and poor product quality are further deterrents to hotels and resorts increasing their reliance on local supplies (Meyer 2007; Timms and Neill 2011).

Analysis of food supply chains in developed countries suggests that local sourcing can reduce firm efficiency and effectiveness as it 'can take time and may involve negotiations with numerous small vendors in order to ensure prompt delivery and adequate quantities' (Murphy and Smith 2009: 213). In the context of the Global South, Trejos and Chiang maintain that, in order to 'maximise the benefits of tourism development for rural communities, ways must be found to increase the utilization of local food products and, where feasible, agriculture' (2009: 373). In some instances, hotels in developing countries that have purchased local agricultural products have 'had substantial enough impact to lift farmers above the poverty line' (Ashley *et al.* 2007: 17). To address the leakage of tourism income, the management of some all-inclusive hotels and resorts in the Caribbean have launched specific initiatives to strengthen linkages with local suppliers (Meyer 2006, 2007). Since 1990, the Four Seasons Resort in Nevis, in a partnership with the local Department of Agriculture, has engaged in a series of initiatives designed to encourage local farmers to become more oriented towards commercial agriculture and involved in the supply chain of the new five-star hotel. During 1996, the Sandals Group of hotels established a programme in Jamaica to improve the production of local farmers (Meyer 2006; Rhiney 2011). This particular initiative includes both management teams from the hotels hosting workshops for farmers in respect of produce quality and marketing and farmers' visits to hotels in order to understand the specific requirements for their products (McBain 2007: 28).

In order to encourage take-up of local foods by Caribbean hotels and resorts, special guides or toolkits have been issued to encourage partnerships between hotels and local farmers (IICA 2008; Joshua 2008). Further notable initiatives designed to increase local producers' access to tourism markets include the establishment of a buffer fund or revolving loan facility in order to address the long delays of up to seventy days that small producers often face in receiving payments from hotels. Capacity and institutional weaknesses in agro-tourism value chains are addressed through improved communication and information systems targeted to support strategic and operational decision making (Kelly 2008). Berno points out that the Jamaican Farmers Programme, implemented and supported by the Sandals Group of all-inclusive resorts, 'is an oft-cited example of a successful farm to fork initiative' (2011: 90). Nonetheless, as evidence that international tourism stimulates local or domestic agriculture is limited, certain scholars contend that 'given their reliance on local food, numerous small tourism establishments may be more important than large hotels or resorts' (Trejos and Chiang 2009: 373). In developing tourism economies smaller hospitality firms or budget backpacker forms of accommodation are shown to source a much higher proportion of their food products locally than larger establishments or resorts (Berno 2011).

Notwithstanding the multiple acknowledged benefits from enhanced tourism–agriculture linkages and local food sourcing, findings from research in the developing world show only limited linkages between tourism and agriculture sectors. The major trend is for most tourism establishments to source their food from wherever is cheapest, most reliable, most easily accessible and of assured quality (Torres and Momsen 2004). Across the experience of Caribbean resorts, Cancun and Lombok it was observed that a high proportion of imported foods is served in hotels. The predominant pattern is for high-end tourism establishments to source required food from distant and mainly large suppliers rather than from local small enterprises or poor entrepreneurs. The implications of sourcing food products from distant large-scale suppliers for local economies are reduced impacts for local development and most especially limited pro-poor impacts (Torres 2003; Torres and Momsen 2004; Meyer 2007; Rueegg 2009). In the work of Mitchell and Ashley (2010) the results of agriculture–tourism linkage initiatives are generally considered as disappointing.

Across the existing international experience, it is evident that 'there is no simple formula for increasing the use of local agricultural products in the tourism industry' (Berno 2011: 90). In understanding these disappointments, one must turn to analyse the results of empirical research on barriers to tourism–agriculture linkages. Over the quarter century since Belisle (1983: 509) identified the 'paucity' of research on tourism and agriculture linkages, this knowledge gap has been addressed through an array of rich empirical investigations mostly undertaken in Mexico, Indonesia and the Caribbean (Telfer and Wall 1996, 2000; Torres 2003; Torres and Momsen 2004, 2011; Timms 2006; Rhiney 2011).

Table 10.1 Influences on agriculture–tourism linkages

Demand-related factors	Supply-related factors	Marketing and intermediary factors	The role of government
Type of visitor accommodation	Physical/ environmental limitations	Marketing constraints	Planning bias towards tourism and neglect of other sectors
Maturity of tourism industry	Quantity of local production	Infrastructure shortcomings	Tourism planning focused on growing volume rather than intersectoral linkages
Type of tourist	Quality of local production	Supply poorly adjusted to demand	Planning bias against domestic agriculture with focus on export agriculture
Lack of promotion of local foods/ cuisine	Costs of locally produced food	Spatial patterns of supply	Lack of credit and micro-finance support
Health and safety considerations	Technological and processing limitations	Role of middlemen	Limited training and education

Source: Adapted from Meyer *et al.* (2004); Meyer (2007); Mitchell and Ashley (2010).

The available material on agriculture–tourism linkages demonstrates the existence of a variety of different factors that can shape patterns of food supply procurement and constrain backward linkage development (Table 10.1). The characteristics and depth of such linkages are considered as associated with several demand-related, supply- or production-related and marketing or intermediary factors (Meyer 2007; Rogerson 2012). Government policy support interventions or lack thereof are a further important set of considerations. In terms of demand-side factors, much significance attaches to the nature of tourism development, which can mould patterns of procurement. The type of accommodation, whether foreign-owned or managed enterprises, the type of tourist and the training and nationality of chefs are factors that can result in high levels of food imports and the corresponding establishment of only weak local linkages (Torres 2003; Meyer 2006; Rueegg 2009). Concerning the upper end of international tourism markets, health and safety issues and the high expectations of guests in terms of food quality (freshness) are key determinants of hotel food purchase patterns, 'making imports inevitable in most developing countries' (Konig 2007: 29).

Core production-related factors include environmental constraints, the nature of local farming systems, high prices of local products, supply inconsistencies, absence of the local production of certain goods and specifically of the types and quality of foods demanded by international tourists (Meyer 2007; Rhiney 2011).

Additionally, local tourism–agriculture linkages may be restricted by lack of inter-action between the two sectors from marketing constraints, deficient distribution infrastructure, kickbacks paid to local chefs by large food suppliers, and inexperi-ence of local producers in marketing (Rueegg 2009). Often the weak channel of communication between the tourism and agricultural sectors 'means that there is generally limited awareness of what is required by tourists and what can be produced locally to satisfy the demands of the tourism sector' (Meyer 2006: 31). Some scholars point to the limited communication channels between key stakeholders, which precipitates mistrust between buyers and potential suppliers (Torres and Momsen 2004; Meyer 2006; Rhiney 2011). In certain instances, this mistrust is based on socio-cultural, ethnic or racial differences that obstruct linkage formation or consolidation (Torres 2003; Rueegg 2009).

Lastly, the absence of any coherent policy focus by national governments for energising tourism–agriculture linkages is another critical issue in the Global South (Torres and Momsen 2004, 2011). Commonly the growth of, and policy development for, tourism and agriculture are considered as separate rather than interconnected issues (FAO 2012). Further, tourism policy is often focused mainly on accelerating visitor volumes to the neglect of encouraging intersectoral collaboration and constructing bridges between agriculture and tourism (Rogerson 2012). By contrast, the innovation of supportive government policies can potentially assist local agricultural producers through interventions such as the provision of micro-credit finance, training or mediation efforts between the agriculture and tourism sectors (Konig 2007).

Agriculture–tourism linkages in rural southern Africa: the safari lodge sector

As underlined by the above discussion, the bulk of existing academic research around agriculture–tourism linkages so far has been pursued in Mexico, Indonesia, the Caribbean and most recently the Pacific Islands. Within each of these tourism destinations, the main focus has been upon coastal beach developments. This study breaks new ground, therefore, in terms of its different geographical focus on southern Africa, the laboratory for much early theory and evolving practice concerning pro-poor tourism (Ashley and Roe 2002). Nevertheless, while the linkage between tourism and agriculture was acknowledged in regional pro-poor scholarship, it failed to attract detailed empirical attention. The primary focus of early pro-poor tourism research in southern Africa has been improving access to, and direct participation in, business opportunities for the poor in accommodation, craft or cultural services rather than in the supply chain of tourism establishments (Ashley and Haysom 2008).

The research here also breaks from existing literature because of its sectoral concentration on safari tourism, which is an element of alternative tourism. Wildlife viewing or safari tourism contributes to the economic growth and employment creation of many countries in southern Africa (Bresler 2011: 67). Massyn and Koch observe that safari lodges are a distinctive form of tourism accommodation as they offer 'the preserved remnants of Africa's charismatic mega fauna and biological diversity in a global context, which is experiencing waves of species extinction elsewhere' (2004: 103). The safari lodge represents a distinctive African contribution to the different forms of tourism lodging as analysed by Timothy and Teye (2009). Safari lodges offer an inclusive experience (luxury accommodation, gourmet cuisine and non-consumptive game viewing) at a remote wilderness location. Because of their remote locations no other options exist for tourists to access food services; the three main pillars for marketing high-end safari lodges are luxury accommodation, spectacular game viewing and gourmet food. Often the drawcard of 'romance' is used, with lodges also marketing their products by focusing on the created legends and imagery of Wild Africa (Massyn and Koch 2004). Typically, at Hippo Lodge in Zambia, lodge guests are invited to 'an experience of a lifetime' in which they 'escape from the reality', can indulge in 'something for gourmets' and luxuriate in secluded thatched accommodation 'with a breathtaking view of the river frontage and wildlife' (Hippo Lodge 2009).

Methodologically, this project was organised into two major phases of work (Hunt 2010). The first phase involved the construction of a database of luxury safari lodges for each of the three study countries – Botswana, South Africa and Zambia. For the purposes of this study, the category 'luxury safari lodges' was defined as establishments offering non-consumptive game-viewing experiences and charging a daily rate (during 2008–9) of at least USD 200 per person per night. The second phase involved conducting interviews with a sample of lodges that sought to reflect their spatial distribution within each of these countries. In total, information was obtained in 2009 for eighty lodges in South Africa, twenty-eight in Zambia and twenty-six in Botswana. Interviews were conducted with decision makers concerning details of food sourcing at the lodges with comparative material collected across the three countries relating to procurement arrangements for food and the respective barriers to the development of local linkages between tourism and agriculture. Both qualitative and quantitative information was obtained in the interviews.

The aim in this discussion is to undertake a broad comparative analysis of the overall 'macro-level' findings emerging from the three country case studies on agriculture–tourism linkages in rural Botswana, South Africa and Zambia. Here, special attention is paid to the extent of, and limits to, developing local linkages between tourism and agriculture. The detailed case studies and micro-level findings for each country are presented elsewhere (Hunt 2010). Importantly, in terms of comparative analysis, it must be appreciated that certain commonalities exist, but also important differences can be noted in the policy and institutional environment surrounding the development of tourism and agriculture linkages. In all three case countries, the significance of agricultural development is highlighted and policy development to support the commercial development of this sector has been energetically pursued, albeit within the environmental constraints of a global sub-region that is negatively affected by climate change and global warming. During the past two decades, all three countries have embraced tourism's importance as a driver for national economic development and potential contribution for poverty alleviation. In South Africa, tourism is targeted as a priority sector for job creation within the country's New Growth Path (Rogerson 2011). Likewise in Botswana, tourism is identified as a key sector for economic diversification away from the traditional dominance of the mining sector. Within Zambia national government support for tourism development is also part of strategies for economic diversification, albeit the sector has not been elevated in local development discourse to the same extent as in either Botswana or South Africa (Rogerson 2003).

What is notably absent in either the Botswana or Zambia case is any effort to establish coherent policy initiatives through national or local governments in order to strengthen linkages between the tourism and agriculture sectors in synergistic fashion. The situation in both countries is that sectoral planning for agriculture and tourism has been essentially separate. By contrast, the position in South Africa is of a policy environment in which certain (limited) efforts have been made through government policy since the 1994 democratic transition to encourage intersectoral linkage development. One central dimension of national tourism planning during the post-apartheid period has been to nurture 'responsible tourism' practices and use tourism as a vehicle to advance the livelihoods of communities previously disadvantaged under apartheid (Spenceley 2008). The 1996 White Paper on the Development and Promotion of Tourism encouraged the development of responsible and sustainable tourism approaches and identified the supply of food to tourism establishments as a potential opportunity for involving poor communities (Republic of South Africa 1996). This policy commitment made to enhance the pro-poor impacts from tourism has been a continuous thread during the post-apartheid era (Rogerson 2006). Especially significant has been government's encouragement of expanded local procurement by the tourism industry in terms of the 2002 national Responsible Tourism Guidelines. These guidelines encourage private sector tourism businesses in South Africa to 'buy local' wherever quality, quantity and consistency permits (Spenceley *et al.* 2002).

Across southern Africa many safari lodges adhere to these principles of 'responsible tourism' and have introduced corporate social responsibility initiatives to benefit local communities. As observed by Snyman, 'High-end ecotourism operations in protected areas often claim to share the benefits of ecotourism with surrounding local communities and to ensure a "trickle down" effect of the revenues that result from such operations' (2012: 395). Throughout the region, safari lodge operations have responded to consumer shifts towards a stronger emphasis on social consciousness and international traveller demands for forms of tourism that 'give back' to the communities and environments they visit. Many lodges are marketed as more 'authentic' by using responsible tourism best practice as their unique selling point (Hunt 2010). The marketing of Wilderness Safaris, one of the largest safari operators in southern Africa, proclaims:

> Wilderness Safaris is a responsible ecotourism and conservation company. The reason we exist is to protect pristine wilderness areas and the flora and fauna – or biodiversity – that they support. We believe that in protecting these

areas, and including the local communities in this process, we will make a difference to Africa and ultimately the world. In short, we believe that the world's wilderness areas will save humankind.

(Wilderness Safaris 2010)

It is against such a policy backdrop, and the imperative of lodge operators to secure a social licence to operate, that the demands of these lodges for quantities of fresh food produce offer opportunities for linking tourism with agriculture, and in so doing avert the dangers of polarised development, which is often a consequence of tourism-led development anchored in the luxury tourism segment.

The essential geography of luxury safari lodge activities is mapped in Figure 10.1. The analysis identified a total of 363 luxury safari establishments operating in 2009. These were distributed between these countries as follows: 235 in South Africa, 65 in Zambia and 63 in Botswana. The detailed spatial arrangement of lodges occurs in terms of clusters that emerge around the major protected areas, or game reserves that have been established in each of the three countries. In South Africa, the highest concentration of luxury safari lodges are in northeastern parts of the country in the two provinces of Limpopo and Mpumalanga, which have the largest amount of land set aside for wilderness conservation purposes. In particular, major clusters of lodges exist around the Kruger National Park. Other significant concentrations of lodges are recorded near to Addo Elephant National Park, the Isimangaliso Wetland Park, Madikwe and the Waterberg. Each of these enterprise clusters involves private game reserves that offer non-consumptive game-viewing experiences and house a range of different safari lodge operations. In Botswana, the leading focus for luxury safari lodge activities is in the surrounds of the Okavango Delta, Moremi Game Reserve and Chobe National Park. In Zambia, safari lodge operations occur mostly around Luangwa National Park, Kafue National Park and the Lower Zambezi National Park.

As discussed earlier, much international scholarship points to the significance of ownership and control of tourism accommodation as influential upon local impacts and in particular the establishment of local linkages (Lacher and Nepal 2010). In terms of ownership and control, considerable differences emerge between the status of the safari lodge industry in South Africa as opposed to that in Botswana or Zambia. In South Africa, the research disclosed that the vast majority of safari lodges are locally owned and controlled. Levels of foreign ownership in the South African safari lodge industry are low and confined to four companies (Virgin Ltd, Mantis Collection, Beyond and Red Carnation), all of which had booking offices in the country. By contrast, the safari lodge economies of both Botswana and Zambia exhibit high levels of foreign ownership and control. In both these countries, although safari lodge enterprises may be registered in Botswana or Zambia, the operations are essentially under external control. For example, the American-based luxury safari company Ker and Downey operates through a Botswana-based public enterprise (Chobe Holdings), which is the owner of several lodge operations. Of note is the expansion of the operations of South African-based safari enterprises into both Botswana and Zambia. The high levels

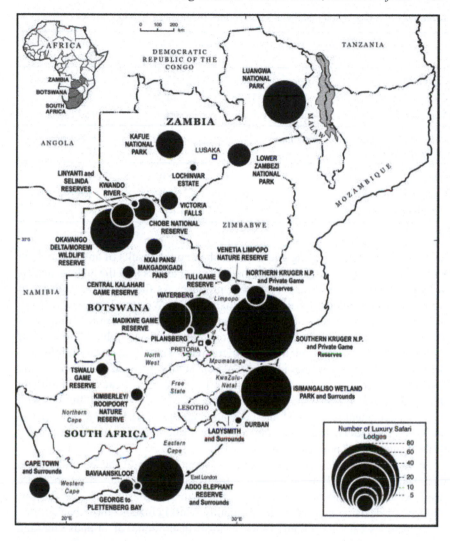

Figure 10.1 The spatial patterns of luxury safari lodges in South Africa, Zambia and
Botswana.

of foreign ownership of lodge operations in the Okavango Delta region of northern
Botswana prompted Mbaiwa (2005) to stylise the local safari industry as a form
of 'enclave tourism'.

For the establishment of linkages between tourism accommodation establishments and local agriculture, considerable significance attaches to decision-making
processes regarding food offerings and food sourcing at the lodges. According to
Torres (2002), tourist food consumption and preferences can be major drivers of
hotel food purchasing in the developing world. In the case of safari lodges most
enterprises frame their decision-making and procurement policies on the perceived

Table 10.2 Food decision making at safari lodges in southern Africa

Individual responsible for decisions on foods served and menus	South Africa (%)	Zambia (%)	Botswana (%)
Chef	42.5	7.1	3.8
Chef and management	31.25	14.3	3.8
Management	26.25	78.6	92.3
Individual responsible for decisions on where foods are sourced	South Africa (%)	Zambia (%)	Botswana (%)
Chef	10	0	0
Chef and management	30	0	3.8
Management	60	100	96.2

demands of their high-paying guests rather than on the results of any research on tourist food preferences. It is essential that cuisine at lodges is of the highest quality, is hygienic and offers a variety of fresh produce. As the majority of guests at safari lodges are international tourists, mainly from Western Europe and North America, lodge management considers that guest preferences are for 'European-style' dishes, requiring that food decision makers access reliable sources of traditional European-style, high-quality ingredients. Table 10.2 reveals differences between the three case studies in respect of who are the decision makers regarding food at safari lodges. In South Africa the role of the chef is far more important than in the cases of Botswana or Zambia, where the major responsibility lies with lodge management or the food and beverage manager. Importantly, however, in all three countries chefs assume only a marginal role in decision making relating to food sourcing or purchasing for lodges.

Table 10.3 provides an overview of respondent profiles of the key individuals responsible for food decision making at safari lodges. Important differences are disclosed between the three case studies. In South African safari lodges, the vast majority of decision makers are local (mainly white) citizens whose background often includes catering training either at local institutions, or in-house through structured internships or at international institutions. By contrast, in Zambia and Botswana the largest share of decision making is in the hands of expatriates or non-nationals, in Zambia mainly UK citizens, and in Botswana mainly South African nationals. The absence of established local tourism training institutions in Botswana and Zambia as compared to training in South Africa is of note. Of importance are the linguistic skills of decision makers and especially their capacity to communicate in local languages. Once again, marked differences emerge across the three case studies. In South Africa, there was a much higher capacity of food decision makers to communicate in local African languages (beyond Afrikaans) than was the situation in Botswana or Zambia. The lack of ability of decision makers to speak local languages is potentially significant in making decisions on food sourcing. In the case of Zambia, while English is the national language, the

Table 10.3 Profile of key food decision makers in the safari lodge industry

Nationality and languages	South Africa (%)	Zambia (%)	Botswana (%)
Respondents who speak a national language other than English	80	17	8
Respondents who are nationals of the countries they work in	82	17	8
Catering training	South Africa (%)	Zambia (%)	Botswana (%)
No official training	43	75	59
In-house training programmes	16	0	8
Trained in national academic establishments	32	0	0
Trained in overseas academic establishments	9	25	33

country has at least forty different local languages and, in the remote rural areas where lodges are situated, the ability of local communities to speak English is often limited. What this means is that the level of potential communication between food decision makers and local communities, who are the potential food suppliers, is reduced. This situation is further reinforced by high staff turnover levels of key decision makers at these rural safari lodges. As shown in research on Indonesia by Telfer and Wall (2000), a new manager (or chef) can potentially have significant impacts on the purchasing policies of hotels, with the consequence that local supplier relationships and trust necessarily have to be rebuilt with the appointment of new personnel. It was revealed that in all three countries there was a high level of staff turnover at lodges, with the significant food sourcing decisions commonly made by individuals who had been in their current managerial positions for five years or less.

The organisation and geography of sourcing food supplies was a central theme under scrutiny with the safari lodge survey. Table 10.4 reveals key issues in terms of the extent of national sourcing of food supplies. At a national scale, it was found that the vast majority of food served at South African lodges was sourced from national suppliers, a finding that reflects the well-developed character of the country's agricultural sector. With the less-developed agricultural economies of Zambia and Botswana, greater leakages were evident in both countries with imports, mainly from South Africa, of a range of food items. In South African lodges, the extent of imported foods is negligible, mostly confined to small luxury items such as caviar or salmon. In terms of local food sourcing, the survey sought to determine the proportion of food supplies that were obtained from sources within a 40 km radius of the lodge. The caveat should be noted that defining 'local' is problematic in cases where lodges were located more than 40 km distant from

Table 10.4 The geography of food sourcing

Details	South Africa	Zambia	Botswana
Percentage of safari lodges surveyed that source the bulk of their *vegetables from within a 40 km radius* of their location	38	11	8
Percentage of safari lodges surveyed that source the bulk of their *fruit from within a 40 km radius* of their location	36	4	8
Average distance from safari lodge to nearest local community	24 km	44.3 km	110 km
Percentage of safari lodges surveyed that source the bulk of their *vegetables from within a 120 km radius* of their location	74	21	8
Percentage of safari lodges surveyed that source the bulk of their *fruit from within a 120 km radius* of their location	75	11	8

neighbouring communities, as occurs in much of Botswana and Zambia and even parts of South Africa.

It is evident from Table 10.4, however, that the actual current extent of local sourcing of food products is limited even in the South African case and in Botswana and Zambia local supplies are minimal. In all three countries, it was revealed that safari lodges procured the largest proportion of their supplies from distant urban markets rather than from local food producers. A common finding across all three country case studies was the critical role assumed by intermediary supplier organisations in determining and articulating sourcing arrangements for food supplies. In order to source the range of food supplies, it was found in all three case studies that the majority of safari lodges procure their food produce through an intermediary supplier. The decision to use an intermediary supplier was made on grounds of convenience: as one South African interviewee observed, 'it is easier to go through a middleman who does all the bartering, sourcing and delivery for you'. In the supply chain of food to these rural tourism establishments, the research in Botswana, South Africa and Zambia highlighted the role of the intermediary supplier in decision making regarding choice of food supplier as well as in establishing standards that local producers must attain if they wish to enter the supply chain.

It was shown that patterns of sourcing were found to vary between the different geographical clusters as well as between different kinds of food products. For example, in South Africa a much higher degree of local sourcing of fresh food supplies was evidenced from the cluster of safari accommodation establishments situated in Western Cape as compared to those around Kruger National Park, mainly because of their proximity to a well-established local and diversified agricultural sector supported by good local infrastructure. Overall, in terms of tourism-agriculture linkages the most significant indicator of supplier relationships relates to sourcing of fresh vegetables. It was disclosed that 38 per cent of safari lodges surveyed in South Africa sourced the bulk of their vegetables from within a 40 km radius as compared to only 11 per cent in Zambia and 8 per cent in the case of the environmentally constrained conditions of arid Botswana.

The most striking research finding was that the overwhelming majority of safari lodges do not source the bulk of their fresh vegetable requirements from proximate local communities. Instead, the largest segment of supplies is channelled through urban-based distributors or sources. In South Africa, a vital role in the safari food chain is played by the Fresh Produce Market in Johannesburg, which is the source for purchases by the key intermediary suppliers. In Zambia, a parallel role is assumed by Lusaka, which is the hub for purchasing by the major Zambian intermediary supplier to the lodges. Commonly, even in circumstances where local fresh produce is available, the majority of this is not sold directly to safari lodges but, rather, is first channelled to urban markets before returning back to the lodges via the intermediary supplier. This arrangement clearly adds greatly to the carbon footprint of these establishments and conflicts with commitments made to responsible tourism practices. Typically, the purchasing of local food is mainly either as 'top-up' supplies for lodges or more commonly for use as staff food. In reviewing the limits of local supplier development to the safari lodge sector elsewhere, Massyn observes:

> the inherent asymmetry between the needs of high-end lodge operations and the capacity of underdeveloped local economies to supply the sophisticated goods and services needed to service the needs of the urban elites making up the bulk of the lodges' clients.
>
> (2004: 7)

Only in isolated pockets of southern Africa (such as Madikwe in South Africa, Mfuwe in South Luangwa, Zambia, and areas surrounding the southern Kruger National Park) has the safari lodge industry stimulated groups of small local producers that service the food supply chain of lodges and correspondingly generate substantial local benefits (Massyn 2004).

The empirical findings from the three case studies lend further support to the complex of factors that have been identified in other international research as constraining the development of intersectoral linkages between tourism and agriculture. The following responses capture some of the 'voices' of the interviewees from the South African research, seeking to explain the reasons for limited local sourcing and the constraints of linkages between tourism and agriculture:

- 'Locals are unfortunately not reliable enough to rely on. There is no guarantee of consistency.'
- 'There is no reliability or consistency with local producers.'

- 'We would rather buy locally but consistency and reliability is a problem.'
- 'We have changed suppliers due to better service provision. Service provision is more important to us than price. And anyway prices differ little between suppliers. Locals don't provide reliable service.'
- 'The quality of the produce is not the same as a commercial farmer, it is also not dependable at all.'
- 'Our supplier is very expensive but is reliable and that is what's most important.'
- 'The climate is very marginal and it's very difficult to grow products at the boundaries of Sabi Sands and Timbavati.'
- 'It is very humid and hot here so that affects the success of crops.'
- 'We tried to start a project but the money was stolen.'

Similar sets of responses were reported from the Botswana and Zambia research investigations (Hunt 2010). Overall, the three-country investigation points to several factors that underpin the existence of limited backward linkages of tourism establishments to local food suppliers. In all three countries, the safari lodge interviews emphasise the inability of (most) local agricultural producers to offer consistent and reliable supplies of food products. In particular, a key factor is that local communities/producers are unable to provide the high-quality standards of food produce that are demanded by the safari lodges. In certain regions, issues of environmental constraints and transport logistics exacerbate the difficulties of local food sourcing.

The qualitative responses listed above indicate very importantly the existence of a lack of trust between purchasers at lodges and local producers. This problem is worsened by the observed levels of high staff turnover at lodges and often also the inability of key decision makers to communicate the requirements of lodges to local communities. In particular, the high staff turnover makes difficult the building of trust or solid relationships for local sourcing between lodges and local producers. In all three countries, disappointments were aired concerning efforts that had been made by several lodges to promote local agricultural food production to supply lodges. Overall, it was disclosed that projects to encourage local food sourcing had been ineffectual and, in most cases, short-lived. In explaining these failures, several factors must be noted, including issues of project management, poor communication of the needs of lodges to local farmers, and under-capitalisation of local producers, often in the absence of availability of micro-finance. Finally, in all three countries the weakness of government support for the building of linkages between agriculture and tourism must be noted. This weakness applies even in the South African case where much policy discussion surrounds the rhetoric of promoting responsible tourism.

Conclusion

Telfer (2009) maintains that one of the major challenges of using tourism as a driver of economic development is its potential for high leakages, especially in relation to luxury international tourism. This chapter has examined issues relating to the development of backward linkages from tourism to the agriculture sector in the context of safari tourism in three southern African countries. It is argued that the successful evolution and strengthening of local linkages between tourism and agriculture are vital to avert the dangers of polarisation, which can accompany tourism-led economic development in the Global South. Our analysis supports the contention of Torres and Momsen (2011) that such linkages represent a vital, important potential mechanism through which to achieve pro-poor tourism objectives. Arguably, the first step both to maximise pro-poor impacts and to avert polarisation is 'to understand why such linkages rarely materialise and to identify the conditions necessary for them to do so' (Torres and Momsen 2004: 296). In the context of tourism–agriculture linkages, while the evidence from southern African safari lodges is mixed and reveals variations between the three countries, it discloses certain common threads concerning barriers that are production-related, demand-related, or caused by intermediary factors and critical issues of policy neglect by government. Existing food supply chains in southern Africa are organised mainly by a network of intermediary suppliers who source the bulk of supplies from urban wholesale markets rather than local agricultural producers. In order to change this established pattern of sourcing and to encourage a greater depth of tourism–agriculture linkage (including local sourcing), national governments and the tourism private sector together must recognise the importance of encouraging backward linkages. More specifically, what is required is a carefully crafted and coordinated set of integrated actions to address the cluster of demand, supply and intermediary factors that presently constrain the formation or continuation of these local supply linkages.

Acknowledgements

Thanks are due to the University of Johannesburg for research funding support and to Wendy Job for producing the figure. The inputs of Teddy and Skye Norfolk are also acknowledged. Earlier versions of this chapter were presented at the International Geographical Union Commission Meeting, September 2010, Stellenbosch, South Africa, and at the International Tourism Sustainability Conference, September 2011, Balaklava, Mauritius.

References

Ashley, C. and Haysom, G. (2008) 'The development impacts of tourism supply chains: increasing impact on poverty and decreasing our ignorance', in A. Spenceley (ed.) *Responsible Tourism: Critical issues for conservation and development*, London: Earthscan, pp. 129–56.

Ashley, C. and Roe, D. (2002) 'Making tourism work for the poor: strategies and challenges in southern Africa', *Development Southern Africa*, 19: 61–82.

Ashley, C., De Brine, P., Lehr, A. and Wilde, H. (2007) *The Role of the Tourism Sector in Expanding Economic Opportunity*, Corporate Social Responsibility Initiative report No. 23, Cambridge, MA: Kennedy School of Government, Harvard University.

Belisle, F.J. (1983) 'Tourism and food production in the Caribbean', *Annals of Tourism Research*, 10: 497–513.

Berno, T. (2011) 'Sustainability on a plate: linking agriculture and food in the Fiji Islands tourism industry', in R. Torres and J. Momsen (eds) *Tourism and Agriculture: New geographies of production and rural restructuring*, London: Routledge, pp. 87–103.

Bresler, N.C. (2011) 'On safari in Botswana: describing the product', *Tourism Analysis*, 16: 67–75.

Britton, S.G. (1982) 'The political economy of tourism in the Third World', *Annals of Tourism Research*, 9: 331–58.

Brohman, J. (1996) 'New directions in tourism for Third World development', *Annals of Tourism Research*, 23: 48–70.

Food and Agriculture Organization (FAO) (2012) *Report on a Scoping Mission in Samoa and Tonga: Agriculture and tourism linkages in Pacific Island countries*, Apia: FAO Sub-regional Office for the Pacific Islands.

Hippo Lodge (2009) *Zambia, the Real Africa: For a unique safari experience – Hippo Lodge*, promotional brochure, Kafue National Park, Zambia: Hippo Lodge.

Hunt, H. (2010) 'African safari lodges food supply chains: the potential for establishing "pro-poor" linkages', MA thesis, Department of Tourism, University of the Witwatersrand, Johannesburg.

Inter-American Institute for Cooperation on Agriculture (IICA) (2008) *The Farmer–Hotel Partnership Tool Kit: From soil to sauce*, Bridgetown: IICA.

Jenkins, C.L. and Henry, B.M. (1982) 'Government involvement in tourism in developing countries', *Annals of Tourism Research*, 9: 499–521.

Joshua, P.A. (2008) *Strengthening of the Tourism Sector through the Development of Linkages with the Agricultural Sector in the Caribbean: Farmer–hotel partnership workshop report*, report of workshop organised by the Inter-American Institute for cooperation on Agriculture and the Organization of American States, Accra Beach Hotel, Barbados, 26–27 March.

Kelly, C. (2008) 'Strengthening the St Kitts farmers cooperative's capacity to deliver direct sales to the tourism sector', unpublished project investment profile prepared for the Inter-American Institute for Cooperation in Agriculture, Basseterre, St Kitts.

Koelble, T.A. (2011) 'Ecology, economy and empowerment: eco-tourism and the game lodge industry in South Africa', *Business and Politics*, 13(1).

Konig, D.A. (2007) 'Linking agriculture to tourism in Sierra Leone – a preliminary research', MA thesis, Sustainable Tourism Management, University of Applied Sciences of Eberswalde, Germany.

Lacher, R.G. and Nepal, S.K. (2010) 'From leakages to linkages: local-level strategies for capturing tourism revenue in northern Thailand', *Tourism Geographies*, 12: 77–99.

Latimer, H. (1985) 'Developing-island economies: tourism v agriculture', *Tourism Management*, 6: 32–42.

Lejarraja, I. and Walkenhurst, P. (2007) *Diversification by Deepening Linkages with Tourism*, Washington, DC: The World Bank International Trade Department.

McBain, H. (2007) *Caribbean Tourism and Agriculture: Linking to enhance development and competitiveness*, Port of Spain: United Nations ECLAC Sub-regional Headquarters for the Caribbean.

Massyn, P. (2004) 'Safari lodges and rural incomes: some key South African trends', retrieved 6 February 2010 from http://hdgc.epp.cmu.edu/misc/Massyn.pdf.

Massyn, P. and Koch, E. (2004) 'African game lodges and rural benefit in two southern African countries', in C.M. Rogerson and G. Visser (eds) *Tourism and Development Issues in Contemporary South Africa*, Pretoria: Africa Institute of South Africa, pp. 102–38.

Mbaiwa, J.E. (2005) 'Enclave tourism and its socio-economic impacts in the Okavango Delta, Botswana', *Tourism Management*, 26: 157–72.

Meintjes, C., Niemann-Struweg, I. and Petzer, D. (2011) 'Evaluating web marketing of luxury lodges in South Africa', *African Journal of Marketing Management*, 3(9): 233–40.

Meyer, D. (2006) *Caribbean Tourism, Local Sourcing and Enterprise Development: Review of the literature*, London: Pro-Poor Tourism Partnership.

Meyer, D. (2007) 'Pro-poor tourism: from leakages to linkages: a conceptual framework for creating linkages between the accommodation sector and "poor" neighbouring communities', *Current Issues in Tourism*, 10: 558–83.

Meyer, D., Ashley, C. and Poultney, C. (2004) *Tourism–Agricultural Linkages: Boosting inputs from local farmers*, Programme Paper No. 3, London: Pro-Poor Tourism Pilots (Southern Africa).

Mitchell, J. and Ashley, C. (2006) *Tourism Business and the Local Economy: Increasing impact through a linkages approach*, briefing paper, London: Overseas Development Institute.

Mitchell, J. and Ashley, C. (2010) *Tourism and Poverty Reduction: Pathways to prosperity*, London: Earthscan.

Murphy, J. and Smith, S. (2009) 'Chefs and suppliers: an exploratory look at supply chain issues in an upscale restaurant alliance', *International Journal of Hospitality Management*, 28: 212–20.

Mwaijande, F.A. (2007) *Understanding Barriers for Agriculture–Tourism Linkages: Setting policy agenda for agricultural growth*, Fayetteville, AR: University of Arkansas.

Republic of South Africa (1996) *White Paper for the Development and Promotion of Tourism in South Africa*, Pretoria: Department of Environmental Affairs and Tourism.

Rhiney, K. (2011) 'Agri-tourism linkages in Jamaica: a case study of the Negril tourism industry', paper presented at the International Centre for Tropical Agriculture, Cali, Colombia.

Richardson-Ngwenya, P. and Momsen, J. (2011) 'Tourism and agriculture in Barbados: changing relationships', in R. Torres and J. Momsen (eds) *Tourism and Agriculture: New geographies of production and rural restructuring*, London: Routledge, pp. 139–48.

Rogerson, C.M. (2003) 'Developing Zambia's tourism economy: planning for "the real Africa"', *Africa Insight*, 33: 48–54.

Rogerson, C.M. (2006) 'Pro-poor local economic development in South Africa: the role of pro-poor tourism', *Local Environment*, 11: 37–60.

Rogerson, C.M. (2009) 'Tourism development in southern Africa: patterns, issues and constraints', in J. Saarinen, F. Becker, H. Manwa and D. Wilson (eds) *Sustainable Tourism in Southern Africa: Local communities and natural resources in transition*, Bristol, UK: Channel View, pp. 20–41.

Rogerson, C.M. (2011) 'Niche tourism policy and planning: the South African experience', *Tourism Review International*, 15: 199–212.

Rogerson, C.M. (2012) 'Strengthening agriculture–tourism linkages in the developing world: opportunities, barriers and current initiatives', *African Journal of Agricultural Research*, 7(4): 616–23.

Rogerson, C.M. and Rogerson, J.M. (2011) 'Tourism research within the southern African development community: production and consumption in academic journals, 2000–2010', *Tourism Review International*, 15: 213–24.

Rueegg, M. (2009) The impact of tourism on rural poverty through supply chain linkages to local food producers in the Bolivian Altiplano, unpub. M.Sc. (Development Studies) dissertation, London School of Economics and Political Science.

Sandbrook, C. (2010) 'Local economic impact of different forms of nature-based tourism', *Conservation Letters*, 3: 21–8.

Seif, J. and Rivett-Carnac, K. (2010) 'Editorial: tourism impacts: lessons for policy, programmes and projects', *Development Southern Africa*, 27: 627–8.

Snyman, S.L. (2012) 'The role of tourism employment in poverty reduction and community perceptions of conservation and tourism in southern Africa', *Journal of Sustainable Tourism*, 20: 395–416.

Spenceley, A. (ed.) (2008) *Responsible Tourism: Critical issues for conservation and development*, London: Earthscan.

Spenceley, A. (2010a) *Tourism Product Development Interventions and Best Practices in Sub-Saharan Africa: Part 1: Synthesis*, report to The World Bank Tourism Industry: Research and Analysis Phase II, Nelspruit.

Spenceley, A. (2010b) *Tourism Product Development Interventions and Best Practices in Sub-Saharan Africa: Part 2: Case studies*, report to The World Bank Tourism Industry: Research and Analysis Phase II, Nelspruit.

Spenceley, A. and Meyer, D. (2012) 'Tourism and poverty reduction: theory and practice in less economically developed countries', *Journal of Sustainable Tourism*, 20: 297–317.

Spenceley, A., Relly, P., Keyser, H., Warmeant, P., McKenzie, M., Matboge, A., Norton, P., Mahlangu, S. and Seif, J. (2002) *Responsible Tourism Manual for South Africa*, Pretoria: Department of Environmental Affairs and Tourism.

Telfer, D.J. (2002) 'The evolution of tourism and development theory', in R. Sharpley and D.J. Telfer (eds) *Tourism and Development: Concepts and issues*, Clevedon, UK: Channel View, pp. 35–77.

Telfer, D.J. (2009) 'Development studies and tourism', in T. Jamal and M. Robinson (eds) *The Sage Handbook of Tourism Studies*, London: Sage, pp. 146–65.

Telfer, D.J. and Sharpley, R. (2008) *Tourism and Development in the Developing World*, London: Routledge.

Telfer, D.J. and Wall, G. (1996) 'Linkages between tourism and food production', *Annals of Tourism Research*, 23: 635–53.

Telfer, D.J. and Wall, G. (2000) 'Strengthening backward economic linkages: local food purchasing by three Indonesian hotels', *Tourism Geographies*, 2: 421–47.

Timms, B. (2006) 'Caribbean agriculture–tourism linkages in a neoliberal world: problems and prospects for St Lucia', *International Development Planning Review*, 28: 35–56.

Timms, B.F. and Neill, S. (2011) 'Cracks in the pavement: conventional constraints and contemporary solutions for linking agriculture and tourism in the Caribbean', in R. Torres and J. Momsen (eds) *Tourism and Agriculture: New geographies of production and rural restructuring*, London: Routledge, pp. 104–16.

Timothy, D.J. and Teye, V. (2009) *Tourism and the Lodging Sector*, London: Butterworth-Heinemann.

Torres, R. (2002) 'Toward a better understanding of tourism and agriculture linkages in the Yucatan: tourist food consumption and preferences', *Tourism Geographies*, 4: 282–306.

Torres, R. (2003) 'Linkages between tourism and agriculture in Mexico', *Annals of Tourism Research*, 30: 546–66.

Torres, R. and Momsen, J. (2004) 'Challenges and potential for linking tourism and agriculture to achieve pro-poor tourism objectives', *Progress in Development Studies*, 4: 294–318.

Torres, R. and Momsen J. (2011) 'Introduction', in R. Torres and J. Momsen (eds) *Tourism and Agriculture: New geographies of production and rural restructuring*, London: Routledge, pp. 1–9.

Trejos, B. and Chiang, L.-H.N. (2009) 'Local economic linkages to community-based tourism in rural Costa Rica', *Singapore Journal of Tropical Geography*, 30: 373–87.

Wilderness Safaris (2010) 'About us', retrieved 5 February 2010 from www.wilderness-safaris.com.

11 Ethnic tourism in Kaokoland, northwest Namibia

Cure for all or the next crisis for the OvaHimba?

Jarkko Saarinen

Introduction

Tourism is a global scale activity that is both a product and a vehicle of globalisation influencing the lives of numerous people – many of them having no direct connection to the industry, no ability to be mobile in touristic ways or no idea what tourism is about. The global tourism industry and related actors bring together different people and cultures, move capital, knowledge, labour and services, construct physical and mental landscapes of distant and nearby places, and distribute impacts, among many other things, on various geographic scales. The increasing complexity of the industry has made it difficult to conceptualise what tourism is and how it operates and creates changes in the global–local nexus.

In spite of the uncertainties in managing the impacts of global tourism locally, the industry has become a key target for governments and regions searching for economic development and employment creation. Especially in developing countries the increase in the demand for tourism is seen as highly beneficial. Sinclair and Stabler (1997) have suggested that increasing tourist demand has a much more significant impact on developing rather than developed countries' economies. However, Sinclair (1998) has also stated that the economic aspects of tourism should be placed in an equation consisting of both the advantages and disadvantages of tourism-related development. Therefore the economic costs, such as inflation, land use changes, security needs, crime and increases in domestic prices should be considered along with the known or estimated benefits. In addition, opportunity costs are rarely discussed in local or regional tourism development discussions. Tourism development also causes cultural, social and environmental changes and impacts that may have economic implications and, thus, eventually create costs or even crises for host countries and regions. However, in spite of the risks, tourism development is increasingly seen as a promising tool for economic growth and diversification, especially in peripheries where there are few other alternatives (Hall 2005; Saarinen *et al.* 2009).

This chapter will focus on the role and relations of tourism with local communities. Traditionally the role and development impacts of tourism and related patterns of mobility and non-local consumption have been governed by

the market-driven industry and/or state authorities and other public sector institutions. Since the 1990s, however, there have been practically and theoretically
driven attempts to transfer tourism growth towards the principles of sustainable
development (Butler 1999; Holden 2007), and several models aiming for the
devolution of power in development responsibilities have been proposed. These
models try to give more authority to local actors, for example communities and
other local institutions (see Hulme and Murphree 2001; Long 2004). The aim is
to minimise negative impacts and maximise positive outcomes by providing local
control over tourism development and resulting benefits. Especially in the Global
South, tourism has been given an important role as a policy tool for community
development, providing jobs and economic benefits for the poor and previously
disadvantaged peoples (see Ashley 2000; Binns and Nel 2002; Rogerson and Visser
2004). This kind of emphasis has highlighted the role of community-based natural
resource management (CBNRM) and especially community-based (Tosun 2000;
Okazaki 2008) and pro-poor tourism (Ashley and Roe 2002; Meyer 2008)
initiatives. These models are based partly on different assumptions, but in general
they aim to promote the participation of local communities in tourism development.

Based on this background, the chapter briefly evaluates the current main ideas
and challenges of participation and benefit sharing in tourism development by
utilising the basic premises of community-based tourism (CBT) and pro-poor
tourism (PPT). The following empirical examples are based on previous studies
focusing on tourism operations and impacts in Kaokoland, northwest Namibia (see
Saarinen 2011, 2012). The aim is to discuss the role of local people in tourism
and the nature of tourism operations based on ethnic village tourism and the
attractiveness of the OvaHimba (Himba). OvaHimba communities have faced
several environmental and socio-political crises in the past decades, which have
made them vulnerable in nationally and internationally driven development
processes. Here vulnerability refers to the degree to which a community is
susceptible to, or even unable to cope with, opposing effects of change, and the
effectiveness of certain adaptive mechanisms as bases for adaptive capacity (see
Smit and Wandel 2006). Thus, vulnerability influences the ability to adapt tourism
and related changes and vice versa, and the relation between vulnerability and
adaptation is defined by power issues between the industry and communities, for
example.

Tourism, global change and local communities

Tourism and global change

The idea of global change or the considerations of its local outcomes do not
academically represent any dramatically new way of thinking. Marsh (1965)
published his seminal work *Man and Nature*, in which he challenged the notion
of limitless resources of the earth, in 1864. Outside the natural resources and
environmental processes, the issue of global change is often equated with
globalisation, referring to the increasing mobility of goods, knowledge, values,

products and services, among many other things, and the deepening interconnected-
ness and dependency of distant places and actors (see Harvey 1996). Although
tourism as a geographical system – covering origins, destinations and routes in
between them – has been global almost from the very beginning of modern tourism,
presently the industry, its destinations and host communities are transformed much
more rapidly and on a more non-local basis than ever before. Thus, the current
processes of globalisation offer a view to reflect the impacts of global change
on local communities and how the relation between the global-scale industry
and local-scale communities are organised in different places (Mowforth and
Munt 1998).

According to Britton (1991: 455) the production system of tourism is simultaneously a mechanism for the accumulation of capital, the private appropriation
of resources and wealth, the extraction of surplus value from a labour force, and
the capturing of income from goods that are often public by nature. Although
the touristic production system has a great potential to contribute positively to the
socio-economic basis of destination areas, it can also fail while growing in visitor
numbers and revenue. Based on this 'ambivalent characteristic' of tourism, there
has been a long tradition of discussion about the costs and benefits of tourism
impacts (see Turner and Ash 1975; De Kadt 1979). Especially, the peripheries of
developing countries, where tourism-driven socio-economic development may
often be characterised by enclavisation, dependency, inequalities and revenue
leakages (see Britton 1991; Mowforth and Munt 1998), are facing the serious
challenges of growing tourism (Scheyvens 2011). Indeed, the economic growth
of the globally driven tourism industry has not always turned into economic and
social development on a local, regional or national scale. Thus, instead of shared
benefits, the development has been characterised by inequalities and uneven
power relations. In this respect, Harrison has stated that the tourism industry in
Africa has traditionally been developed by 'colonialists for colonialists' (2000:
37). In order to change this tendency, many commentators and policy makers
nowadays underline the need for the industry to refocus and benefit the local
community (see Goudie *et al.* 1999; Rogerson 2006). This has turned out to be a
challenging task in practice. However, the aim to refocus in tourism development
has created discourses and policy efforts aiming to stabilise or harmonise the
relationship between the tourism industry and local communities, and search for
sustainable – and more locally beneficial – tourism-related growth models, such
as CBT and PPT initiatives, which will come into view next.

Community-based tourism and pro-poor tourism: between global change and host communities

The need for more locally beneficial tourism-based growth has created new
forms and ideas of tourism and tourism development. In addition to the general
notion of sustainable development in tourism (Butler 1999), an increasing body
of literature and projects are focusing on ideas such as the aforementioned
community-based natural resource management (CBNRM), community-based

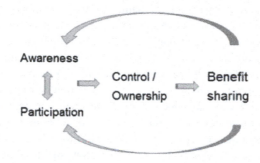

Figure 11.1 Idealised model of community-based tourism: increasing local participation and awareness in tourism support each other, and with an element of control or ownership the tourism operations on a local scale lead to better benefit sharing between the industry and communities, which fosters participation and awareness in tourism.

tourism (CBT) and pro-poor tourism (PPT) (Adams and Hulme 2001; Scheyvens 2002; Jones and Murphree 2004). In general, CBNRM aims to involve local communities in natural resource management by stating that they must have direct control over the uses and benefits of adjacent resources. By securing the control and benefits, local people are assumed to value, use and manage natural resources in a sustainable way (Blaikie 2006). CBT initiatives are based on the same line of argument as CBNRM: local communities need to benefit from the use of their environment and/or their culture and heritage in tourism. In order to safeguard the resources, effective benefit sharing, local participation, awareness and control over tourism development are said to be needed (Figure 11.1) (Holden 2007; Stronza 2007). In a positive situation, increased benefits will lead to deeper participation and better awareness of tourism. However, what needs to be safeguarded is the element of control.

The CBT aims to balance the local–global relations in tourism development and potentially uneven relations between hosts and guests by providing a control mechanism and sense of – or actual – ownership of tourism resources (Scheyvens 2002). The element of control, however, does not refer only to the use of material resources or intangible traditions, but also to how local people are used and depicted in tourism promotion, for example (Saarinen and Niskala 2009; see also Del Casino and Hanna 2000). This issue is important, especially when local communities, indigenous peoples or other ethnic and tribal groups, for example, are the main tourist attractions (Hinch and Butler 1996). In this respect Telfer and Sharpley (2007) have stated that CBT should also embody respect for local people, cultures and traditions. Thus, local people should be used and depicted in a way that is ethically acceptable and sustainable (Saarinen 2011).

In the context of globalisation, the need for more equal benefit sharing is a timely issue in the southern African tourism development scene. The majority of the region's tourism industry, perhaps except in South Africa, is dominated by international businesses and actors reflecting global forces shaping the production and consumption of tourism. At the same time, the majority of the region's tourism strategy documents refer to a necessity for local participation, ownership and benefits from tourism (see Republic of Namibia 1994; Government of South Africa 1996). In Namibia, tourism development policies (e.g. Ministry of Environment and Tourism 2005a, 2008) recognise the basic premises of CBT and the Ministry of Environment and Tourism (2005b) has initiated a specific CBT policy that aims to explore ways in which communities can benefit from the tourism industry and that promotes social and economic development and conservation in peripheral communal areas (i.e. conservancies) (see Massyn 2007; Lapeyre 2010). According to the Namibian CBT policy, tourism should be developed in a way that people can benefit from tourism and participate in tourism planning and development; people will be encouraged to develop tourism enterprises; tourism on communal land must be acceptable to the people living there; businesses are encouraged to work with people in communal areas; and tourism will work hand-in-hand with conservation of the environment (see also NACSO 2008). Thus, by involving local communities the benefits of tourism are expected to trickle down to the local level where tourist activities take place. On a community level, however, further challenges are the scale of benefits and how they are distributed (Saarinen 2012).

The CBT model can be seen to be applicable in almost any given community setting. In contrast to this the PPT focuses specifically on developing countries' contexts and the creation of net benefits for the poor (Goodwin 2009). The benefits created in PPT may go beyond the economic and include social, environmental and cultural issues (Ashley and Roe 2002; Meyer 2008), and on an ideological level, the PPT has links to the goals and targets of the United Nations' Millennium Project (Millennium Development Goals – MDGs), aiming to halve extreme poverty by 2015 (see Holden 2007; Telfer and Sharpley 2007; Scheyvens 2011). Related to the UN MDGs, tourism could be used as a tool for poverty reduction, ensuring environmental sustainability and the empowerment of previously neglected communities and social groups, for example.

In general, the models of CBT and PPT aim in the same direction: to benefit local people through tourism operations. However, in the literature the relation between PPT and CBT is somewhat problematic or even contradictory. According to Goodwin (2009), the early discussion papers (e.g. DFID 1999) on PPT did not refer to CBT or related initiatives. He states that at the time 'the radicalism of the PPT approach was seeking to use main stream tourism to achieve the objective of poverty elimination' (2009: 91). As such, PPT was seen as the outcome of a private sector venture and industry and market-oriented development strategy with an aim to mitigate the negative local impact of tourism growth. In contrast to this, CBT was seen as a small-scale and public-oriented development approach without a real capacity to contribute to wider poverty reduction in developing countries. Although CBT initiatives can often refer to small-scale and donor-driven community projects in practice (see Blackstock 2005), the strict conceptual juxtaposition may be overemphasised as the idea of CBT is not necessary limited to (1) non-private sector collaboration and (2) a single small community. In addition, PPT initiatives cannot be floating in the global neoliberal markets without much-needed local structures integrating business actions with communities in practice.

In Namibian communal conservancies, for example, CBT collaboration between private and public sectors can vary from private sector- to public sector-driven developments, where the private sector partner represents international mainstream tourism businesses (e.g. Wilderness Safaris) with a wide variety of community connections in the country and elsewhere in southern Africa (see Massyn 2007; Lapeyre 2010; Bandyopadhyay *et al.* 2011). In addition, the access to and sustainable use of natural resources in developing countries play a key role in poverty reduction and the achievement of the MDGs. Therefore, the CBNRM aspect can be seen as crucial not only for CBT but also for PPT development in the Global South. Next, after contextualising the case study, the chapter evaluates the contribution of tourism to benefit local OvaHimba communities in northwest Namibia and how the current tourism operations relate to the models of CBT and PPT discussed.

Ethnic tourism in northwest Namibia

From crises and isolation to tourism-led development hopes

The past few decades have been characterised by several crises in northwest Namibia and especially in the lives of the OvaHimba: the apartheid era and the Namibian War of Independence, numerous major and minor droughts, and political isolation and marginalisation in the independent Namibian regional development. Before independence in 1990, in northwest Namibia, the current Kunene region (115,000 square kilometres) and its northern parts (Kaokoland) was an 'operational area' (i.e. a war zone) between South African Defence Forces and the South West Africa People's Organization (SWAPO) representing the main Namibian political group in the Namibian War of Independence (1966–88). Due to the war, public and business access was restricted to Kaokoland (see Bollig and Gewald 2000; Henrichsen 2000), but the region was already isolated before the war: northern Kunene was, and still is, demarcated by a veterinarian fence preventing the movement of livestock, meat and related diseases from north to south and, thus, affecting past, current and future economic development possibilities in northern Namibia as large-scale livestock herding is not an economically viable option due to the risks and restrictions in trade. In addition, the arid climate and relatively common droughts hinder the viability of traditional livelihoods, which has also turned some OvaHimba communities towards tourism.

The OvaHimba are often described by using terms referring to the past, and nostalgia, for example as 'a people caught up in a time warp' (Jacobsohn 1998: 9). Their culturally distinctive features can be explained by their strong inner values and traditions and/or geographical isolation. Related to the former explanation,

Jacobsohn states that the 'Himba strategy to generally reject outside values was made possible by their economic independence' (1998: 9). According to this view, before the early 1980s serious drought (in 1977–82) and the loss of about 80 per cent of northern Kunene's cattle stock, the OvaHimba purposefully 'rejected' outside elements from their culture and way of living. While strong social cohesion may potentially explain the existence of traditions and other cultural features in northern Kunene, and elsewhere in the world, the OvaHimba, their cattle and customs are also locked deeply in socio-spatial networks and not all decisions are in the hands of the OvaHimba themselves.

Although no culture is totally isolated or has evolved in a vacuum but is rather a product of interaction with other cultures and people, the OvaHimba have lived, and still live, in a rather harsh and remote area where contacts with other cultural groups have been relatively limited. Historically, living in a remote part of the region may have served security needs in order to protect livestock from other groups such as the Namas (see Jacobsohn 1998; Bollig and Heinemann 2002). Even today, the OvaHimba are still largely isolated in Namibian society (see Mupya 2000), which does not necessarily reflect strong cultural cohesion and values among the OvaHimba, but a political situation originating from a specific historical context and processes. As previously stated, until the end of the apartheid period, Kaokoland was an 'operational zone' for the South African military against SWAPO-led forces. At the time, many OvaHimba served the South African Defence Forces against the Ovambo-dominated SWAPO or they rejected joining either of the parties. After independence, the SWAPO became, and has remained, the dominant political party in the country, which has kept the OvaHimba and many other ethnic groups in Namibia at the periphery (e.g. in resourcing, education and politics). This has partly left Kaokoland economically underdeveloped. Thus, the modernisation of Namibia is still on its way in Kaokoland.

The OvaHimba and tourism

The OvaHimba form an ethnic minority group that mainly lives in northwest Namibia and southwest Angola. Strictly defined, they are not an indigenous group as they have not lived in the region they inhabit longer than some other cultural groups (see Barnard 2006), but according to the United Nations' definitions and principles, the terms 'indigenous' and 'tribal' can be used as synonyms 'when the peoples concerned identify themselves under the indigenous agenda' (2004: 3). Thus, their tribal and marginalised status can be seen 'politically' as equivalent to that of an indigenous people and, like many other tribal groups, the OvaHimba have used their 'indigenous' or 'native' character both culturally and politically (e.g. against hydro-power plant construction processes – see Friedman (2000) and Kanguma (2000)).

In the national tourism system, Kaokoland in the northern Kunene represents a 'periphery of a periphery' (Weaver and Elliott 1996). This peripheral location with poor accessibility means that the total numbers of tourists in the region are relatively modest. Rothfuss (2000: 135) has estimated that in 1999 about 9,000 tourists visited the region. Relating to the current situation, Novelli and Gebhardt indicate that 'north-west Namibia has experienced considerable tourism growth over the last decade' (2007: 450). However, there are no statistics to indicate the current visitation level.

Although the OvaHimba are geographically, politically and socio-economically still somewhat isolated, their images and representations are widely used in Namibian tourism promotion (Saarinen 2011). According to Saarinen and Niskala (2009), the OvaHimba are represented as passive, primitive and exotic objects for Western (male) tourists to gaze at: the majority of the images depict 'half-dressed' Ovahimba women, or women with children, while Ovahimba men are rarely included in the tourism promotion material (see also Kanguma 2000; Echtner and Prasad 2003; van Eeden 2006) – their role as indigenous or tribal people is to stay as good natives (see Neumann 2000). This kind of primitivisation or zoo-ification of indigenous and native people has been a typical feature of Western travel literature since the colonial era and contemporary place promotion in tourism is a continuation of that process (see Edwards 1996; Wels 2004).

The main touristic attraction elements and sites in Kaokoland are based on the wilderness characteristics of the region and the OvaHimba culture. In addition, the Eupupa Falls as a single attraction site, located on the Kunene river and the border of Namibia and Angola, forms a well-known tourist hot spot in the region. There are also historical war sites that attract some tourists from South Africa. Relatively recently established communal conservancies in the region (such as Marienfluss, Orupenbe, Sanitatas, Okondjombo, Puros and Kunene River) support nature conservation, local communities and their relation. From a community perspective, the conservancies, which are part of the Namibian CBNRM programme, could offer an institutional framework for communities to manage wildlife and tourism resources and thus benefit directly from tourism (see Long 2004; Massyn 2007).

The OvaHimba have distinctive cultural features, and especially the female clothing and their tradition of using a mixture of ochre, butter fat and herbs to cover their skin are recognisable and are widely targeted in Namibian tourism promotion. The OvaHimba are mainly traditional pastoralists, but recently some communities have also turned towards tourism-related activities (see Novelli and Gebhardt 2007; Saarinen 2011). The importance of tourism has increased due to the growing numbers of visiting tourists and the establishment of communal conservancies in northern Kunene.

Community benefits from tourism

The following empirical case examples are based on a combination of previous studies by the author on host–guest relations and community benefits from tourism in Kaokoland (Saarinen 2011, 2012; see also Saarinen and Niskala 2009).

The research materials are based on thematic interviews from 2007 and 2010 in four communities near the town of Opuwo, the administrative centre of the Kunene Region. In 2007 two of the interviewed villages were located relatively close to Opuwo (less than 20 km from the town), while the remaining two case study sites were located further (about 35–40 km) from the town. In 2010, the two case villages were selected based on the earlier experiences and sites: one from close to Opuwa and the other one further away from the town. For ethical reasons, and to protect the identity of interviewed people, including chiefs and headmen, these communities are named Village I and Village II. The interviews were done with the headmen of the villages and/or their representatives and other households in the communities. Altogether ten interviews were held in 2007 (two or three per community) and seven in 2010 (three or four per community).

According to the community members interviewed, tourism benefits people: the role of tourism was seen as beneficial by all those interviewed. The main referred benefits from tourism were based on food supplies and souvenir payments. In addition, tourists were reported to provide medicine, tobacco, small direct money donations and occasional photography payments (see Saarinen 2011, 2012). Tourism benefits based on foodstuffs are not usual for ethnic tourism operations but they are characteristic of ethnic village tourism in Kaokoland. In the early 1990s, after Namibian independence and the region's opening up for international tourism, visitation fees to the villages were based on direct monetary payments but, by the late 1990s, the payments were noted to create conflicts among the community members. The monetary payments were received by the chief or headman of a community and, thus, it was difficult for other community members to know the level of payments and control the equal distribution of tourism benefits in the community, which as a whole was the attraction and reason for tourists to come. In contrast to money, foodstuffs were seen to be more visible and controllable. After receiving the foodstuffs from visitors, the different supplies are distributed equally to every woman-led household in the community.

According to the interviewees, the main supplies received were maize meal (flour), sugar and cooking oil (Table 11.1). Based on the results, Village I, located closer to Opuwo, received a slightly larger number of 'gifts', namely foodstuffs, on average per visiting tourist group, than Village II. The former community is larger and it also receives larger tourist groups, which both have an effect on the scale of the gifts organised by the guides bringing the tourists to the villages. Thus, the total number of received gifts is much higher in Village I, as it is more frequently visited, than in the more distant community from the town of Opuwo (Saarinen 2012).

The levels of received foodstuffs per tourist group were reported relatively similarly among the interviewees in the same village. However, the total economic impact of tourism on the interviewed OvaHimba communities is rather difficult to quantify exactly. It was obvious that the community members have also received benefits other than foodstuffs from tourists, which they perhaps did not want to report as openly or in as much detail as the shared items. Still, based on the

Table 11.1 The amount (average) and selection of foodstuffs tourists bring to the two village communities in Kaokoland

Village	Maize meal (kg)	Sugar (kg)	Oil (ml)
Village I, close to Opuwo (3 interviews, 15 households)	25	7.5	750
Village II, further from Opuwo (4 interviews, 11 households)	20	5	750

Source: Saarinen (2012).

participant observations focusing on visiting tourists in the villages, the scale of benefits other than foodstuffs was quite modest. However, small monetary payments from souvenir sales were considered valuable since money can be used for several purposes, including hospital and medical payments or for pleasure consumption when visiting a town.

If the foodstuffs alone are counted, with the estimation of the yearly or seasonal visitor group numbers given by the headmen and community members, the value of received shared gifts equals 11,220 Namibian dollars (approximately 1,100 euros in 2009) in Village I and 710 Namibian dollars (approximately 70 Euros in 2009) in Village II, using 2010 price levels. Thus, although tourism was perceived to be beneficial, the financial contribution of tourism was not very significant, which was also noted by some of the community members after the interviews. However, the interviews did not reveal any major problems caused by tourism and, as there were no major evident or perceived problems, all the interviewed community members shared the view that more tourists would be beneficial for the villages in future: this would perhaps lead to a more substantial level of benefits. However, the community members did not have awareness of the tourism system, and therefore did not know how to increase the number of tourists visiting their village. In this respect, the communities were dependent on the industry and the tourist guides, who are mostly non-local, selecting the communities for tourist groups to visit.

Although the interviewees did not know how to actively influence the markets, many of them had an understanding of why tourists want to visit the villages: to see the OvaHimba culture and their way of life (Saarinen 2012). Thus, some interviewees stressed the importance of maintaining the OvaHimba traditions as a tool for attracting tourists. The traditions considered to be important were mainly focused on women and how they dress. In order to maintain the tradition assumed to be valued by the tourists, some community members interviewed indicated that they were reluctant to send children, especially girls, to school as the educated children would lose the attractive 'habitus' and/or they would not stay in the village but in towns in the future. In addition, the children were needed to take care of the livestock.

Discussion and conclusions

In many developing countries, and especially in their peripheral parts, the tourism industry is increasingly seen as beneficial for local and regional development. While tourism has grown and also transformed towards products focusing on specific cultural and ethnic groups, the indigenous and tribal communities and their socio-economic environments are also under processes of change – or they have already dramatically changed. Indeed, in many places in the Global South, traditional livelihoods have lost or are losing their ability to provide economic survival and well-being for the people. As a result, the future viability of traditional livelihoods is seen as being challenged by the communities, which have made tourism-related activities increasingly attractive to them. In addition, the general modernisation of the surrounding societies has created external and internal pressures and needs for communities to be involved with ongoing socio-economic development processes. In the case of the OvaHimba, for example, the community members interviewed recognised the impacts and the lure of the modernisation process of Namibian society. In contrast to the general tendency described above, however, some of them seemed to prefer to stay in 'isolation' (i.e. outside the education processes) because of tourism and their role in the tourism system.

The interviewed OvaHimba communities valued and perceived tourism as being beneficial for them. Thus, if possible, they were willing to host more visitors in future – even though the received contribution was relatively modest: in Village I, the annually received amount of foodstuffs represents approximately three to four weeks' consumption needs, while in Village II the people would survive a week or less based on the amount of tourist 'gifts' received during the past twelve months (see Saarinen 2012). In addition to the modest scale of tourism benefits in the form of foodstuffs, the main problem may be that the small contribution received is based on and supports the uneven structures of the tourism–community nexus and the marginalisation of the OvaHimba in Namibian society. In order to satisfy the known or assumed motivations of tourists to visit their villages, the OvaHimba are trapped and willing to play, or actually stay, as an unchanged, 'primitive' and exotic culture referring to a past in order to meet the expectations and needs of international visitors. Therefore, instead of a cure for all the historically constructed challenges and current socio-economic problems in their lives and in regional development, the tourism industry may just represent the next crisis the OvaHimba are facing, making them even more vulnerable.

Obviously, the current system of ethnic village tourism in Kaokoland does not operate the same way as, or result in outcomes that are referred to by, international agencies, such as the UNWTO, WTTC or the Overseas Development Agency (ODI), when promoting tourism as a path to development or for solving problems such as poverty in the peripheries of the Global South. Tourism in the OvaHimba villages is based on the direct relationship between the communities and the mainstream tourism operators, which is often referred to as the main premise and 'radical innovation' of PPT (see Goodwin 2009). Naturally, that element alone does not make any regional tourism system a pro-poor one. However, the key question is: why would mainstream tourism go beyond the current practices in their ethnic tourism operations in Kaokoland? Absolutely speaking, the industry receives multiple times more benefits than the communities when they organise visits to the 'authentic OvaHimba communities' (see Saarinen 2012). In addition, while in Namibia and Kaokoland, tourists need accommodation, food and transits etc., which creates more benefits for the industry. Nevertheless, at the same time, the local OvaHimba communities also seem to be satisfied with their share. Thus, it is difficult to see why the mainstream tourism industry would go beyond the current benefit-sharing system and levels in the region.

Indeed, Regina Scheyvens has critically asked why we should assume that the tourism industry 'has some ethical commitment to ensuring that their businesses contribute to poverty-alleviation?' (2009: 193; see also Hall 2007). It is a good question and can also be linked to the CBT model. However, in the context of CBT, (1) there is a built-in need to empower local communities by giving them a sufficient level of control over the tourism operations based on their living environments and/or cultures, and (2) there is often a mediating actor or structure in between the mainstream industry and the community. From the mainstream tourism perspective, both of these dimensions can be seen as hindering growth in tourism. In addition, the latter dimension is often also seen to be negative by PPT advocates as it can lead to so-called donor dependency in local communities, but the dimension of control should be integrated with PPT as well. However, it is not automatically in the hands of local communities when tourists arrive, but needs to be arranged – and if the community has a low level of awareness of the tourism system, it may be a challenging and long-term process.

In contrast to this, the CBT model involves a moderating agency and/or government-regulated structures such as communal conservancies, as in Namibia, which provide to the communities a level of control over and also ownership of the resources used in tourism. However, in the context of global poverty alleviation aims, the outcomes of CBT projects are seen as fairly modest and mostly disappointing. Thus, many PPT advocates state that true poverty alleviation cannot be achieved without the mainstream industry's involvement (Goodwin 2009). There is no doubt that, if a major part of the global tourism industry and policy makers get involved with ethically driven tourism development ideas, it can reduce extreme poverty and hunger, contribute to education and the gender equality faced by millions of people, and lead to truly sustainable and PPT (Telfer and Sharpley 2007). But is it realistic to expect that major parts of the global industry will follow the path leading to the UN MDGs? At the same time, mainstream tourism development may also bring a spectrum of risks as discussed in the chapter – and not only in theory but also in practice. Therefore, instead of the active aim to confront the CBT and PPT models in tourism development discourses, more heterogeneous and even hybrid approaches may be needed by acknowledging that tourism may work as an effective response to crises, but it can also increase communities' vulnerability and turn into crises in local development. In a global economic crisis situation, tourism itself is also a highly vulnerable and insecure industry, which makes it a risky partner in development.

References

Adams, W.M. and Hulme, D. (2001) 'If community conservation is the answer in Africa, what is the question?', *Oryx*, 35: 193–200.

Ashley, C. (2000) *The Impacts of Tourism to Rural Livelihoods: Namibia's experience*, ODI Working paper 128, London: Chameleon Press.

Ashley, C. and Roe, D. (2002) 'Making tourism work for the poor: strategies and challenges in southern Africa', *Development Southern Africa*, 19(1): 61–82.

Bandyopadhyay, S., Humavindu, M., Shyamsundar, P. and Wang, L. (2011) 'Benefits to local communities from community conservancies in Namibia: an assessment', *Development Southern Africa*, 26(5): 733–54.

Barnard, A. (2006) 'Kalahari revisionism, Vienna and the "indigenous peoples" debate', *Social Anthropology*, 14: 1–16.

Binns, T. and Nel, E. (2002) 'Tourism as a local development strategy in South Africa', *The Geographical Journal*, 168(3): 235–47.

Blackstock, K. (2005) 'A critical look at community based tourism', *Community Development Journal*, 40(1): 39–49.

Blaikie, P. (2006) 'Is small really beautiful? Community-based natural resource management in Malawi and Botswana', *World Development*, 34(11): 1942–57.

Bollig, M. and Gewald, J.-B. (eds) (2000) *People, Cattle and Land: Transformaton of a pastoral society in Southwestern Africa*, Cologne, Germany: Köppe.

Bollig, M. and Heinemann, H. (2002) 'Nomadic savages, ochre people and heroic herders: visual presentation of the Himba of Namibia s Kaokoland', *Visual Anthropology*, 15(3): 267–312.

Britton, S.G. (1991) 'Tourism, capital, and place: towards a critical geography of tourism', *Environment and Planning D: Society and Space*, 9: 451–78.

Butler, R. (1999) 'Sustainable tourism: a state–of–the–art review', *Tourism Geographies*, 1(1): 7–25.

De Kadt, E. (1979) *Tourism: Passport to development?*, New York: Oxford University Press.

Del Casino, V.J. Jr and Hanna, S.P. (2000) 'Representation and identity in tourism map spaces', *Progress in Human Geography*, 24(1): 23–46.

Department for International Development (DFID) (1999) *Tourism and Poverty Elimination: A challenge for the 21st century*, London: HMSO.

Echtner, C.M. and Prasad, P. (2003) 'The context of third world tourism marketing', *Annals of Tourism Research*, 30(3): 660–82.

Edwards, E. (1996) 'Postcards: greetings from another world', in T. Selwyn (ed.) *The Tourist Image: Myths and myth making in tourism*, Chichester, UK: Wiley, pp. 197–222.

van Eeden, J. (2006) 'Land Rover and colonial-style adventure', *International Feminist Journal of Politics*, 8(3): 343–69.

Friedman, J.T. (2000) 'Mapping the Epupa debate: discourse and representation in a Namibian project', in G. Miescher and D. Henrichsen (eds) *New Notes on Kaoko*, Basel, Switzerland: Basler, pp. 220–35.

Goodwin, H. (2009) 'Contemporary policy debates: reflections on 10 years of pro-poor tourism', *Journal of Policy Research in Tourism, Leisure and Events*, 1: 90–4.

Goudie, S.C., Khan, F. and Kilian, D. (1999) 'Transforming tourism: black empowerment, heritage and identity beyond apartheid', *South African Geographical Journal*, 81(1): 21–33.

Government of South Africa (1996, June) *White Paper: Development and promotion of tourism in South Africa*, Pretoria: Department of Environmental Affairs and Tourism.

Hall, C.M. (2005) *Tourism: Rethinking the social science of mobility*, Harlow, UK: Prentice Hall.

Hall, C.M. (2007) 'Pro-poor tourism: do "tourism exchanges benefit primarily the countries of the South"?', *Current Issues in Tourism*, 10(2/3): 111–18.

Harrison, D. (2000) 'Tourism in Africa: the social and cultural framework', in P. Dieke (ed.) *The Political Economy of Tourism Development in Africa*, New York: Cognizant, pp. 135–51.

Harvey, D. (1996) *Justice, Nature and the Geography of Difference*, Oxford: Blackwell.

Henrichsen, D. (2000) 'Pilgrimages into Kaoko: Herrensafaris, 4x4s and settler illusion', in G. Miescher and D. Henrichsen (eds) *New Notes on Kaoko*, Basel, Switzerland: Basler, pp. 159–85.

Hinch, T. and Butler, R. (1996) 'Indigenous tourism: a common ground for discussion', in R. Butler and T. Hinch (eds) *Tourism and Indigenous Peoples*, London: International Thomson Business Press, pp. 3–21.

Holden, A. (2007) *Environment and Tourism*, London and New York: Routledge.

Hulme, D. and Murphree, M. (eds) (2001) *African Wildlife and Livelihoods*, Cape Town: David Phillip.

Jacobsohn M. (1998) *Himba: Nomads of Namibia*, Cape Town: Struik.

Jones, B.T.B. and Murphree, M.W. (2004) 'Community-based natural resource management as a conservation mechanism: lessons and directions', in B. Child (ed.) *Parks in Transition*, London: Earthscan, pp. 63–103.

Kanguma, B. (2000) 'Constructing Himba: the tourist gaze', in G. Miescher and D. Henrichsen (eds) *New Notes on Kaoko*, Basel: Basler, pp. 129–32.

Lapeyre, R. (2010) 'Community-based tourism as a sustainable solution to maximise impacts locally? The Tsiseb Conservancy case, Namibia', *Development Southern Africa*, 27: 757–72.

Long, S. (ed.) (2004) *Livelihoods and CBNRM in Namibia*, Windhoek: Directorate of Environmental Affairs and Ministry of Environment and Tourism.

Marsh, G.P. (1965) *Man and Nature or Physical Geography Modified by Man*, New York: Charles Scribner.

Massyn, P.J. (2007) 'Communal land reform and tourism investment in Namibia's communal areas: a question of unfinished business', *Development Southern Africa*, 24(3): 381–92.

Meyer, D. (2008) 'Pro-poor tourism – from leakages to linkages. A conceptual framework for developing linkages between the tourism private sector and "poor" neighbours', *Current Issues in Tourism*, 10(6): 558–83.

Ministry of Environment and Tourism (2005a) *A National Tourism Policy for Namibia* (first draft, February 2005), Windhoek: Government of Namibia.

Ministry of Environment and Tourism (2005b) *Community Based Tourism Policy*, retrieved 21 January 2008 from www.met.gov.na/programmes/cbnrm/cbtourism_guide.htm.

Ministry of Environment and Tourism (2008) *National Tourism Policy for Namibia* (draft, September 2007), Windhoek: Government of Namibia.

Mowforth, M. and Munt, I. (1998) *Tourism and Sustainability: A new tourism in the third world*, London: Routledge.

Mupya, W. (2000) 'Political parties and the elite in Kaoko', in G. Miescher and D. Henrichsen (eds) *New Notes on Kaoko*, Basel: Basler, pp. 207–19.

Namibian Association of CBNRM Support Organizations (NACSO) (2008) *Namibia's Communal Conservancies: A review of progress and challenges in 2007*, Windhoek: NACSO.

Neumann, R. (2000) 'Primitive ideas: protected area buffer zones and the politics of land in Afrida', in V. Broch-Due and R. Schroeder (eds) *Producing Nature and Poverty in Africa*, Stockholm: Nordiska Afrika Institutet, pp. 220–42.

Novelli, M. and Gebhardt, K. (2007) 'Community based tourism in Namibia: "reality show" or "window dressing"?', *Current Issues in Tourism*, 10(5): 443–79.

Okazaki, E. (2008) 'A community-based tourism model: its conception and use', *Journal of Sustainable Tourism*, 16(5): 551–29.

Republic of Namibia (1994) *White Paper on Tourism*, Windhoek: Cabinet, Republic of Namibia.

Rogerson, C.M. (2006) 'Pro-poor local economic development in South Africa: the role of pro-poor tourism', *Local Environment*, 11: 37–60.

Rogerson, C.M. and Visser, G. (2004) 'Tourism and development in post-apartheid South Africa: a ten year review', in C.M. Rogerson and G. Visser (eds) *Tourism and Development Issues in Contemporary South Africa*, Pretoria: Africa Institute of South Africa, pp. 2–25.

Rothfuss, E. (2000) 'Ethnic tourism in Kaoko: expectations, frustrations and trend in a post-colonial business', in G. Miescher and D. Henrichsen (eds) *New Notes on Kaoko*, Basel, Switzerland: Basler, pp. 133–58.

Saarinen, J. (2011) 'Tourism, indigenous people and the challenge of development: the representations of Ovahimbas in tourism promotion and community perceptions towards tourism', *Tourism Analysis*, 16(1–2): 31–42.

Saarinen, J. (2012) 'Tourism development and local communities: the direct benefits of tourism to OvaHimba communities in the Kaokoland, north-west Namibia', *Tourism Review International*, 15(1–2): 149–57.

Saarinen, J. and Niskala, M. (2009) 'Local culture and regional development: the role of OvaHimba in Namibian tourism', in P. Hottola (ed.) *Tourism Strategies and Local Responses in Southern Africa*, Wallingford, UK: CABI, pp. 61–72.

Saarinen, J., Becker, F., Manwa, H. and Wilson, D. (eds) (2009) *Sustainable Tourism in Southern Africa: Local communities and natural resources in transition*, Bristol, UK: Channel View.

Scheyvens, R. (2002) *Tourism for Development: Empowering communities*, Harlow, UK: Prentice Hall.

Scheyvens, R. (2009) 'Pro-poor tourism: is there value beyond the rhetoric?', *Tourism Recreation Research*, 34(2): 191–6.

Scheyvens, R. (2011) *Tourism and Poverty*, London: Routledge.

Sinclair, T. (1998) 'Tourism and economic development: a survey', *Journal of Development Studies*, 34(5): 1–51.

Sinclair, T. and Stabler, M. (1997) *The Economics of Tourism*, London: Routledge.

Smit, B. and Wandel, J. (2006) 'Adaptation, adaptive capacity and vulnerability', *Global Environmental Change*, 16(3): 282–92.

Stronza, A. (2007) 'The economic promise of ecotourism for conservation', *Journal of Ecotourism*, 6(3): 210–30.

Telfer, D. and Sharpley, R. (2007) *Tourism and Development in the Developing World*, London: Routledge.

Tosun, C. (2000) 'Limits to community participation in the tourism development process in developing countries', *Tourism Management*, 21: 613–33.

Turner, L. and Ash, J. (1975) *The Golden Hordes: International tourism and the pleasure periphery*, London: Constable.

United Nations (2004) The Concept of Indigenous Peoples, New York: UN Department of Economic and Social Affairs, retrieved 12 December 2011 from www.un.org/esa/socdev/unpfii/documents/workshop_data_background.doc.

Weaver, D. and Elliot, K. (1996) 'Spatial patterns and problems in contemporary Namibian tourism', *The Geographical Journal*, 162(2): 205–17.

Wels, H. (2004) 'About romance and reality: popular European imagery in postcolonial tourism in southern Africa', in C.M. Hall and H. Tucker (eds) *Tourism and Post-colonialism: Contested discourses, identities and representation*, London: Routledge, pp. 76–94.

Index

Please note that page numbers relating to Notes will have the letter 'n' following the page number. References to Figures or Tables will be in *italics*. GFEC stands for 'global financial and economic crisis'.